ON TRIAL

ON TIME

By Norman Sheresky and Marya Mannes
Uncoupling: The Art of Coming Apart

NORMAN SHERESKY

ON TRIAL

Masters of the Courtroom

THE VIKING PRESS NEW YORK

First published in 1977 by The Viking Press
625 Madison Avenue, New York, N.Y. 10022

Published simultaneously in Canada by
The Macmillan Company of Canada Limited

LIBRARY OF CONGRESS CATALOGING IN PUBLICATION DATA
Sheresky, Norman.
On trial.
Includes index.
1. Trials—United States.   2. Lawyers—
United States.   I. Title.
KF220.S5   345'.73'00924   76-49098
ISBN 0-670-52523-5

Printed in the United States of America

Set in VIP Caledonia

Acknowledgment is made to the following for material quoted.

Chappell & Co., Inc.: From "When I'm Not Near the Girl I Love." Copyright © 1946 by Chappell & Co., Inc., copyright renewed, all rights reserved. Reprinted by permission.

Chicago Daily News: From "For Strong Grand Juries," June 23, 1971, from several articles by Mike Royko. Reprinted by permission.

Chicago Sun-Times: From "Barney Badgered All the Way" by Tom Fitzpatrick, August 5, 1971. Reprinted by permission.

Harper & Row, Publishers, Inc.: From *Against the Law* by Leonard Levy. Reprinted by permission.

McIntosh and Otis, Inc.: From *King of the Courtroom: Percy Foreman* by Michael Dorman. Copyright © 1969 by Michael Dorman. Reprinted by permission of McIntosh and Otis, Inc.

To Brooke With Love

PREFACE

Much has been written by and about our great trial lawyers, but little has been said about the breed in general. Who and what kind of people are they? What distinguishes these gladiators of the trial arena from the run-of-the-mill lawyers?

The names of some of the more illustrious legal luminaries have become familiar to us—Edward Bennett Williams, Louis Nizer, Percy Foreman, F. Lee Bailey. . . . There are also many others—known mostly to "the trade"—who may be classified as truly great advocates. I think of such giants as "grand masters" of the courtroom. I wouldn't venture to say how many are to be found among the hundreds of good trial lawyers in the United States; suffice it to say that they are rare.

The grand masters I have chosen to write about in no way constitute a totality of the breed; they merely exemplify it. Some have been omitted because their stories are already well known; some because their "nominations" as grand masters would trigger off unintentional controversy. Others are not mentioned because they practice the same type of law, with the same kind of magical skill, represented by my five candidates. Still others have been omitted because I don't know them and have never heard of them. The genius of the trial lawyer knows no geographical bounds. He is to be found in every city and in many small towns.

I have interviewed each of the grand masters about whom I have written. All of them have given kindly and unsparingly of their time and knowledge; entire trial records were made available to me. With varying degrees of enthusiasm, they approved of and encouraged my project, because they, as I, believe that the trial lawyer is largely misunderstood and unappreciated.

I hope to be able to describe here what, in part, separates these supermen from the boys at the trial bar. Any judgment as to the good or evil inherent in their activities must be left to the reader or to students of jurisprudence.

CONTENTS

Preface   ix

Introduction   1

THE TRIAL ARENA   9

EDWARD BENNETT WILLIAMS   19
A Subcommittee's Subterfuge   33

VINCENT HALLINAN   63
A Gentle Dissenter v. The City of San Francisco   68
The Case of the Unconscious Killer   89
Revenge in Purgatory   97

BARNABAS F. SEARS   105
Conspiracy in Blue   110
Sears v. The State's Attorney, the City of Chicago,
    Public Apathy, and Judicial Ineptitude   121

ALFRED JULIEN   139
The $50,000 Lunch   143
The Operation Was a Success, but the Patient Is Now
    Deaf   146
Divorce, Julien Style   192

MELVIN BELLI   199
The State of Texas v. Jack Ruby, and Melvin Belli v. The
    City of Dallas   206

ET AL.   221

THE SEARCH FOR TRUTH   233

Index   239

ON TRIAL

INTRODUCTION

Since civilization began, the grand masters of law have made history—and often changed it. They have fought political power with the power of passionate belief and have plunged in to prosecute or defend where lesser men feared to "make waves."

In 70 B.C. a relatively unknown trial lawyer named Marcus Tullius Cicero sought to bring to justice the governor of Sicily, Gaius Verres. His opposing counsel, Quintus Hortensius, thought him quite mad—an upstart who seemed bent on putting an end to the career of his client, a rich and ruthless leader who could not only afford the best counsel but whose name struck terror in the minds of the five hundred senators constituting the jury. Cicero attacked the courts of Rome and told the jurors that it was they who were on trial, they who had to prove to the world that they were truly just and not just a part of the "system." The trial never reached a conclusion. Before even making his summation, Cicero won and Gaius Verres fled into exile.

In 1820 another trial lawyer, Henry Peter Brougham, found himself defending Queen Caroline before the House of Lords. The queen was charged with adultery and the penalty, if she was found guilty, was her head. This partisan jury was reluctant to offend the wishes of their king, George IV, the alleged cuckold. The outlook for the defense was grim; the alleged lover had been seen entering the queen's bedchamber.

But, as the result of skillful cross-examination and impassioned pleas, which at once upheld the lords' respect for their queen and subtly hinted at the well-known and undisputed infidelities of the king,

Queen Caroline was acquitted. Happily, there was no alternative. . . .
When pressed for details, the witness who swore he saw the lover (and who surely would have remembered such circumstances had he truly observed them) simply mumbled on and on, "I do not remember. I do not remember."

In America, in 1846, Mary Bickford was found at 3:00 a.m., her head almost severed and her bedclothes on fire. The murder weapon, a razor, was nearby. The accused, Alfred Tirrell, had been observed visiting his paramour that evening and he was apprehended while walking around in a daze.

Rufus Choate, one of America's greatest trial lawyers, proved that at the time of this murder, his client was sleepwalking. In proving that Tirrell had been a victim of somnambulism all his life, Choate gave his client the perfect alibi—the perfect excuse for not taking the stand in his own defense. When asked if Tirrell would go on the stand, Choate replied, "Our client was asleep that night and therefore cannot assist us."

In 1926, Clarence Darrow undertook the defense of Henry Sweet, one of eleven blacks who had been arrested and charged with first-degree murder. The defendant was the younger brother of a successful black gynecologist who had moved his family into a white neighborhood in Detroit, Michigan. From the moment the Sweets moved in, gangs of whites surrounded their house venting their outrage. The second night of their occupancy of the house (armed friends and relatives were now with them), shots were fired and one white man was killed and another wounded. The prosecution contended that the crowd merely consisted of the curious; the defense maintained that the crowd was part of the "Waterworks Improvement Association," whose function it was to drive blacks out of white neighborhoods.

Detroit's black population had grown from six thousand to about seventy thousand in fifteen years, and the blacks found themselves unable to live outside black ghettos.

Darrow put the City of Detroit, the concept of bigotry in the United States, and each of the jurors on trial, along with his client. In his summation, he said:

> I insist that there is nothing but prejudice in this case; that if it were reversed and eleven white men had shot and killed a black while protecting their home and their lives against a mob of

blacks, nobody would have dreamed of having them indicted. I know what I am talking about, and so do you. They would have been given medals instead. Ten colored men and one woman are in this indictment, tried by twelve jurors, gentlemen. Every one of you is white. At least you all think so. We haven't one colored man on this jury. We couldn't get one. One was called and he was disqualified. You twelve men are trying a colored man on race prejudice. . . .

You don't want him. Perhaps you don't want him next to you. Suppose you were colored. Did any of you ever wake up out of a nightmare dreaming that you were colored? Would you be willing to have my client's skin? Why? Just because somebody is prejudiced! Imagine yourself colored, gentlemen. Imagine yourselves back in the Sweet house on that fatal night. That is the only right way to treat this case, and the court will tell you so. . . .

Gentlemen, you were called into this case by chance. It took us a week to find you, a week of culling out prejudice and hatred. Probably we did not cull it all out . . . but we took the best and the fairest that we could find. It is up to you.

Your verdict means something in this case, something more than the fate of this boy. It is not often that a case is submitted to twelve men where the decision may mean a milestone in the progress of the human race. But this case can mean just that. And I hope and I trust that you have a feeling of responsibility and that you will take it and do your duty as citizens of a great nation and as members of the human family, which is better still . . .

This case is about to end, gentlemen. To them, it is life. Not one of their color sits on this jury. Their fate is in the hands of twelve whites. Their eyes are fixed on you, their hearts go out to you, and their hopes hang on your verdict.

I ask you, on behalf of this defendant, on behalf of these helpless ones who turn to you, and more than that—on behalf of this great state and this great city which must face this problem and face it fairly—I ask you, in the name of progress and of the human race, to return a verdict of not guilty in this case!

The defendant was acquitted.

And Robert H. Jackson, in his closing address at the Nuremberg trials, responding to the defenses of Hermann Göring, Joachim von Ribbentrop, Albert Speer, and other war criminals that they were only acting under orders, said:

> It is against such a background that these defendants now ask this tribunal to say that they are not guilty of planning, executing, or conspiring to commit this long list of crimes and wrongs. They stand before the record of this trial as bloodstained Gloucester stood by the body of his slain king. He begged of the widow, as they beg of you: "Say I slew them not." And the queen replied, "Then say they were not slain. But dead they are. . . ." If you were to say of these men that they are not guilty, it would be as true to say there has been no war, there are no slain, there has been no crime.

In 1975 former Secretary of the Treasury John B. Connally was put on trial by the U.S. government, accused of a tawdry bribe-taking scheme. Decades of public service, an untarnished reputation, and the former secretary's freedom were at stake.

Edward Bennett Williams, in defending Mr. Connally, reminded the jury of a visit he had once made to the oldest courthouse in all England. He said: "I found myself down in the basement of that building, and there inscribed on the wall were some words which I have never forgotten. The words were: 'In this hallowed place the Crown never loses because when justice is done to the lowliest subject in England, the Crown wins.' "

He reminded the jury that the same rule applied in federal courthouses in the United States: "It never loses in a criminal courtroom, because when justice is done any man, to any one of us, the United States wins." Connally was acquitted.

Although the art of advocacy is an ancient one, there has never been an era in which the practitioner was particularly appreciated or trusted. While people have always been captivated by a trial lawyer's accomplishments professionally, they (perhaps justifiably) continue to be suspicious of him personally.

Even in England, after the Magna Carta of 1215, lawyers were extremely unpopular. As late as 1300, only forty men were allowed to be practitioners in that country. In 1305 these men formed the Inns of Court. Up until the fifteenth century, lawyers were banished from Parliament. It was not until the next century that the dual system of barrister and solicitor became established in England.

Early settlers in the United States were just as unkindly disposed toward lawyers. They wanted their new world to be corruption-free and felt they could accomplish it best without this tricky breed. Witch trials were perceived by many to be as good a way as any to determine the truth, better than relying upon lawyers who were paid only to deceive. Indeed, there were long periods in America's history when lawyers were not permitted to plead cases in court. Lawyers were not allowed to practice at all in Massachusetts. They were forbidden to become members of the Assembly in New York and in Rhode Island. They were forbidden to become legislators, "their presence being found to be of ill-consequence."

Were it not for the rapid growth of trade and mercantilism, it is hard to predict what would have happened to the legal profession. Lawyers finally became not only accepted but necessary to implement the evergrowing sophistication of commerce.

Even in the comparatively civilized nineteenth century the fear persisted that the art of advocacy, as practiced by some, bore a closer resemblance to witchcraft than to the more honorable pursuit of persuasion. And that fear still seems to persist.

Rare is the lawyer who hasn't heard comments from his relatives or friends such as: "Oh, you're just being a lawyer"; or "Stop arguing like a lawyer"; or "Stop cross-examining me, I'm not on a witness stand." And surely most of us, at one time or another, have asked or been asked the equivalent of: "Do you think Foreman will get him off?" or "Do you think F. Lee Bailey will win this one?" The trial lawyer is regarded as a magician of sorts. We watch him produce the rabbit out of the hat. But was it really a rabbit? Did it really come out of the hat? Was it a trick? How did he *do* it?

Of course, lawyers are not the sole target of suspicion in the judicial system. Corruption in government and bureaucratic overzealousness, dishonest judges and biased juries, prejudice and minority persecution, mass hysteria and public apathy—all these factors continue to lead to a general antipathy toward the legal trial system. The all-powerful state, with its vast financial and investigatory resources, makes it virtually impossible for anyone—except extremely wealthy people—to have a fair or equal criminal trial.

These influential forces have always existed and will continue to exist. They are constant social infections that threaten to disrupt and destroy the notion of a just "day in court" for every litigant. Every day the innocent are convicted, injured victims go uncompensated, and injustice prevails even in the best judicial systems.

Because of these very imperfections, it is all the more essential that we have a courageous trial bar—the kind of bar exemplified by the grand masters, few as they are. For when a great trial lawyer is inspired to take up the cudgel on a client's behalf, he can be a powerful and effective antidote to injustice and judicial abuse. It cannot be denied that throughout history the innocent, the wronged, the maligned, and the underdog in search of justice have found it only through the labors of the great trial lawyers.

These heroic lawmen are reminiscent of the fabled gunfighters of the early West. Their self-image is that of the crusader, many notches above the ordinary lawyer. Once a grand master accepts a client, the client becomes a Cause; and the Cause becomes the foundation upon which the entire system of justice either stands firm or collapses.

He is a fascinating mixture of genius and fraud, of healer and medicine man, of evangelist and devil. He illuminates the truth, vindicates the innocent, and avenges the victim. He also obfuscates facts, twists the law beyond its endurance, sets free the guilty, punishes the victim, and rewards the transgressor. When his client has killed, the victim deserved to be killed. When his client is accused of committing adultery, the spouse, the detective, the friends, and the relatives who observed it are liars. When his client has breached a contract, either there never was a contract to begin with or the other side made him do it. Justice itself sits as co-counsel with every grand master; the other side sits alone, or alone with the facts and the witnesses.

No single work could adequately cover all that goes into the makings of a great trial lawyer. Passion coupled with empathy for a cause or a client . . . emotion . . . the ability to enlist fellow citizens in a rare opportunity to serve humanity—these are just some of the basic ingredients.

Guts are a *sine qua non* of the grand master, as are grace, timing, ego, and sincerity. Is it important to have a pleasant voice? It can't hurt; but it can't make a trial lawyer a great one if he doesn't know exactly what to say and what not to say. If there is in the grand master a fundamental departure from the qualities possessed by other lawyers, it is that during the process of a trial, he loses all sense of objectivity while appearing to maintain it.

Vincent Hallinan claims he has no problem maintaining objectivity. When you discuss with him his current roster of clients, they are all angels. What about some of those he has represented in the past? Well, he admits, they had their faults and foibles.

Hallinan told me that the only time he was ever ashamed of himself professionally was when he refused to defend a man who had killed a child, propped its eyes open with toothpicks, and sent the body back in a box to its parents. "A man so aberrated," he said, "could not possibly be guilty under the law and was entitled to a defense."

In the area of criminal law, particularly, any lawyer—or any one, for that matter—would be hard put to describe some defendants as likable or even as acceptable human beings. In such a case, the lawyer becomes focused on and passionately immersed in the Cause.

Edward Bennett Williams is one of the all-time masters at wrapping his clients in the American flag or the United States Constitution. It is how we treat the worst in our society that gives security to the best. The Williams theory is that a jury who would deprive his clients of their liberty would be risking its own; and his clients are simply not worth it!

It can be fairly said that the greater number of great trial lawyers and grand masters developed as individual practitioners, or from having practiced out of small law offices with few associates. Trial work is a lonely business; only one man can effectively try a case. Success or failure is by no means assured by committee work upon which the litigation departments of the large firms rely so heavily. The fact that a case has been prepared by a group of associates does not always help but may hurt the client's cause.

There are exceptions, of course, and Louis Nizer is certainly one. He often tries cases that have been prepared for the most part by others, relying as well upon notes passed to him in the courtroom by his associates.

As in most professions, there is a great deal of rivalry among trial lawyers. As much as they may like and admire each other, they rarely agree on who among them are the best. There is one thing, however, on which there is unanimous agreement: A great trial lawyer can try any kind of case before any kind of court or jury.

While a trial lawyer may very well possess many of the endowments described here, he still might not qualify as one of the greats. For, above all, he must be steeped in and fortified by experience. He must be a master technician and have the ability to speak to jurors of vastly different backgrounds. There has never been a born trial lawyer; there are no prodigies. The successfully seasoned trial man emerges only after years of marinating in a well-blended mixture of cases and courtrooms.

Recently I was discussing the subject of trial lawyers with a friend who is a distinguished psychiatrist and former professor of psychiatry at Yale. He suggested that a great trial lawyer, like a great psychiatrist, had to be a man (or woman) who could recognize nobility. To him, the ability to convince a jury of the nobility of a client or of a cause is the key talent that distinguishes the master trial lawyer or psychiatrist. The psychiatrist must persuade the nonfunctioning patient that he is worthwhile, that he is a decent person capable of achievement. So too must the trial lawyer persuade a court or jury that beneath or within the evidence there is tragedy, drama, humaneness, and nobility.

And Judge Herbert Stern, a U.S. District Judge in New Jersey, correctly points out: "It isn't the velvet tongue, in my opinion, that makes a man a good trial lawyer. Those days are gone forever. I don't think juries want that. Juries want to do the right thing. They want to come to the right decision. The trick is not to persuade them that you are eloquent but that you are right. If you convey the impression in a courtroom of being too facile of tongue, or even too brilliant—but not right—you may look good but you will go home with an empty basket. The one quality above all others that the trial lawyer needs is sincerity."

THE TRIAL ARENA

The number of television shows and motion pictures devoted to trial lawyers and their cases is certainly indicative of the American public's fascination with the subject. But the theatrical image created by these media bears little resemblance to the real-life trial lawyer or to the trial process itself as an art.

A courtroom trial, for the average spectator (as seen from his living room), consists of the maligned defendant represented by the starring attorney, who always wins; the relentless prosecutor; the black-robed judge, who gavels the courtroom to attention periodically with: "One more outburst of this kind and I shall instruct the bailiff to clear the court"; and the mute jury, coached to look dispassionate, sits in its box and does its limited best to make some kind of individual showing for the folks at home.

The trial is over in an hour (of prime TV time, or two, if it's a movie) when the courtroom doors swing open and the surprise witness is brought in. She was driving by the scene of the crime and heard a funny noise. She peered through the bushes and eyewitnessed the real murderer in the act. It is not the defendant after all; it's that woman in the fourth row who leaps out of the spectators' section shouting, "I shot him because I loved him!" The culprit is carried off with arms flailing, and counselors close with a no-hard-feelings handshake. And that's the way it goes—on film.

In the real-life courtroom, the dynamics of the trial process are a great deal subtler, at times invisible, far too slow to suit a television producer, and far more fascinating. Often, it begins when the grand master is selected, as this means that we have a case which is instantly exciting and prestigious. For the opposing counsel, the challenge, though formidable, promises great rewards: If he scores a victory against one of the giants, his reputation will take on new dimensions; he will probably earn a large fee and enough ego satisfaction to last him a lifetime. But, in the meantime, he is likely to be scared out of his wits. And the grand master, knowing this, will exploit the fact.

I have witnessed dozens of instances in which the mere fact that a grand master is going to participate in a trial results in severe psychological disadvantage to the other side. These psychological minuses have a way of proliferating and sometimes ruining the other client's willingness to wage a fight-to-the-finish courtroom battle. The ultimate damage, of course, is often seen in a premature settlement out of court—the tendency of the intimidated to compromise rather than risk a go-round with a master.

Usually the mere prospect of opposing a famous or highly reputable advocate is enough to set in motion a maelstrom of misgivings and anxieties in the average trial lawyer: What has he found out that I haven't? What trick is he going to play? What witness will he call first? Maybe I should go read some records of some of his other trials. Maybe I should try to get some sleep. With *him* in the offing, who can sleep? As a result, he begins to inundate himself in a morass of irrelevant detail and overprepares his client's case. The public, however, rarely gets to see or hear any of the drama of pretrial strategic warfare.

The everyday trial lawyer is also aware and fearful of the grand master's remarkable ability to "get across" to a jury, to bridge the credibility gap so that his "side" becomes the just and honest one. There is a delicate skill involved in communicating with a jury, and the grand master has refined it to a high art form. Instinctively, he is able to convey to them this kind of message: Trust me; I know you, I understand you, I respect you, I like you, and, most important, I will not mislead you. I know the law, I know what justice is and what it should be. I need your help. Justice depends upon you. Justice is with my client. Your duty is to do justice, as is mine.

The process by which a jury is selected is a fascinating facet of trial work, again, unseen on the screen. The men and women who are

THE TRIAL ARENA

going to be the supreme judges of the facts in a case come from every walk of life. Who they are, how they interact with each other, and how they may respond in a given case are of crucial concern to the litigants. The theory behind jury selection is that the parties should be permitted to weed out prejudice. Normally, both sides are given a certain number of "peremptory" challenges by which they may excuse prospective jurors without any cause at all. They are also permitted to excuse jurors "for cause"—that is, if they can demonstrate to the judge that such jurors are unable, by reason of some fixed belief, prejudice, or religious view, to weigh the facts objectively in a case.

This notion of ferreting out bias is admirable enough; and the experienced trial lawyer—well aware that a jury is much more interested, responsive, and alert at the beginning of a trial, and well aware of the importance of first impressions—uses the process to begin currying favor with the jury. He uses jury selection as his first opportunity to get rid of possible enemies and start making friends. For that reason, in many states and in the federal system, jurors are not questioned by the lawyers but by the presiding judge. In those instances, attorneys are permitted to submit to the judge the questions they would like him to ask the jurors.

The system of jury selection by a judge has been widely criticized by the trial bar. The argument is forceful: Prejudice is subtle and underground. Prospective jurors rarely come out and say that they are prejudiced, or rarely volunteer facts that would lead to the uncovering of such prejudice. As Belli has said, "My client hired me for the whole goddamn case, not just for part of it. He is entitled to rely upon *me* to get him a fair trial, not on the judge." Other trial lawyers are just as critical.

No matter who does the questioning of the prospective jurors, the process of selecting them and exercising peremptory challenges against the unwanted may very well be vital to the outcome of a case. Experienced trial counsel rely on their years of experience with hundreds and thousands of juries to tell them who they want and do not want in a given case. Prosecutors, for example, tend to excuse Jews—too emotional and sympathetic, they say. Personal-injury lawyers tend to excuse accountants, statisticians, employees of large companies, and employees of all utilities. These people, the theory goes, are only comfortable with facts that can be put down on a piece of paper. They are uninclined and, frequently, unwilling (as opposed to artists, salesmen, and performers) to translate human suffering and pain into dollars. A lawyer trying a matrimonial case in which the "guilt" he wishes to prove was adultery or cruel and inhuman treatment would want to exclude from the jury the more mature women, Catholics, Chinese, and other staid groups. These people, he fears, would tend to feel, We stuck it out, why can't this plaintiff? Often, when there are two or three prospective women jurors and one is exceptionally good-looking, the first lawyer to question the prospective panel might excuse the attractive woman, almost immediately and brusquely, in the hope and expectation that the others will say to themselves, He is not taken in by *her.*

Many trial lawyers make a habit of staring at prospective jury panels not only before their case is called but during recess and before it is finally empaneled. By then, they can see which jurors seem to be the leaders and which the followers. Particularly in cases involving minority groups, they want to make sure in excusing a certain juror that his jury-room friends are also excused.

In some states it is possible to acquire a "dope sheet" on a prospective juror who has sat in other cases which details how he voted in each case. Most trial lawyers avail themselves of the dope sheet, but the grand master has no use for it. He would say, "I am interested in how these jurors will vote for me; and that depends upon how they answer my questions and what happens when I look them in the eyes."

Even when the judge is doing the questioning, the trial lawyer will find some way to say something so as to appear affable and likable, and demonstrate to the jurors that he is there to be helpful. Anything to curry favor with them—anything that the judge will let him get away with.

Once, during the course of a trial in New York City during early summer, Bruno Schachner, an old and respected trial warrior, arose and suggested to the court that the jury would be more comfortable if they were permitted to remove their jackets. The trial judge became infuriated and told the jury that the suggestion was improper; that Mr. Schachner could not care less if the jurors fried in hell, and that he was only trying to solicit their favor. The tirade was so stern that I, as associate counsel, felt the perspiration pouring down my sleeves. Schachner replied, "Your Honor, I had no idea that my suggestion would be considered improper, but if it was, I most respectfully apologize to you and particularly to this jury." Upon which he sat down and whispered in my ear, "Screw him, look at the jury; they love me."

As soon as the jury is empaneled, they are twelve people apart, separated from the rest of the courtroom by the jury box and rail. How to climb into that box and become the thirteenth juror now becomes the trial lawyer's mission. If you approach that jury rail too quickly, you can actually see the jurors recoil. So you walk by it and occasionally touch it, even leave a piece of paper on it for a second, then you pick it up. And sooner or later—if you have tried enough cases, had enough experience, possess all the qualities of a great trial lawyer, and know what will please *this* jury—you, the grand master, will be permitted (figuratively) inside the jury box.

The first day, perhaps you've touched that rail only once; you may have walked around to the side of the box and questioned a witness with phrases such as, "Tell *us* . . . "; "*We* would like to know . . ." But you are careful to do that only once or twice, because your friendship and subsequent love affair with the jury must develop slowly. As the trial progresses, the jury and how they sit will tell you (if you are a grand master and can read the signs) when you are one of them. Then you will make greater use of "we" and "us," and you will project your voice from beside the jury box so that more and more your voice will seem to be coming from it. As you approach the jury box, the arms of the people in front will no longer be folded as though to exclude you. As you touch the jury rail, there will be no shifting in the seats. You will look from juror to juror and they will not look away. If you are too tall or your voice is too overpowering, you will never be permitted near the jury box and will have to develop other techniques.

In some courts the presiding judge will not permit trial lawyers to move about; they are directed to sit. To hamstring lawyers in their efforts to persuade hardly seems to fit into the theory and the system. As Belli said when we were discussing the problem, "Pretty soon we will be mailing in our arguments."

The jury system (according to one source*) was started in Europe by Charlemagne's son, the Holy Roman Emperor Louis I, called le Débonnaire. This jury was designed to participate in cases involving royal rights and, like subsequent juries in England and the earliest juries or assemblies in Egypt and Greece, it acted not only as the arbiter of disputes, but as the witness for or against the litigants. The

---

* Various sources differ as to the origin of the jury system in time and place.

members were chosen for their familiarity with the facts in dispute and were to give evidence instead of hearing it.

The jury system in the twentieth century, whatever its vices, is superior to any previous system in its attempt to resolve disputes between litigants and arrive at the truth as closely as it can be determined. We could not possibly have an effective trial bar without it.

Anyone who has ever stood accused of a crime, or been fearful of being accused, will know how precious is the right to submit the controversy to an impartial body of men and women, rather than to an individual judge who is closely associated with the government. Even in a civil case, it is extraordinary to observe the relief on the face of a litigant when he realizes it is not this one judge—with his own prejudices and predilections and very busy calendar to clear—who will investigate into the facts and decide his fate but it will be twelve interested fellow citizens.

There doesn't seem to be any really satisfactory explanation as to how twelve people (or a lesser number in jurisdictions where smaller juries are authorized), from entirely different prejudices and experiences, are so often able to become amalgamated into an effective fact-finding unit. But, as Belli has said, "When this jury returns its verdict, right or wrong, one seeing this picture is at once satisfied with the result; yet he would not be tried by any one of these twelve individually." We are loath to trust our lives and our property, our futures and our well-being to the mind of any one man, regardless of how bright, honest, or fair he is.

A jury, of course, adds up to a lot more than the mere sum of the twelve people who constitute it, no matter how ordinary or uneducated or diverse they are individually. They form a common body devoted to performing an unusual (for them) function. It is an uplifting, important, and selfless experience, and each one takes his responsibility seriously and wishes to perform it well.

What kind of argument should be made to *this* jury? What will *this* jury accept? What experiences in my own life can I bring to bear that will be persuasive to this jury? Will any one of those experiences offend any member of this jury? A witness has testified that my client has a prejudice against Italians. That will not sit well with juror number 6 and juror number 8. What can I do to counteract it? What story can I tell, what experience can I relate that will prove to jurors numbers 6 and 8 that my client does not have that prejudice—or, if they won't buy that, that *I* don't have that prejudice, and that I understand my client and believe in him, even though I abhor his prejudice?

"There has been testimony here, ladies and gentlemen, that my client has dealt unfairly with people simply because of their ethnic backgrounds. I don't know why my learned opponent brought it up, unless he wanted to prejudice you in a case where prejudice should play no part. This case involves a breach of contract, and if we are going to ask ourselves, in an American court of law, whether or not we like one side or the other, then pretty soon we will be deciding cases on who is the prettiest, or who is the smartest or tallest."

A grand master not only knows what to say but he feels what he says. And what he says to one jury, he wouldn't dream of saying to another. (Except Perry Mason, who hasn't changed his style in over thirty years.)

To sit down and plot what you will say is fine; but it is not enough. The grand master has the instantaneous reflexes of a fighter in counteracting his opponent's moves.

Many years ago, I remember telling two experienced trial lawyers about the success I had been having in telling jurors that I was just a young lawyer, afraid that when they retired to render a verdict they might penalize my client because of my inexperience, not to mention my opponent's much greater experience and eloquence. The first lawyer said, "Why, if you ever did that to me, I would pop up and say, 'Ladies and gentlemen, I am personally very disturbed that Mr. Sheresky has the slightest qualms about his ability as a trial lawyer. I think you will agree with me that he has tried this case as ably as it could be tried; and if, because of his youth, he has made contentions here that he has not been able to prove, we all know that it may have had something to do with his inexperience in evaluating a case, but not his ability in presenting it.'" The other lawyer said, "I would simply get up and tell the jury that I was getting just a little fed up with Sheresky and his appeals to juries' sympathy, and I was particularly fed up with it since it is the third time I heard him say that this month." I never said that again.

Alfred Julien loves to invite jurors to make an investigation of the facts along with him. He might say, for example, "Let's examine the facts of this case together as though you were in my living room or I in yours. Let's discuss this matter as though we were friends trying to resolve a dispute between people we knew. . . ." His technique is so well known among his colleagues that he once found himself trying a case against a former student ("Mr. Brown") who invited the jury into *his* living room before Julien could. When he concluded, smiling in smug satisfaction, Julien arose and said:

"Why, I couldn't believe my ears when I heard Mr. Brown invite you into his living room. This isn't a tea party, this is a court of law. I couldn't believe it when Mr. Brown virtually leapt over the jury rail and into your laps. Does he think he can get away with that sort of thing? Does he think you are going to be taken in for one second because he has invited you, or worse, because he has invited himself into your living room? Does he think because his client's story won't hold any water in this temple of justice, it is going to sound any better in your room or in his?"

It is important, of course, to be able to use, memorize, and recall set patterns of attack and counterattack; but it is absolutely essential that you are able to think on your feet, and to think innovatively and dramatically and be right. In trial work, as in chess, there are too many possibilities for any lawyer to be able to foretell what will occur. Once, during a murder trial, the only criminal trial in which Julien participated, there came that classic, cliff-hanging moment so often portrayed theatrically, and so often actually used by prosecutors, when the eyewitness is asked, "Do you recognize in this courtroom the man who killed the deceased?" The witness said his "I do," and the prosecutor, according to script, then said, "Will you stand up and identify him?"

Julien jumped to his feet: "Wait a minute. Before this miraculous identification is made, may the record reflect that there is only one black accused of this crime, and only one black sitting in front of this rail, and he is sitting next to me, and I am the defense lawyer, and behind him is an armed guard. Now go ahead. Who do you say did it?"

The eyewitness, of course, pointed to Julien's client, but whatever dramatic impact there would have been was either lessened or destroyed.

The opening address to the jury, the direct examination of witnesses, the cross-examination, the summation of counsel, the charge to the jury, and the verdict have all been well documented and the public is aware that these are the basic visible components of the trial. While many trials are mechanical and tedious, the productions put on by the grand masters rarely are. They are carefully designed and orchestrated, so that each day the jury is left hungering for more, looking forward to the denouement. The opening address promises and hints and tantalizes, the testimony builds, and the suspense is maintained. But in order to appreciate these fascinating, complicated techniques and their ultimate accomplishment, the trial must be observed from beginning to end. Few of us, however, can devote the time necessary for watching a whole trial (unless we are involved in it).

Similarly, the mere reading of a trial transcript cannot possibly give you the full story with all its innuendos. It is never so accurate that all the advocates' words are recorded correctly; and, more important, voice inflections are not recorded. The hesitation of a witness, his sudden perspiration when he is befuddled, his fear and apprehension, his recoiling movement as the cross-examiner bears down upon him, cannot be read.

While the mechanics of the jury trial have been observed by us all in the broadest outline in the entertainment media, few of us have been privileged to see what the truly great trial masters accomplish every day. When the ordinary lawyer practices trial advocacy, he hopes to win by his powers of persuasion. The grand master wins by the art of seduction. His achievements are not born of magic or miracles; they are the fruits of hard labor, executed with extraordinary talent and a touch of genius. There has never been a successful trial lawyer who was not an indefatigable worker.

Wonder-worker, seducer, master of psychology and timing—the grand master is a fascinating, many-faceted artist. He belongs to a special and fearless breed of men ready to undertake any cause that they believe in. They refuse to pander to the will of the majority when they believe they are right. They kowtow to no judge. They are nobody's man but their own. And once you meet such a man, you will never forget him.

EDWARD BENNETT WILLIAMS

Among the distinguished members of the trial bar in the United States, few are better known to the public than Edward Bennett Williams. Even among the grand masters, this extraordinary man has few, if any, detractors. Early on, the press, dazzled by Williams' wizardry in the courtroom, took him to its bosom, and just about every national magazine and newspaper has done a major piece on him.

Surely no other trial lawyer has achieved as much unanimity of acclaim. Judges, fellow lawyers, law professors, and a long list of grateful clients, with rare consistency, attest to his skills of advocacy. So recognized are his skills that his enemies and competitors have not hesitated to call on him when they themselves got into trouble. Williams, for example, headed President Richard Nixon's "enemies list." The Watergate tapes showed that in a conversation in the Oval Office on September 15, 1972, Nixon told John Dean and H. R. Haldeman, "I wouldn't want to be in Edward Bennett Williams' position after this election. I think we are going to fix the son-of-a-bitch." Yet Williams was asked to defend the former President. He refused.

He also was asked to, and did, defend John B. Connally, former Secretary of the Treasury, for perjury. The former secretary went on trial on April 2, 1975, charged with lying when he testified that in 1971 he did not solicit and receive a $10,000 payoff for helping the dairy industry. Connally's indictment had also grown out of the Watergate scandal. Even more recently, Williams represented former CIA Director Richard Helms, who, together with others, was under investigation by the government for "possible criminal liability under federal Civil Rights statutes."

Indeed, "anybody who is anybody" tries to get Williams first. The Hearsts tried to hire him to represent Patricia. Patrick Cunningham, one of New York City's most influential political leaders, has hired Williams to defend him in connection with a grand jury investigation into political payoffs in New York City. The Governor of Maryland, Marvin Mandel, tried to hire Williams in connection with an investigation of charges of accepting payoffs.

A list of Williams' famous clients is almost endless: *The Washington Post,* Georgetown University, the Democratic National Committee, Castro Convertible Corp., Hugh Hefner, Robert L. Vesco, the Motion Picture Association, Angie Dickinson, Burt Lancaster, Joe DiMaggio, and many, many others. Then, of course, there are the Cabinet members, diplomats, senators, and other big-shots who call him constantly, either in connection with real or "anticipated" problems, and every bit as meaningful, there are the frequent calls from lawyers who find themselves in trouble with the law.

All that is in addition to being active president of the Washington Redskins and treasurer of the National Democratic Party. There is no question that Williams is one of the power-brokers in Washington.

Williams was born in Hartford, Connecticut, on May 31, 1920. His family was this side of impoverished (which he claims is totally irrelevant to his success). A graduate of Holy Cross, he obtained his law degree from Georgetown University in 1945—he was an honor student all the way. His first job, with one of Washington's most prestigious law firms, lasted four years, and he spent virtually every day from September to June trying cases. Next, he opened his own one-room office in Washington and tried every kind of case imaginable. From 1946–58 he was professor of criminal law and evidence at Georgetown University Law School. In 1954 he was guest professor on criminal law at the University of Frankfurt in Germany. And in 1973 he was a guest lecturer in constitutional litigation at Yale University. Since then, he has lectured at numerous other universities and colleges.

From the time he first set his sights on becoming a trial lawyer, Williams was destined to become a public figure; yet he remains a very private person. It had taken me several months to arrange an interview with him, and he agreed to see me only as an accommodation to a mutual friend. There was perhaps another "only": I was a fellow lawyer earnestly trying to write about that group whom Williams regards as the most affable and interesting of them all, the trial bar.

His office, like the presence of the man himself, is massive. It is tastefully decorated and replete with awards, plaques, testimonials, and autographed pictures of the most eminent of the eminent. Although he is younger than most grand masters, Williams is the most impressive. I was struck at once with what has been described by many writers and courtroom buffs as his boyishness (emanating from a two-hundred-pound man!).

Williams let me know straight away that he really cherishes his privacy and assiduously avoids granting interviews to the press, appearing on television programs, and the like. He simply changed, he said. Although in the past he had delighted in seeing his name in print, it now means nothing to him.

As is true of most people whose business it is to be appealing and fascinating, Williams has an engaging smile and an easy way with anecdotes and jokes. But when it comes to his craft—the law—there is an instant personality change; he is sober and contemplative, the most serious of scholars.

At first we conversed about our mutual friend and exchanged the usual pleasantries. When we turned to the subject of my visit, Williams immediately became "all-business." He reviewed the names of the grand masters I had chosen to write about and thought there were "glaring" insufficiencies in the list. I rationalized that some of the men he named were not being included because I felt that the nature of their trial work would not be of general interest to anybody but specialists. It didn't quite satisfy him. According to Williams, a great trial lawyer must have the capacity to try all kinds of cases with equal skill in virtually every field and every kind of court.

The reputations of many so-called great lawyers are based, he said, on the "simple stuff" they tried, admittedly with "consummate skill." He does not believe, for example, that a lawyer whose sole expertise is in trying crimes of violence or negligence deserves to be called great, skilled as he may be. Those areas of trial work, though interesting and headline-making, hardly manifest any growth on the part of the lawyer.

He said: "I think you have to be able, to try complex antitrust cases . . . to master difficult economic facts. You have to be able to master crafts and arts that are wholly different from the ones in which you have expertise. Unless you are able to do all those things—and then even take the case on appeal and make a superb appellate argument in a tribunal like the Supreme Court of the United States—I don't regard you as a great advocate. A lot of people are hailed in the press as great trial lawyers who can't do any of those things. . . . There's no way they can do them. There are other trial lawyers, probably unknown outside of the profession, who meet those qualifications."

Williams feels strongly that it is every lawyer's right *and* obligation to defend causes as well as people, no matter how unpopular they happen to be. He has been criticized for defending thieves, Communists, murderers, embezzlers, and scoundrels of all sorts; but he insists that his responsibility is as an advocate, not as a judge or jury.

Time and again, he has waged courtroom war against frustrated government prosecutors and others who, unable to prove any real crimes which they feel have been committed, resort to trumped-up charges for which the transgressor *can* be convicted. Not only do some prosecutors proceed on bogus charges but they do so on evidence received from plea bargaining or other dangerous solicitation of perjured or tainted evidence.

The public, unfortunately, tends to associate the lawyer with the cause espoused by his client, when in fact the counselor is concerned solely with the legal issues involved in the case. As Williams points out, doctors are not maligned or deprecated for performing their specialty on criminals or other "undesirables." Why should lawyers be condemned for representing unpopular people or causes? The Constitution and the laws of this country must be applied equally to all citizens.

Williams wrote: "This is a basic rule of logic, finding expression in the Sixth Amendment to the Constitution of the United States, which makes it the obligation of a lawyer, in my opinion, to afford his counsel to anyone who seeks it, so long as it is sought within the limits of integrity and decency.

"I say it is an obligation for this reason: When the founding fathers wrote the Bill of Rights and it became a part of the Constitution, they gave to every accused the right to counsel, no matter what the accusation might be, and no matter who the person might be. It does not say every accused except a Communist, or every accused except a narcotics peddler, or every accused except a murderer—it says that *everyone* has the right to counsel.

"This is true, and must continue true, no matter how obnoxious an individual may be personally, no matter how offensive he may be politically. . . . It is true also of any person accused of violence, regardless of the nature of his crime or how strongly the evidence may point to his 'guilt.' It is especially true when he has already been convicted in the court of public opinion. This man, and every man, has the right to trial and it is the obligation of his lawyer to raise for him every possible defense that is authorized by the law of the land.

"Now, rights and duties, as I understand them, are correlative ideas. There cannot be a right for one person without a corresponding duty on the part of someone else to respect it. I am convinced that a man's right to a trial and to counsel bespeaks the duty on the part of my profession to afford that counsel whenever it is honestly sought.

"You may ask: What is 'honestly sought'? I mean that a lawyer is always called on to defend a man, but never called on to accept and use weapons of fraud. Suppose a man comes and says, 'I am charged with bank robbery. I know that you are the best advocate in the country and I want you to represent me. I will pay you a big fee because I don't want to go to jail for thirty years. Now I did it, but I want you to get me off. I'll get a couple of witnesses who will produce an alibi for me and, of course, I'll take the stand and deny it.'

"These are weapons of fraud, outside the standards of honesty, and the lawyer cannot take that case. Here is a man who wants to commit perjury and suborn perjury. The lawyer can only turn him down and refuse his case; in fact, throw him out.

"But there is no reason why this same man cannot have a defense, provided it is an honest defense. He has every right to ask for the aid of a lawyer, provided he simply wants his constitutional right of trial and wants the government's case tested in the crucible of cross-examination, while he himself stands silent and offers no evidence.

"In such a case, which may very well seem to the layman to be a complete paradox of justice, we must immediately make the fundamental and essential distinction between *moral* guilt and *legal* guilt. As we use the term 'guilt' here, we are concerned with it only as a legal term. It is essential that this fact be understood; that always we are talking of guilt only within the law. The making of moral judgments is beyond us, and should be, for they are within the exclusive jurisdiction of God." *

I asked Williams what particular quality, in his opinion, is vital to the make-up of a great trial lawyer. "The 'affidavit' quality," he said (by which he meant the ability to seem sincere or truthful to a court or jury). "It must appear very often that what he says is true simply because he says it is true."

Such a quality requires the advocate to avoid overstating, and sometimes it requires him to do or say things that seem counterproductive to his interests. He has to tell the jury about the weaknesses of his case as well as the strength: "You have to have all of the cosmetics of fair play; and I have found over a quarter of a century that, certainly, the best way to have all the cosmetics of fair play is to *do* fair play."

Williams and I found ourselves in a friendly controversy over the percentages of success in cases handled by grand masters as compared to those by run-of-the-mill lawyers. His notion is that the grand master makes only a twenty-per-cent difference.

"I think that the facts are so powerful in some cases," he said, "that it doesn't make any difference who the advocate is. There are certain areas in which the most effective advocate can't bring about the desired results—just as the greatest surgeon can't perform a successful operation in some cases and he loses his patient. I think that in the kinds of cases I deal in, which are hotly contested, hard, often complex cases of importance, the advocate may swing a twenty-per-cent difference. And, of course, if you are the client, you'll want the advocate who'll get you the three-to-two edge, instead of one with a three-to-two edge against you."

The average person, he says, really has no comprehension of what the end result is in a great majority of criminal cases across this country. Each year, about thirty-five thousand federal criminal cases are instituted, and Williams says: "Suppose you went down now with your tape recorder and interviewed the first ten people who walked up the street and you said, 'Now, I'm the inquiring photographer. There are thirty-five thousand criminal cases brought by the U.S. government every year. How many of those people do you think end up convicted?' You would hear estimates ranging from ten to forty per cent. 'Oh, everybody gets off,' you'd hear. 'About ten per cent get convicted.' The

* A. Love and S. J. Childers, *Listen to Leaders in Law* (New York: Holt, Rinehart & Winston, 1963).

EDWARD BENNETT WILLIAMS

fact of the matter is—I can guarantee to you as a result of long and careful study on this subject, on all its facets, jury trials, nonjury trials, defendants who took the stand, defendants who didn't take the stand—that about ninety per cent of all those persons who were charged with crimes end up convicted. Of course, you have a large number of guilty pleas, but you've got a tremendous percentage of convictions."

Paradoxically enough, Williams' batting average may be lower than those of many grand masters, although he is a superior lawyer. For the most part, however, the others deal in fields far less complicated than those plowed by Williams. In many of his cases, the fact patterns and the evidence are so overwhelming that even his skill cannot overcome them. By the time he is called into an antitrust case, for example, or a complicated securities-fraud case, the government may have amassed tens of thousands of pieces of evidence pointing to the guilt of Williams' client. It is not easy to argue with years' and sometimes decades' worth of records. It is a lot easier in a murder case—where it is the cops against the bad guys—to turn the matter around and call the cops the bad guys, the eyewitnesses brainwashed, and the defendant a "setup."

"Curiouser" still—on the subject of Williams' batting average—is the fact that much of his trial practice is against inexperienced young assistant U.S. attorneys of indisputably inferior ability. These young men, however, are armed with the full resources of the government's power and money, can investigate the facts of a case, collate the material, and come to trial well prepared.

Who among the grand masters is the best? Courtroom buffs argue the point in much the same way that sports fans argue about their athletes. Champions of one or the other grand masters—whose forte is, say, the negligence field—will argue that while Williams is struggling against inept prosecutors, *their* man is often pitted against an equal; therefore, his triumphs are more fairly and harder won.

There is one point on which all grand masters firmly agree, and that is that a great trial necessarily involves great art. Williams said, "I think the trial of the case is the most challenging creative art there is. I had a debate one time with a fellow named Robert Ross, who made the best motion picture I ever saw. He said the greatest thing in life was to be able to produce, direct, and write a motion picture because nothing could tax so many talents. I said I thought that the greatest creative art was to try a major criminal case in which you are circumscribed by the facts; you have no retakes; you have no backdrops; you have no lights. You really are all at once the producer, director, and writer because you can take the same facts, you can take the same answer, which is a truthful answer, and you can create a positive impression or you can do something that is wholly neutral or negative.

"I have seen it happen a hundred times. I do it every time in my cases. The most important preparation in our trials is to work with the principal actor, namely, the defendant in a criminal case. We prepare him for hours and hours and hours. We subject him to the most grueling cross-examination that you can conjure up with the longest flight of your imagaination. We just work and work and work with him so that everything that could possibly be asked of him he is prepared to answer. And if an answer that is truthful is disadvantageous to him, we try to put it in the best possible light—and there are hundreds of ways to do that."

When asked whether or not this "preparation" furthered the cause of justice, Williams replied, "It furthers the cause of the defendant that I am representing and the adversary system. It furthers the administration of justice, in my judgment. It is my responsibility in that courtroom to represent this defendant.

"You take a witness and he comes in here and sits in that chair and I'm preparing him for his cross-examination. It's a brutal scene. I had prepared Adam Clayton Powell to be cross-examined in New York one time. I remember that we were working in my apartment and I was really letting him have it with all guns blazing. And Faye Emerson, the television actress, dropped by because we were all going to P. J. Clarke's for drinks and she sat there because we hadn't quite finished. I went at him for about forty-five minutes, and after a half-hour, she burst into tears and left. She said, 'I didn't know what kind of a son-of-a-bitch you were. This is the worst thing I've ever seen!' "

The ethics and propriety of trial "preparation" often provoke lively disputes. Just about every trial lawyer with even a modicum of experience instructs his client to answer "yes" if asked, "Did you discuss this case or your testimony with your attorney before appearing in court today?" That should be fairly obvious, since no jury would believe a witness who denied consulting his own lawyer about his own case. The courtroom setting, its illusion of spontaneous answers to spontaneous questions, is at best misleading. All lawyers use cosmetics on the testimony of their clients and witnesses, to the extent that they are permitted to do so.

Williams wanted me to imagine a trial in which where he was on a particular date was relevant. If I asked the question, and he answered it with "I don't know," the jury certainly would not consider that answer a "plus," and it might not even consider it a "minus." Perhaps the jury would simply say they didn't know where they were on that date, either. "But," Williams added: "if I say to you in response to that question: 'Mr. Sheresky, I thought you were going to ask me that, and I have racked my recollection to try to ascertain where I was. I have searched my records because I want to help. I want to help you ferret out every last fact in this case, and I want the jury to know all the facts. For the life of me I cannot find out where I was that night. I'm sorry, but I just can't find out. I have no independent recollection.' That is a very different answer but it's the same truth, isn't it? That is the difference between a good advocate and a bad advocate. A good advocate tells his witness how to answer. That may be just a little vignette out of a long drama, but it's a plus. And you keep getting plusses and plusses and plusses and you win! Or, you get nothing and nothing and nothing and you lose."

While the example can hardly be argued with, if the jury is impressed by a witness who seems to have racked his brain searching for a date in order to be helpful to them, a favorable but misleading impression has been made, even on the facts hypothesized by Williams. It was Williams who impressed the jury by telling his client what to say. And a client who scores points or plusses by *seeming* to answer questions spontaneously and truthfully, but in a manner suggested by his lawyer, is still fooling the jury.

The only full and truthful answer to "Where were you on the date in question?" would be: "I don't know where I was, but my lawyer said I should tell you that I have searched my records and want to help the jury, et cetera, et cetera."

Trial lawyers in general, and the grand masters even more specifically, tend to regard themselves as ministers of justice. It is useless to argue with any of them that what they do in any way perverts rather than promotes justice. The infinite skill with which they cosmeticize testimony and stage the presentation of their cases seems to require first and foremost their belief that what they are doing is right. There is no way to convince Williams that if Frank Costello couldn't hire him, our system of law would not have collapsed. His analogy that even a criminal with a serious disease is entitled to a doctor, and therefore an attorney, is obviously imperfect. As Judge Herbert Stern points out, a criminal who gets a disease gets it honestly. The criminal's need for a lawyer is something else again.

So, too, with the other grand masters. There is no way to convince Louis Nizer that his oft-repeated statement—"I am ineffective in representing clients in whose causes I do not passionately believe"—is almost a shibboleth. Nizer has represented clients, as has every grand master, whose causes were nonexistent and whose life-style merited scorn instead of the bounty which is a Nizer defense. Williams and Nizer are great personal friends. It is rather telling and amusing how they regard each other's philosophy, however. Williams says that Nizer's notion that he has passionately to believe in a client's cause is "a lot of bunk." He points out that Nizer represents corporate clients on annual retainers, that he represents them whether he passionately believes in them or not. He said that he's seen Nizer represent clients whose causes were so without merit that he had to scratch his head and wonder how he did it.

On the other hand Nizer, who appreciates Williams' talents as much as any other trial lawyer, thinks that some of Williams' notions, such as the supposed duty of a lawyer to represent anybody, no matter how distasteful the cause, are equally self-deceptive. The fact is that trial lawyers are no more perceptive about themselves than are any of the rest of us. Their talents do not seem to include the ability to analyze themselves. Perhaps one of the reasons that they are so likable and affable is their ability to make heroes not only of their clients but of themselves, and they have had years of experience in playing the parts they have created.

But whatever makes Williams tick, it's nothing short of fascinating to watch him operate.

I asked Williams how he was able to convince the government not to prosecute former CIA Director Helms, who concededly authorized the clearly questionable entry of CIA agents into a private photo studio. I

EDWARD BENNETT WILLIAMS

told him that I was particularly surprised that the Justice Department would announce its decision in an atmosphere in which press and public, in the aftermath of the Watergate scandals, were crying for some more top-level blood.

Williams told me that he simply told various top-level government officials that if his client Helms were indicted, he was going to use the Freedom of Information Act in a way it was never used before. Williams said he would demand, on Helms's behalf, disclosure of every illegal wiretap, every illegal entry, every violation by government officials of citizens' rights for a period of at least five years. He then said that he was going to take that information to Assistant Attorney General J. Stanley Pottinger, head of the Civil Rights Division of the Justice Department, and the same attorney general whose obligation it would be to prosecute Helms.

Williams said, "I told Pottinger: if you indict Helms, I'm going to make you the busiest assistant attorney general in the history of America. I'm going to take all those cases that I learn about under the Freedom of Information Act, and I'm going to ask you to prosecute every one of them. And if you don't, I'm going to make a motion to dismiss any indictment of Helms on the theory of selective prosecution." With the same alert twinkle in his eye that he always gets when discussing his cases, he explained that the government can prosecute anyone that it wants to under existing statutes, but it can't selectively apply this to just one instance and ignore a host of others. Obviously, Williams' tactics were successful, since the government almost immediately thereafter announced its decision to drop the Helms case.

Williams is deeply troubled over the role of lawyers in the political community. When he delivered the commencement address at Suffolk University Law School, where he was awarded a doctoral degree, he told the prospective lawyers that it was time for attorneys "to clean out our house before it becomes an Augean stable." He said, "It's time for grave introspection. The reputation of our profession has been battered unmercifully by the score of lawyers who have been convicted or indicted for felonious conduct in the highest positions of the executive branches of government." Speaking of the Watergate scandals, he said that the community had been "offered the dismaying spectacle of lawyers in the highest reaches of government conspiring to obstruct justice, plotting to pay hush money to convicted burglars, contriving to suborn perjury, and planning vendettas against their political opponents by the use of the machinery of government. . . . I ask you passionately, for the sake of yourselves, your profession, and the administration of justice, never to compromise your principles."

As much as Williams abhors the "Watergate mentality" which infected the government under Nixon, he seems to dislike the bureaucratic hypocrisy which has grown out of that scandal even more. Speaking, for example, about the hue and cry about disclosures that various members of the intelligence community may have been less than candid under oath to various Senate committees. Williams expresses a good deal of outrage.

He scoffs at the notion that there is any justice in prosecuting government servants for dedicated service under rules that they never made, probably didn't like, and wouldn't have followed were it not necessary to do so. When they came to Washington these men were told—by the same coaches who want their scalps today—that in Washington "you are free to do anything in the lexicon of crime except rape and sodomy." Now, with two minutes left in the fourth quarter, the rules are being changed and the same people who laid down those rules are claiming that they were violated. While Williams' argument has a good deal of plausibility, in the sense that it seems unfair for government officials to complain about their own rules, it leaves much unanswered. The public knew nothing about the rules, and it is for them that the laws prohibiting such rules were legislated. While it would have been unfair for Hitler to have complained about von Ribbentrop's conduct, it doesn't seem unfair for the German people to have complained. "They made me do it" is an all-too-familiar and abhorrent refrain in the law.

The more one watches Ed Williams operate, the less apocryphal seems the after-dinner story told about him by his good friend, Washington columnist Art Buchwald. In describing why Williams became a lawyer, Buchwald told a law-school audience, "One day, while he was walking home from school, he saw a man being led out of an insurance-company building in handcuffs, surrounded by FBI agents. Williams asked what the man did and he was told that he had embezzled twenty million dollars from women and children, and he was going to end up in prison. Incensed by the injustice of it all, Edward Williams vowed then and there that he would become a trial lawyer and," concluded Buchwald, "no swindlers have gone to jail since then."

Although he enjoys the image, as other grand masters do, of himself as a guardian of the underdog, he is more realistic than many of the others in regarding the job of advocacy as an art and not a sacred calling. I reminded him of a recent case when, after pleading one of his enormously wealthy clients guilty of violations of criminal statutes, Williams made a passionate, eloquent, and somewhat irrelevant plea to the judge, before sentencing, about how the man had suffered enough. While it may be true that the man had suffered, I pointed out to Williams that the plain unvarnished facts were that his client had violated the statutes more flagrantly than had anyone else, including some who had been put in jail, and he hadn't hesitated to involve many innocent parties. I asked Williams whether he didn't feel a little queasy about the fact that the judge simply fined the man and imposed no jail sentence. He said he didn't and that he simply had done the best he could.

Williams has a good sense of humor. At a dinner honoring Joe DiMaggio at the time of the Watergate scandals, he told the audience, "If I'm nervous it's because I am a Washington democrat and this is the first time in two years that I have talked into a microphone that I can see." And referring to former Attorney General John Mitchell, he said, "He's done for all future campaign managers what the Boston Strangler did for door-to-door salesmen."

During one of our interviews, Williams told me that Richard Nixon had twice asked Rabbi Baruch Korff (the former President's stanchest ally, fund raiser, and friend) to try to induce Williams to defend Nixon in the post-Watergate litigation which has been plaguing the former President. When I asked him why Rabbi Korff loaned himself to some of the asinine statements made by him and on behalf of Nixon, Williams said that the rabbi reminded him of Judge Mike Musmanno. The judge used to carry out outlandish feuds with other judges which enraged the public, the press, other lawyers, and appellate judges, and managed to get his name in the paper every day. After one such feud, one of his friends asked him, "Mike, why do you have these damned-fool arguments that end up in the newspapers?" The judge replied, "Well, ten years ago when I walked across the street against the red light, people would say, 'Look at that dumb son-of-a-bitch walking against the red light.' Now, when I do the same thing, people say, 'Look at that dumb son-of-a-bitch Judge Musmanno, walking against the red light.' "

The trouble with Ed Williams is that there is too much to say about him. As a grand master he is without peer. He is presently thinking about going into public service. He seriously considered running for senator in Maryland but was persuaded from doing so because of the 1976 Presidential campaigns and his obligations as treasurer of the National Democratic Party. But he thinks sooner or later he will enter politics more formally.

I suggested to him that I would like to write a biography of him. "Yeah," he said, "but I don't want any of those cosmetic, authorized jobs." He made it clear that he would be interested—but only if the biography was a lot more than the self-serving "garbage" that usually gets written about famous personalities who are still alive. But it would be a loss to the public and to the legal profession if all that has been written about this grand master is what is in the press, in *Who's Who*, in assorted magazine pieces, and in these few pages. Consider, just as a sampler, Williams' genius in *U.S.* v. *Icardi*. . . .

A SUBCOMMITTEE'S SUBTERFUGE

Thumbing through the trial transcripts of cases tried by Edward Williams is pretty much like rummaging through the pages of Ernest Hemingway or listening to the records of Enrico Caruso. They are all exceptional. Although some may be better than others, the Williams touch, that special gift or genius, is always there. When people talk about his work, involving people of equal or lesser fame, different "favorites" usually emerge; but invariably and without exception, everyone will marvel at his craftsmanship.

One of Williams' masterpieces was the 1956 *U.S.* v. *Icardi* case, in which this strategist supreme soft-pedaled his way to victory by "psyching out"—and totally wiping out—the opposition. Completely unaware that they were being disarmed, government counsel was left holding the biggest bag of unfired ammunition that Williams had come up against in years.

The story had its beginnings in September 1944, when a Major William Holohan and four other men (one of whom was Lieutenant Aldo Icardi) were selected by the Office of Strategic Services (OSS) to go on what became the famous "Chrysler Mission." These five volunteers were dropped behind enemy lines in Italy as part of the U.S. effort to bring unity and cohesion to several competing Italian underground movements. Their mission was to coordinate these partisan groups with the Allied drive, to supply necessary funds and leadership, and to prevent open conflict among the competing factions.

On December 6, 1944, at a critical point in the mission, Major Holohan mysteriously disappeared. The mystery deepened when it was later learned that he was killed on that date. Subsequently, various fingers of suspicion were pointed at Icardi, and volumes of "evidence" were amassed against him—all this long after his discharge from the army.

By 1951 certain "facts" began to emerge concerning the major's disappearance and death. But there was one fact for sure: There was no effective way at that time of prosecuting Icardi for his alleged crime. There was simply no existing legislation that would permit the prosecution of ex-servicemen, after their discharge, for crimes committed during service. Early in 1951 (largely as a result of the Icardi case and the work of the House Armed Services Committee) such legislation was passed. However, since the law did not exist at the time of Holohan's murder or of Icardi's severance from the service, it would be impossible to bring Icardi to trial retroactively.

The new law did not satisfy Congressmen W. Sterling Cole from New York and Carl Vinson of Georgia, who was the head of the House Armed Services Committee. According to them, there was a possibility that further legislation might be necessary; and as a result, a special subcommittee was appointed and duly constituted under the Eighty-second Congress. It consisted of Congressmen Cole and Paul J. Kilday of Texas.

In December 1951 and January 1952 this subcommittee met and received oral testimony from Michael Stern, a foreign correspondent for *True* magazine, and from Henry Manfredi, who was chief agent of the U.S. Criminal Investigation Division. It also received statements of several persons in Italy and of Sergeant Carl LoDolce, one of the original Chrysler Mission members. All the testimony fixed responsibility for Holohan's death upon Icardi.

The subcommittee had also received information from the files of the OSS and the Criminal Investigation Division, including Icardi's own version of the events leading up to Holohan's death. Icardi had denied any implication of guilt in the major's murder, and pointed out that, because of the particular circumstances surrounding the Chrysler Mission, there were many people who had reason to kill the major—some of whom had supplied the information tending to implicate Icardi.

Public hoopla over this case continued to be generated in the press and elsewhere to the point that more than a year later—in March 1953—a special subcommittee (again, Cole and Kilday) was again constituted to investigate the Holohan affair. They invited Icardi to appear in Washington for questioning on March 26.

Icardi appeared voluntarily and was warned that anything he said might be used against him in future proceedings; but he testified freely, nonetheless. He was the only witness questioned at that time. (Some two months later, it should be noted, testimony was taken from Colonel Ralph Pierce, who had conducted a lie-detector test of Icardi in 1947. From that test, he had concluded that Icardi did not kill Holohan, and that he probably did not know who did.)

As a direct result of the March 26, 1953, hearing, Lieutenant Icardi found himself indicted for perjury for allegedly lying to the subcommittee about his involvement in Holohan's death. Williams then undertook to defend Icardi and found himself once more pitted against the government in a fascinating major criminal case, in which all the resources of the government and its investigatory branches were massed against him. The army and the subcommittees had been collecting data relating to the Chrysler Mission for years and years prior to any crime's having been attributed to Icardi. The government had files swelling with evidence: Icardi had only Williams.

From the very beginning, it was basic to Williams' strategy in defending Icardi that there might exist a technical defense, and a very good one. What on earth was the legislative purpose of holding *any* hearings some nine years after Holohan's death, when (a) there already existed legislation recommended by the very same subcommittee that had conducted those earlier hearings, and under which a crime such as that alleged to have been committed by Icardi could now be prosecuted, and (b) when all the evidence relating to Holohan's death, including Icardi's own statements, had already been collected and published at prior hearings and during another session of Congress? Was there a *real* legislative purpose—or had the subcommittee simply decided that Icardi was probably guilty of one crime (murder), and since he could not be prosecuted for that, he should be "brought to justice" by being prosecuted for perjury?

There are many constitutional questions involved in the permissibility of conducting legislative inquiries, and they are complex. Surely, congressional committees have been and must be granted wide discretion in the matter of conducting hearings to determine the adequacy of existing legislation and the need for new legislation. It is generally not for the courts to tell the legislative branch how to gather facts, what facts to gather, and what facts they should determine are material and relevant. But since the days of the House Un-American

Activities Committee and McCarthy, the public and the courts have learned to draw the line between legislative witch hunts and legitimate legislative inquiries. Although the matter is heavily weighted, as it must be, in favor of legitimizing the right of Congress to investigate matters upon which it wishes to consider legislation, there is a presumption of validity to government proceedings.

Now, Edward Bennett Williams knew full well in this case that a defense founded frankly upon the technical shortcomings of the perjury indictment and resting on a claim of illegitimate legislative purpose, would have about as much human-interest appeal to a jury as would an advanced course in trigonometry. Also, it might not succeed before a judge. He knew, too, that it would be difficult, if not impossible, to prove his point if he telegraphed his intentions of making a big to-do over his notion that the Cole-Kilday subcommittee's hearing had been without any bona fide legislative purpose. It is always the government's obligation in a criminal proceeding involving perjury before a congressional committee to prove that the witness deliberately lied concerning material facts in a material inquiry. If the government and members of the committee were to know in advance that Williams was going to attack the legitimacy of the congressional investigation, they would certainly have been tempted to ramble on at great length as to why Icardi's testimony was essential to a legitimate inquiry. No, decided Williams, much better to take a back road.

In 1956 the case of *U.S.* v. *Icardi* came on before U.S. District Judge Richmond B. Keech and a jury. Everything that Williams said to government counsel or to the press apparently centered on Icardi's only possible defense: He did not lie to any congressional committee at any time; he did not kill Major Holohan; he did not know who killed the major, but there were plenty of suspects.

Not once did Williams imply that lack of legislative purpose was on his mind. So far as anyone knew, Icardi and Williams were in court to defend the honor of a brave lieutenant who had volunteered for duty behind enemy lines in the service of his country. Williams' opening remarks to the jury were dramatic, well organized—and designed to be distracting as well as totally irrelevant:

> May it please the court, ladies and gentlemen of the jury: What Mr. Woerheide [the prosecutor] said to you yesterday afternoon, as His Honor indicated to you, was his opening state-

ment in this case. It is not evidence in the case. It is a statement of what he hopes to prove to you throughout the course of this trial. And likewise, what I say to you now is the opening statement made on behalf of the defendant. It isn't evidence in the case. Rather, it is a statement of what we expect to prove to you when the opportunity comes to us.

Following the opening statements, under the rules of this court, the government has the opportunity to put in its case first and to call its witnesses and to elicit from them the testimony that they will give to you from the witness stand here in this courtroom; and not until all of the government's case is in does the opportunity come to us to call our witnesses.

And so, at the outset, I ask you only to keep an open mind during the course of this trial, bearing in mind, not until all the prosecution's case is in may we go forward.

(Whether the jury were to keep its mind open or shut "during the course of this trial" was hardly of any consequence to Williams, since it was not his intention to pursue the course he had declared.)

Now, much will be said in this trial about an organization known as the Office of Strategic Services—the OSS. We will show you that the OSS came into existence by order of President Roosevelt during World War II in 1942. We will show you that it was a secret government agency, created for a twofold purpose: first, to get information about the enemy and, second, to sabotage the war potential and the morale of the enemy.

(And a little more of Williams' window-dressing):

It was headed up by a man named General William J. Donovan of New York, more familiarly known as General "Wild Bill" Donovan of World War I renown. Its personnel was comprised of members of all three branches of the military services as well as civilians. It was called the "Cloak and Dagger" outfit of World War II, and it worked in conjunction with the underground movements in Italy, in Germany, and in occupied France.

As a newly commissioned officer, up from the ranks of corporal, fresh off the campus of the University of Pittsburgh, twenty-three years old, Aldo Icardi, the evidence will show, was asked by his commanding officer at Camp Edwards, Massachusetts, if he would volunteer for a dangerous mission, perhaps behind enemy lines.

We will show you that he was slated then for service with the OSS. We will show you that at that time, by reason of the fact that he spoke the Italian language fluently, he was scheduled for a mission in Italy.

We will show you further that, without hesitation, he volunteered. He was sent to Washington, D.C., and from there to a secret hiding place in the hills of Maryland where he was exhaustively and intensively drilled and schooled in espionage, in sabotage, and in just the plain business of keeping alive behind enemy lines.

Now, in order to understand fully the significance and the implications of the bizarre facts that will be unfolded before you from this witness stand throughout the course of this trial, it is necessary that you have a knowledge of the situation that existed in war-ravaged Italy in late 1943 and in 1944. It is necessary that you know the backdrop of the dramatic facts that make up this case.

And so we shall show you, members of the jury, what that situation was, because it forms a vital part of this case.

Williams, the master storyteller and technician, then proceeded to provide the "necessary" knowledge by painting a vivid picture of the situation in war-torn Italy. He "showed" the members of the jury—via painstakingly precise historical flashbacks complete with dates, names, titles, and maps—what had happened to Italy politically, militarily, and emotionally from July 1943 until September 1944, when the Chrysler Mission entered the scene. One got the impression that he was touring over painfully familiar terrain as he dealt dramatically with the bombing of Rome, with Mussolini and Hitler, King Victor Emmanuel, and finally the Allies' landing at Anzio.

From there, he segued into a behind-the-scenes look at the Communist and non-Communist partisan groups which were intent on ousting the Nazis and the Fascists. Williams, the educator, had his student body of jurors (as well as the court and government counsel) listening with cliff-hanging attention as he continued to spin his documentary tale of intrigue and internal conflict:

Now the Allied leaders, as they marched their troops up the peninsula, feared that once the Germans were driven out of north Italy and once the Mussolini government was overthrown, finally, that civil war would break out among these partisans who had just as much hostility toward each other as they had toward the Nazis. They were joined only to drive the Nazis out. . . .

So they decided that a mission had to be formed to go in behind this line [pointing at a map] up into the heart of the enemy, a mission of Americans, to do two things: to provide some form of leadership for these partisans, and to keep in communication with the advancing Allied leaders. . . . And by keeping them advised as to the conditions back there, to prevent the outbreak of open warfare among these partisan groups. . . .

And so there came into existence in September 1944 what was known as the Chrysler Mission. . . . Five men were selected from the American Army to serve in the mission . . . to fly up behind enemy lines, parachute in onto the mountains, do the job for which the mission was set up.

Williams went on to name the five men: Major Holohan, Lieutenant Icardi, Sergeant LoDolce—and a sergeant and a lieutenant (both of whom subsequently disappeared in a Nazi mop-up). He described the briefing they had been given, with emphasis on the partisan movement in north Italy, the terrain, and survival in the Alps. When the mission was finally ready, he said, the men were given money (and the jury was given a breakdown—immaterial, of course—of the various currencies involved). The money was for survival behind enemy lines, but, more important, it could buy information.

Williams proceeded to describe, in exquisite detail, the mission's heroic transfer into enemy territory. His graphic grasp of the facts gave an I-was-there feeling to his story:

In September they came down to North Africa [pointing] . . . and on the dark and moonless night of September 26, 1944, the evidence will show, they took off from Maison-Blanche Airfield in

Algiers in a B-17, a Flying Fortress. There were two Flying Fortresses to carry these men, because they had to jump through the hole in the floor simultaneously, and only four could jump with sufficient speed to get out over the appointed dropping place, and so another bomber had to be supplied for the fifth man. Since they had to supply that bomber anyway for the fifth man, they sent three Italian partisans, who were going up there on other business, along with the mission.

And now, having put parachutes on his entire courtroom audience, Williams faithfully flew them up the Italian peninsula, where "they were fired upon, flak burst around them, but they got through despite the fact that the plane was hit."

Having gotten everyone safely into north Italy, Williams then plunged them into the perilous drop—onto a rough mountain between two lakes:

> . . . When they got over the mountains, they opened the slide and jumped into the night and into the midst of the enemy. . . . But they landed near the signal fires that had been lit for them by partisans who had been alerted to receive them; and on the night of September 26, 1944, they were taken, under cover of darkness, to the village of Coiromonte, and they were housed by friendly partisans who put them up and gave them shelter and food.
>
> We will show you that garrisoned along the western shore of Lake Maggiore were thousands of Nazi troops. Garrisoned along the eastern shore were Fascist troops. So that they were literally surrounded by the enemy on the top of the mountain. Within a radius of two or three miles from this American mission on all sides were enemy troops.

At this point, Williams left our mission at the village and went on to display a staggering knowledge of partisan activities at that time in Italian history. In a series of We-will-show-yous, he dipped into the backgrounds of the leaders of the two partisan groups. On one, Moscatelli, he covered birthplace, schooling, political dedication, his imprisonment and release, his guerrilla campaigns—ending with the important office which he held after the war. About the other, we learned of a dif-

EDWARD BENNETT WILLIAMS

ferent kind of guerrilla warfare and leadership . . . of his seeking assistance from the American mission, which sent two of its members to help, and in the ensuing Nazi action, this leader was killed, and the mission lost the sergeant and the lieutenant referred to earlier.

Williams now returned the jury to the three remaining members of the mission who had been living among the partisans at the village for about a month. The partisans, it seems, had begun to talk loosely "about the presence of the daring Americans behind the lines," and so our intrepid trio decided to move their operation into the safety of the mountains.

Enter Giorgio—that was his battle or partisan name—"about whom Mr. Woerheide indicated yesterday you will hear much in this case." Williams:

Early in the game, Giorgio had offered help to the Americans. He had an intelligence service up here in this area [pointing]. Information was constantly fed to him concerning Fascist and Nazi troop movements. Giorgio had friends all through the area. Giorgio was daring. And so the mission began to rely upon Giorgio. They got information from him. He got their food for them. He got their clothing for them. He changed their money for them, and he provided all those little services so necessary for a band of men living behind the enemy lines. So when they decided to move, because they feared capture, it was to Giorgio that they turned.

And Giorgio said, "I will find you a place to live." True enough: he had a place for them and provided two men as guides and as aides during the move, which of course was fraught with danger. And on October 19 they came down from the mountain. They came down to the east side of Lake Orta and rowed across the lake and went into the foothills of the Alps to a village called Egro, and there Giorgio had a place for them to stay with a partisan family. But the place was not suitable because they could not get radio reception adequate for them there and could not transmit with their radio transmitter from that position; and so, without the lifeline of radio contact, they could not survive. And so [after a few days] they had to move.

Again they turned to Giorgio, and again it was Giorgio who found them a place, the Villa Maria. . . .

Williams' audience was being treated to a picturesque description of the boarded-up villa resort, where our three mission members—and Giorgio's two aides, Mannini and Tozzini—were destined to spend only a few days. Williams, meantime, spent several pages of transcript to help pass the time at the villa. . . . In this segment, the jury learned how the mission had become almost totally dependent on Giorgio—for food, shelter, intelligence about enemy movements, the aides, "both of whom had lived all their lives near the lakes; they knew every inch of the mountains; they knew the lakes, and they were excellent guides; and they did all the laboring chores."

Suddenly, their benefactor turned greedy. "What is in it for Giorgio?" he asked.

> Up to now the members of the mission had thought that he was serving them out of dedication to the partisan cause. . . . They had paid sums of money to him during the weeks he had been aiding them, but it was always for reimbursement of expenses. But now Giorgio says, "What is in it for me? I am risking my life by helping you. The La Franchi Mission in another section of the Alps, a British intelligence unit, has offered me money. I have got to think of myself."

Having no choice in the matter, Icardi and Holohan (the two remaining officers) agreed to cooperate with Giorgio when he suggested they give him some gold coins which he could exchange on the black market for a profit.

At this point in the saga, the courtroom witnessed still another aspect of the grand master's virtuosity as he switched hats from historian and back to currency expert; and in another series of We-will-show-yous, he led his listeners through a maze of official rates of exchange then-and-now, the lira's fluctuating buying power, complete with black-market evaluations. He would show that Giorgio had indeed made a profit out of his partisan activities, and that he became worried about having to explain his sudden wealth to fellow partisans and the authorities; that he asked the mission to draw up a sham contract, stating that the Americans had invested this money in his toy factory in which Icardi had thus become a partner. And Williams would further show that Icardi never received one penny therefrom, "that at no time has he made any profit from this whole transaction which is in dispute

EDWARD BENNETT WILLIAMS

in this case"; and that he had so testified before the Congress in 1952.

The story of the trials and tribulations of the Chrysler Mission was proving to be a long and complicated one; but the court, the jury, and opposing counsel found themselves paying rapt attention to the scholarly storyteller who had done his homework so well. After all, there was a great deal at stake here—a brave soldier's honor and certainly his future. Williams apparently was out to prove Icardi's innocence, and all this documentation surely must be germane to the case he was making. The court listened respectfully, the jury struggled to digest every detail, and the prosecutors' pencils flew as the grand master proceeded to ring up the curtain on the next scene.

Back at the villa . . . We hear rumors of an another impending German mop-up in the area. The mission hurriedly packs and rows out to a small isle where they are hidden in a monastery by two priests.

. . . During the night, Nazi troops rowed out to the monastery. A systematic search was conducted. But the little Italian priests had hidden the mission so well and protected them so zealously that they escaped the Nazis on October 30.

The next day they rowed back to the western shore of Lake Orta, because it had been shown to them that this was not a safe hiding place. They went up into the mountains and lay there one whole night in a driving torrential mountain rain.

On November 1 they abandoned the mountains. They went to the city of Grassona and there one of the same priests hid them again. This time he hid them in his church in a small hole in the roof underneath the ceiling. After they were hidden some Nazi troops came into Grassona. They searched every nook and cranny, and forty of them lived in the church underneath the Americans for five days and five nights.

Finally, the Germans left. The Americans then could come out. They came out and returned that day to the Villa Maria. . . .

On November 25 they moved again, because they dared not stay anywhere for so long as three weeks. This time they moved only a quarter of a mile to the Villa Castelnuovo . . . a large splendid Italian summer home with twenty-two rooms. It was the summer house of a wealthy Italian Fascist who dared not use it during the war. It, too, was boarded up . . . and they [Holohan,

Icardi, LoDolce, and the two aides, Mannini and Tozzini] lived in the basement.

Williams, the artist, continued to smear his courtroom canvas with lurid cloak-and-dagger colors. . . . He drew a pathetic picture of the harassed men who, after only a few days in their new hiding place, learned that the enemy was aware of their presence in the area. On December 5 the two priests who had befriended them earlier came to the villa and told them:

> . . . the rumor was out all over the little town of Orta across the lake that the daring Americans were living at the villa. . . . And the priests implored them to move because they feared this information would fall into the hands of the enemy. We will show you they decided to stay. On the night of December 5, 1944, they did stay. They lay with their eyes open and their guns at the ready throughout that night, waiting for an attack on the villa.

Having brought his listeners, in enviable Alfred Hitchcock style, to the eve of the major's murder, Williams went on to tell how the next day they sent word to Giorgio to get them another place to live, and he sent word back that he was attempting to find such a place. "A light was to be flashed from the Isle of Giulio that night if he located a place." The Americans and the two aides waited. But that evening a fog enveloped the lake and there wasn't a possibility of exchanging signals between the isle and the villa.

> We will show you that in any event the decision was made to leave. . . . They determined that if they had to go back to the hills, they would do so. . . . About nine or ten o'clock that night they had their gear packed.
> We will show you they had a rented boat which was on Lake Orta. It was probably seventy-five or a hundred yards from the edge of the lake to the back of the villa. . . .
> We will show you they carried their equipment down and put it in the boat. They were preparing to leave, and in accordance with their regular habitual plan, one of the partisans was sent back to secure the villa . . . to make sure it was locked and that

EDWARD BENNETT WILLIAMS

there was no evidence left of the fact that the Americans had been there.

Major Holohan, Aldo Icardi, and Carl LoDolce stood on the shore in the fog under cover of dark waiting to shove off; one of the partisans was on the [garden] path and one was closer to the villa.

Suddenly out of the night came the cry *"Chi va la?"*—who goes there?

There was a shot, followed by a blaze of gunfire.

The Americans, pursuant to OSS directives for a mission behind enemy lines, separated instinctively. Their practice was to separate so that all would not be captured and perhaps some could escape.

We will show you that guns blazed at the Villa Castelnuovo. Icardi drew out his .45 and fired. Then he ran north along the lake shore . . . , for as long as his legs could sustain him and as long as he had any wind.

He ran under cover of dark and shrouded by a fog all the way to the village of Capella [to the home of a partisan where Giorgio was living]. He burst in and poured out this story of the attack on the villa.

(At this point, incidentally, and unbeknown to the courtroom audience as yet: exit Giorgio. In his dramatic narrative, Williams had spent much time and description on this seemingly central character, who and he hoped no one would notice, turned out after all to be quite dispensable and "uncrucial" to the ultimate denouement of the story!)

Members of the jury, we will show you that the last time Aldo Icardi saw Major William Holohan, the major was alive, standing at the edge of the water at Lake Orta.

We will show you that the next day LoDolce and Tozzini joined Icardi. They said that they had been at the Villa Maria all night. They had fled together. Mannini did not show up. . . . A search party was instituted to look for the missing men.

The boat wasn't there. The equipment wasn't there. The radio transmitter wasn't there. Holohan and Mannini were missing.

. . . . At the end of the fifth day, Mannini appeared. He said he had been at his home across the lake and that he could not come back because the Fascist garrisons were there and they might see him.

When he came back he did not have the equipment of the mission. . . . He said that he left those in a boat garage belonging to his father. He was sent back to get the equipment.

This time he was missing again for several days and the mission was without its equipment. He finally came back. The search was continued for Major Holohan. But to no avail.

We will show you that after this episode Mannini and Tozzini were not around any more. They disassociated themselves from Chrysler Mission. There were only Icardi and LoDolce.

We will show you that a full report was made by Lieutenant Icardi of this whole incident. . . .

Now, members of the jury, the investigation into the death of Major Holohan did not stop in December of 1944. It did not stop in 1945. We will show you it did not stop in 1946 or 1947. We will show you that it has not as yet stopped.

In 1945 the OSS and the Criminal Investigation Division of the U.S. Army turned loose a number of investigators in northern Italy in the Lake Orta area to learn what they could about the disappearance of Major Holohan.

We will show you that they combed this area and they talked to all the persons who might have knowledge of this subject. They talked to the two aides. . . .

We will show you that Mannini and Tozzini at that time said that the mission was planning to move on the night of December 6. They said that one of them was securing the villa and making sure that there were no traces of the presence of the mission there, and the other was somewhere along the winding path through the garden behind the villa, when a footstep was heard. The challenge was made. A gun blazed. They said that they did not see Major Holohan after that night. They were exhaustively interrogated, members of the jury, and that is what they said.

The Communist partisans, who were the leading partisans in the area, were exhaustively interrogated also as to what they knew about this episode. Moscatelli [their leader] was carefully questioned, as were his men. No one gave helpful information, but inconsistencies began to develop as the investigation grew warmer.

We will show you, ladies and gentlemen of the jury, when the evidence is in, that the United States government, acting through its duly authorized investigative agencies, in 1947, was correct when it concluded: "The disappearance of Major Holohan was a political move engineered by the Communist group headed by Moscatelli, a man of few scruples who was capable of weakening the opposite party in order to enrich his group." We will show you before this case is completed that that conclusion, arrived at by the impartial investigation conducted immediately after the event, was right.

When that report was filed, the investigation was renewed. It was renewed for the purpose, members of the jury, of determining the specific individual responsible for the disappearance of the major.

A man named Henry Manfredi, who is with the Criminal Investigation Division of the U.S. Army, was given the assignment to find out who, which individual, was responsible for this act. We will show you that he marshaled all the information at his command. He examined all the reports that had ever been written on this bizarre episode of World War II history. Then he went back to the scene of the crime. And he began, with the aid of those assigned to help him, a systematic investigation, going over all the steps that had been gone through before, from beginning to end, to double-check the conclusion previously arrived at.

We will show you that the emphasis of the investigation was on the Communist partisans. It was on Vincent Moscatelli and one of his executioners . . . the emphasis was also on Mannini and Tozzini.

And here Williams continued with a machine-gunlike barrage of We-will-show-yous. He would show:

That further inconsistencies developed in the stories of the two aides, and that involvement of the Communist partisans under Moscatelli soon became clear;

That Moscatelli decided to liquidate Holohan after a meeting with him on December 2 because he believed that the major constituted an obstruction to his plans after the war and during the concluding aspects of the war;

That the attack on the villa that fateful night was a simulated one made by Moscatelli's partisans, with the knowledge and assistance of the two aides;

That when the involvement of these Communist partisans became a subject of hot inquiry, Moscatelli hatched a plot to blame the Americans for Holohan's death; and to save the two aides (who, unknown to the mission, were Communist party members), they would say they had been pawns in the hands of the Americans and had acted under their orders;

That, accordingly, the aides had been instructed to change their stories (which, in 1950, they did), but that their new stories, concocted fast and under pressure, did not mesh; and

That Mannini and Tozzini, still clinging to their defense that "the Americans were to blame," finally admitted to having dumped Major Holohan's body into the lake.

And Williams would further show:

The body was taken out of Lake Orta, and lo and behold, there were bullets in the cadaver. The bullets were from Mannini's gun, a gun which he had carefully gotten rid of shortly after the event by selling it to one Edward Molino.

(The buyer's name here is a typical Williams touch, reflecting his predilection for detail.)

We will show you that when the investigation grew warmer, and it was pointing at Moscatelli and his brigands, a defense was devised to shift responsibility for these actions to Aldo Icardi, the American.

We will show you, members of the jury, that an official line of the Communist Party of Italy was promulgated to the effect that Major Holohan was killed on order of the U.S. Defense Department and the U.S. State Department. . . . It was employed as a defense for Mannini and Tozzini, who went to trial in Italy for this crime. It was planned and plotted in 1950.

We will show you that since 1944, this defendant, Aldo Icardi, has answered all questions propounded to him by any responsible official of the U.S. government concerning this matter.

Williams zeroed in now on his client's history of cooperativeness and truthfulness: He would show that Icardi had voluntarily submitted not only to intensive questioning by OSS and CID agents but to a two-day polygraph test "at the hands of the foremost expert in the U.S. military organization"; that he had answered all the questions truthfully "and that this fact was so reported"; that when he received a letter from Congressman Cole inviting him ("not subpoenaing, not requiring, but *inviting* him") to come to Washington to testify, he did so. . . . "He raised his hand, took an oath, all voluntarily, with no demand, no legal requirements to do so"—and he testified, "answering the questions completely and candidly as he did before, and as he has done since 1944.

"We expect to show you, members of the jury, that Lieutenant Aldo Icardi is not a murderer or a thief or a liar. The evidence will show that he was one of the real heroes of World War II. When we show you these things, we will ask, at your hands, at the conclusion of this case, a verdict of not guilty."

It is never the obligation of the criminal defense to make an opening address to a jury. But Williams, like many veteran trial lawyers, believes it is an opportunity never to be missed, since in the opening stages of a trial the jury is fresh, interested, and impressionable.

In the Icardi case, Williams knew that his technical argument (lack of legislative purpose of the subcommittee before whom his client allegedly perjured himself) might be rejected by the court. He knew that he was "blind siding" his government opponent by not letting on that he thought much of his argument. He knew that a jury would probably be unsympathetic to an argument that his client was being harassed by a perjury indictment just because the government was frustrated in being unable to fairly try him for a brutal murder. So Icardi and Williams had everything to gain by leaving out entirely the very point upon which Williams thought the Icardi case rested. In a long opening address to the jury (but tightly condensed on pp. 36), Williams did not reveal by a single word or suggestion the notion that his client was being tried for perjury before a committee that Williams thought had no sound constitutional authority.

The government, of course, believing that Williams had every intention of going forward on the question of whether or not Icardi murdered Holohan, let its guard down in perfunctorily putting in its proof of legislative purpose. At the court's suggestion—and Williams and the prosecution went along with it—the government's proof was to be heard outside the hearing of the jury. It was just too boring, too technical, and too unimportant.

The government's first witness was Congressman Cole, who breezed his way through questions about the formation of his subcommittee and the prior legislation passed by Congress which made it possible to prosecute a member of the military service after his discharge for a crime committed during service. Cole freely admitted that during the course of the Eighty-second Congress, his subcommittee was concerned about public indignation over the Holohan "murder." He testified further that later in 1953—fourteen months after prior hearings in which witnesses were heard and statements taken, including Icardi's—Icardi was invited to Washington to tell his story.

Congressman Cole then told the court that after Icardi's March 1953 testimony, a full report was made and accepted by the Congress, recommending that federal courts at the port of entry of an American citizen returning from abroad would have jurisdiction over any felony committed by that person while abroad. Cole explained that the legislative purpose of that March 26 hearing (when Icardi was alleged to have perjured himself) was in part to afford him an opportunity to tell his story; that the hearing was, in part, "a consequence of the earlier hearings . . . for the purpose of determining any dereliction of duty by the army and making inquiry regarding the death of Major Holohan, apprehension of the guilty person and . . . to inquire whether the law was adequate to cover situations such as this [the Icardi case]."

Edward Bennett Williams then rose to cross-examine. Williams has a special way about him when conducting an inquiry—a way which seems to say, "Whatever has happened to my Constitution? Whatever happened to fair play and decency? Why do people get into these messes? What can we do to make sure that the Law gets applied equally to everybody?"

He is always polite and rarely hostile, although he often seems incredulous. Most of all, he is firm. Williams respectfully approached the distinguished congressman—and slowly led him down the garden path:

W.: Mr. Cole, you are a lawyer, are you not, sir?

C.: I was one some years ago. I am not practicing.

W.: You have never stopped being one, have you?

C.: It depends on the term being a lawyer.

W.: You are still a member of the New York Bar, are you not?

C.: Yes.

All right. So the congressman was going to equivocate. . . . But Williams, when he's after an unequivocal answer, seems to have the patience of a saint and the tenacity of a bulldog.

W.: Now, you have testified that your committee was prompted to look into the disappearance of Major Holohan by virtue of press reports concerning the finding of his body; is that correct?

C.: Correct.

W.: Was there anyone who came to you and asked you to look into this particular incident?

C.: I can't recall that there was.

W.: Did a writer named Michael Stern come to you?

C.: No, he did not.

To Cole's best recollection, no, Stern had nothing to do initially with getting him interested in the case. A news item was called to his attention "by somebody, some news reporter" asking him to comment on it. Williams' attempts to refresh the congressman's recollection about Stern's role in the matter were to no avail. All he remembered was that after reading the article, he was disturbed over the army's apparent laxity in failing to inquire into the case, in its apparent failure to take care of its own; that he was so disturbed, in fact, that he got in touch with Chairman Vinson of the Armed Services Committee urging that an inquiry be made into the Holohan case.

Point Number One. Or as Williams would put it—a plus. Yes, the subcommittee was concerned that somebody murdered the major and was getting away with it, and yes, the congressman had "urged" the chairman of the Armed Services Committee to "look into the Holohan case."

Williams then established that as far back as December 1951 and

January 1952 the subcommittee had held hearings and taken the testimony of Michael Stern of *True* magazine and Henry Manfredi of the CID. He then asked if it was not correct that the purpose of holding these hearings "was to look into the disappearance of Major Holohan." "Correct," said Cole. Williams continued to question him about these two witnesses:

> W.: Neither of them had any firsthand knowledge on the subject, did they?
>
> C.: If by firsthand knowledge you mean eyewitnesses to the death of Major Holohan, they were not. . . .
>
> W.: I don't mean something as narrow as that, Mr. Cole. Neither of them had anything but hearsay evidence to offer to the committee; isn't that so?
>
> C.: That is right, as I understand it.
>
> W.: As you understand it. You were there present; is that right?
>
> C.: Yes, surely I was there.
>
> W.: Now, when you filed your report in the Eighty-third Congress, you said, did you not, over your signature, that the inquiry by the special committee was concerned primarily with whether or not a crime had been committed? Is that right? (Yes, that was right.)
>
> W. (intent on pinning this one down): Is that the fact? Is that what the subcommittee was concerned primarily with?
>
> C.: That was what we stated at that time as being the primary purpose.

Not quite good enough. Again: "Is that the fact?" This time, Williams got the simple "yes" he wanted. Now for the same question, with the slight addition of suggested motive:

> W.: Is it the fact that the primary purpose of your sitting with Mr. Kilday was to see whether a crime had been committed and whether prosecution was possible?
>
> C.: Well, I wouldn't add the latter part of it. . . . We felt it was necessary to know whether a crime had been committed in order to determine the adequacy of the statutes and also the sufficiency of army diligence.

W.: . . . How does whether a crime has been committed or not affect in any way the adequacy of statutes?

C.: Because the circumstances under which a crime may be committed are so variable that it is quite conceivable that the statutes do not cover all circumstances, because they were unforeseen at the time the statute was enacted.

W.: Now you sat, had you not, on the Armed Forces Committee of the Eighty-first Congress?

C.: Yes, I did.

W.: And you were a member of that committee then, weren't you?

C.: Yes, I was.

And now, to wrap up the point:

W.: *You knew, did you not, Mr. Cole, that in the Eighty-first Congress, out of your very committee, there came legislation which made it possible to prosecute a member of the military service for a crime committed during the service after his discharge; isn't that so?*

C.: I made reference to that earlier, yes.

W. (not quite satisfied): *You knew that, didn't you?*

C.: *Yes.*

Williams was quite satisfied now. He had extracted another plus, although nothing in his face or manner indicated that he was either pleased or displeased with the congressman's answers. If anything, he seemed to be displaying a kind of intellectual curiosity about what that subcommittee was really doing. His attitude implied, Oh, come on, Congressman, there's no jury here. Weren't you really just interested in satisfying your and the public's genuine curiosity about a murder case that took place in Italy in 1944?

Williams is a big believer in silent plusses; and they were adding up. His cross-examination of Cole is totally consistent with his view of the art of cross-examination. The object, Williams says, is to think toward the end. "I'm always looking for nuggets to mine, put in the basket, and save for the end for summation. And the best ones to me are the ones that are absolutely concealed, that nobody knows about. The other side doesn't know when he has been hit with such a shot; he is totally oblivious of it. You just stash that away, and you tell him how hard he got hit five weeks later, in the summation. You just take the ring post and hit him over the head with it. That's my idea of the most brilliant kind of cross-examination—when you can work a witness, when you can elicit things from him that are so devastating they're going to win the case for you, and yet they're concealed."

The average trial lawyer, he says, has an enormous tendency to show off. To illustrate his point, he talked about a case he had tried in which he defended a lawyer charged with perjury before a grand jury. The attorney, it was claimed, had testified falsely when he said he had not given television sets as bribes to two different men on two different occasions:

"The only defense we had was that he just didn't remember. There had been an investigation of the RFC [Reconstruction Finance Corps] and they had had six Department of Justice lawyers sitting in the grand jury which had run eighteen months, and they brought in a number of indictments against various people. A lawyer named, let's say, Brown, testified and they asked him whether, under oath, my client told the grand jury that he had no recollection of giving the television sets away. Mr. Brown said, 'Yes, sir.' So I asked him, in what appeared to be a real Dickie-the-dunce cross-examination, 'How long were you working with that grand jury, Mr. Brown?' 'Nine months,' he said. 'Who were the other lawyers working with you?' 'Mr. Green and Mr. Blue and Mr. Black.' So now they bring on Mr. Green, and I Dickie-the-dunced him for fifteen minutes. 'You worked this grand jury for how long?' 'Twelve months,' he said. 'Were there other lawyers from the Department of Justice working with you?' 'Oh, yeah,' he said. 'There was Mr. Brown, and there was Mr. Jones, and Mr. Black.'

"They brought down every single one of those grand jury lawyers before whom my client was supposed to have testified falsely. . . . And each lawyer omitted at least one name, and, in some instances, two names of the lawyers with whom he worked during that grand jury proceeding. The government prosecutor was bewildered—absolutely lost! The whole thing was lost. It looked like an absurd cross-examination designed simply to stall. But, you see, during summation I was able to say, 'Now, they are asking you to return a verdict of guilty against this lawyer who has a peerless reputation up to now—absolutely unstained—on the ground that he forgot something. That is really what it is. Now let's look at Mr. Brown, the prosecutor.' I ticked off the names of each one who had forgotten two names, or one name, and I said, 'Now, if I asked you to return a verdict of perjury against them, you would laugh me down the courthouse steps, because it would be intrinsically absurd. That is what they are asking you to do against my client.' "

Williams, of course, was doing the same kind of mining of Congressman Cole—just storing nuggets, not for a summation, but for the argument he intended to make for a dismissal based on the law. And he would make it sooner than the prosecution ever dreamed. Having already gotten Cole to agree that there was existing legislation covering the fact pattern of the Icardi case at the time of the congressman's investigations, Williams gently continued his cross-examination:

W.: Well, now, what was there about this particular factual situation, sir, that gave you cause, that made you feel it was necessary to have a congressional investigation to determine if it was covered? What was unique about this case that raised a doubt in your mind as to whether or not it was covered by the amendment that had been made in the Eighty-first Congress by your very own committee?

C.: I would say there are two reasons: one, the timing of it, being the first case of this type which was brought to public attention; and the other was because of the enormity of the alleged crime itself. . . .

W.: The enormity of the crime itself interested you?

C.: Yes.

Next, Williams dealt with the witness's previous testimony that his subcommittee was interested in the adequacy of federal law concerning crimes committed by ex-servicemen:

W.: Now, when Mr. Stern testified as a witness, he was not asked any questions about the adequacy of federal laws, was he?

C.: I do not recall that he was.

W.: You wouldn't call him as an expert on that subject, would you? You called Mr. Stern simply to get his hearsay version of what happened in the Holohan disappearance, isn't that so?

C.: Yes, that is so.

W.: And when you called Henry Manfredi, you didn't call him

to get his views on the adequacy of federal laws, did you, sir? (Again, Cole could not recall.)

W.: There wouldn't be any reason to ask Mr. Manfredi his views on the adequacy of federal legislation or military legislation?

C. (conceding): No particular reason, no reason why we should, either.

Plus. And another plus. Then the bombshell questions:

W.: After you heard [the testimony of] Mr. Stern and Mr. Manfredi, you then knew from what they told you about this case that it fell squarely within the statute that you passed in the Eighty-first Congress covering crimes committed by servicemen during their service, holding that they could be prosecuted in army court-martials after their service, did you not?

C. (barely audible): Yes.

W.: You knew that then, didn't you? You knew on January 10, 1952, that existing law covered the Holohan case? (A qualified "*Apparently* covered it" was the best answer Cole could manage here.)

It was certainly beginning to look as though the subcommittee hearings may have lacked a legislative purpose indeed. By now, of course, the congressman and the prosecutor squirmed, knowing full well that this perfunctory hearing, sans jury, to determine legislative purpose was not just some aimless excursion on Williams' part. But it was too late. As Williams had already brought out, Cole's own committee had passed a law that covered trials of ex-servicemen. The congressman had already admitted that his committee was very interested in the dramatic impact of the Icardi case.

Williams next brought out that nothing was done by Cole's subcommittee from January 10, 1952, until March 1953. The congressman's "justification" was as lame as it sounded:

C.: We awaited the outcome of certain other procedures that were in course at the time.

W.: You waited, didn't you?

C. (softly): Yes.

W.: But you didn't do anything, did you?

C.: Well, we were aware of what was developing in the case.

W.: You didn't issue a report?

C.: No. (And no, they didn't hear any more testimony; and no, they didn't hold any meetings.)

When Williams began to press the congressman as to why the committee wanted Icardi's testimony, Cole again tried to get away with a simple explanation that they thought Icardi might help them with his views about existing federal law. His helpless response served to rack up another plus for Williams:

C.: *Only as I recollected it at the end we asked him if he had any comment or evidence or statement that he wished to make, and he apparently had none. I do not recall of any specific inquiry.*

Williams next dealt with the subcommittee's final report, rendered after all its hearings. The congressman agreed, reluctantly indeed, that his committee did conclude that the fact pattern in the Holohan case was covered by existing law, although he would not say so "positively."

Williams finished his cross-examination and sat down, counting on the prosecutor to try and rehabilitate the congressman on redirect examination. (As every grand master will tell you, it is essential that you not only refrain from asking too many questions but that you know your opponent and keep something in your briefcase to hit back with if he hurts you.)

Williams knew that his opponent, Mr. Woerheide, would elicit further testimony from the congressman as to how seriously the committee was taking its job in considering new legislation; and that is precisely what the prosecutor did. Cole testified that his subcommittee's hearings and investigation "pointed to a glaring deficiency in the statutes covering the jurisdiction over offenses committed abroad." And, he triumphantly pointed out, as a direct result of those hearings, he was the sponsor of a bill actually amending the prior statute on the books at the time Icardi testified before his subcommittee.

Williams looked into his briefcase, comforted by the fact that he knew he had not left it empty. If he felt that anything the congressman had added on redirect had hurt his case, he certainly did not show it.

As he rose to cross-examine Cole again, his attitude was one of indignation. His voice now was louder than usual, but he was still fully in control:

W.: Did you talk to anyone, anyone at all, sir, before Mr. Icardi was invited to testify with respect to setting up a perjury case against Mr. Icardi?

C.: I cannot quite subscribe to setting up a perjury case. I can, in response, say that the question of perjury was a subject of discussion.

W.: And that was a subject of discussion before he was called?

C.: Yes, sir, before and after and—

W.: *Before?*

C.: Yes, sir.

W.: With whom did you talk about perjury in the case of Icardi before he was called?

C.: Well, at this date I cannot recollect with certainty the identity of the individuals with whom I did discuss it. I am quite certain it must have been with my colleague member of the committee, counsel for the committee. . . .

W.: Did you talk to anyone at the Department of Justice on this subject?

C.: To my best recollection, I did not.

W.: Do you have knowledge as to whether any member of your committee or anybody on the staff of your committee did it, sir?

C.: I have no recollection that they did.

W.: Did your discussion take this form, sir, that if Icardi could testify or be induced to testify before your committee, that he could be prosecuted for perjury and this would be a way to institute a criminal prosecution against him, since Section 3 of the Uniform Code of Military Justice did not apply to him because it had been passed after 1944?

C.: The question is so conditional that I cannot respond.

W.: You *did* talk in the committee about a perjury case on Icardi?

C.: The subject of perjury in connection with the hearings about to be held by the committee were discussed.

W.: And you did know at that time, because you had said so in your report, that Section 3 of the Military Code of Justice could not apply specifically to Icardi because it had not been passed until the Eighty-first Congress and the events of the Holohan case had taken place back in 1944?

C.: Yes, that's right.

W.: And you did say, if we can get Icardi in here to testify and he will tell the same story that he has told heretofore, it is possible that we can get a perjury indictment against him?

C. (limply): Well, there were further conditions to that . . .

W.: Such as?

C.: If there is adequate and competent proof that the testimony he might give to us under oath was untrue.

W.: But you had discussed this possibility beforehand?

C.: Perjury, whenever we swear a witness before a committee of Congress is for the purpose of eliciting the truth, and the consequences of not telling the truth are perjury. So inevitably the subject of prosecution for perjury is discussed.

W.: But you had discussed a possible perjury prosecution of Icardi *before* he was invited to testify?

C.: I would not say we had discussed a *prosecution*. The subject of *perjury* was discussed.

W.: Tell me what was said about perjury.

C.: I can't tell you exactly.

W.: Tell me the *substance* of what was said about perjury in relation to Icardi before he was called.

C. (getting flustered and bordering on gibberish): The substance of perjury is perjury itself.

W.: Tell me the substance of your conversation, sir.

C.: It would only be repetition. The subject of swearing Mr. Icardi was discussed. It was determined to swear him. He offered no resistance to being sworn as a witness. It is my recollection that the question of prosecution for perjury was entered into the discussion of the question of swearing him under oath. Now I cannot particularize beyond that.

W.: But this was all before he was invited to testify?

C.: Well, it wasn't limited to that time.

W. (determined to hammer his point home): But you did have

this discussion before he was invited to testify?

C.: I can't swear positively that we did. I say it is my best recollection that we must have.

(The bulldog couldn't let go yet, not until his victim said "uncle" loud and clear.)

W.: Didn't you have a conversation with your counsel and with Mr. Kilday during which you discussed inviting Icardi to testify, during which you discussed that you would swear him if he accepted the invitation, and during which you discussed that a perjury case could be spelled out against him if he testified in accordance with the reports that you then had in your committee files obtained from the army?

(Cole could not "deny that that happened." On the other hand, he could not "swear that it did happen." But he "could very readily say that in all probability it did happen.")

W.: And your best recollection here today is that it did happen?

C. (still hedging): It could very well have happened.

W.: It is your recollection that it did, is that your answer, sir?

C.: Yes, sir.

Yessir, the grand master had gotten his "uncle" now. He had all he needed. No further questions. He had mined enough nuggets and piled up enough plusses to make his move. His feet were on solid ground now as he rose and earnestly supported his position that his client was the obvious victim of a legislative setup. He respectfully requested the court, without hearing any further evidence, and without the jury having heard any at all, to direct the jury to return a verdict of acquittal. There was no legitimate legislative inquiry at the time Icardi was invited to testify. It was perfectly obvious, Williams argued, that at the time of the Cole-Kilday hearings and before Icardi testified, all relevant witnesses and documents, including his own client's statements, were before the subcommittee. And even if it had had a legislative purpose, Williams argued, the testimony of Icardi was useless, since they knew he had consistently denied any complicity in Holohan's death. How would Icardi's repeating his denial under oath aid the committee in recommending legislation?

And hadn't the court itself heard directly from the chairman of the committee that the possibility of a perjury indictment and the "dramatic impact" of the Holohan murder were really uppermost in the minds of the committee?

Judge Keech, after listening to arguments from the government, issued a written opinion in which he said:

. . . While a committee or subcommittee of the Congress has the right to inquire whether there is a likelihood that a crime has been committed touching upon a field within its general jurisdiction, and also to ascertain whether an executive department charged with the prosecution of such crime has acted properly, this authority cannot be extended to sanction a legislative trial and conviction of the individual toward whom the evidence points the finger of suspicion.

On the basis of all the evidence before it, the court therefore finds, as a matter of law, that at the time the subcommittee questioned the defendant Icardi, it was not functioning as a competent tribunal.

Assuming, however, that the subcommittee was functioning as a competent tribunal when Icardi gave the testimony upon which the indictment is based, the court holds, as a matter of law, that the false answers defendant is charged with having given did not relate to a "material matter. . . ."

Counsel for the government has suggested that frequently individuals are adjudged guilty of an offense by a congressional committee in the exercise of its functions. This court doubts the accuracy of such statement; but if it be true, such practice should not be condoned, as it denies to the accused the constitutional safeguards of judicial trial.

For the foregoing reasons the defendant's motion to dismiss—which I believe under the new rules I must treat as a motion for judgment of acquittal—must be granted.

I shall ask the marshal to call in the jury and I shall direct a verdict of acquittal for the defendant.*

* 140 Fed. Supp. 383 (U.S. District Court, District of Columbia, 4/19/56).

Aldo Icardi was acquitted. The jury never heard any testimony—although they did get to hear a gripping, if somewhat irrelevant, spy story. The prosecution never got to present its evidence. And Williams, the grand master, had triumphantly orchestrated another technical masterpiece.

VINCENT HALLINAN

Communist or new radical? Crackpot or humanitarian? Vincent Hallinan has been called all that and more. It's a matter of opinion. As a matter of *fact*, he is a former boxer and football star and amateur actor and jailbird, and he is the husband of an author and father of six sons. And there is not a living soul among his detractors or admirers who would deny that whatever else he is, he *is* a living legend.

Hallinan, by self-designation and with the full approval of his wife and children, has always been and continues to be the defender of the oppressed, the protector of the weak, and the sworn enemy of the bully. In the course of his extraordinary trial practice, he has taken on all kinds of civil and criminal cases, and still does if they are important enough politically and socially, and if the client is unable to pay for other counsel. He rarely takes fees, but he always takes sides.

Hallinan is for the underdog. Perhaps it's because of his own beginnings . . . one of many children born of a family with very little money. His father was a streetcar conductor in San Francisco. The young Vincent found himself rebelling against the injustices of society and it came as no surprise to his family, friends, or foes when he decided on the courtroom as his battlefield.

When I first met Hallinan, now one of San Francisco's most venerable and controversial trial lawyers, he treated me to hours of unrestricted dialogue. The thing that comes across strongest in talking with this man is his love for people. He is very family-oriented—his own family and just about everybody else's, it would seem. His wife, Vivian, is a well-known leader of civil rights and radical groups and has spent time in jail for the civil-rights cause. One of his sons, Terence, is a criminal lawyer specializing in civil rights; and, it may be recalled, one of the important clients he was called upon to defend was Patricia Hearst. Another son is a teacher-lawyer. Four of the boys were intramural boxing champions at the University of California, and three were awarded Phi Beta Kappa keys there. One son who carried off awards as well as a scholarship at the University of Pennsylvania abandoned it to join the Communist party in New York. He became the youngest person ever to have been elected to its central committee.

When we discussed some of the scoundrels Hallinan has represented, he said (in his Irish brogue), "Everybody is somebody's little darling. There is some good to us all. I have never been able to say that under some circumstances I would not have committed an act that somebody else has committed. It's getting to know them and trying to find out why they did it that's so difficult."

Nowhere, nohow, have I met a lawyer with more wide-ranging interests. The day of our first meeting, I had with me a Sony tape recorder. That, of course, reminded him of the Japanese economy and he launched into a two-hour dissertation on the subject, complete with the yen's devaluation, the relative merits of the various economic and political systems, and other areas that I am not ashamed to say were way over my head.

His knowledge on the subject of trial lawyers was just as staggering. Hallinan talked at length and with much romance of the great advocates of today and those of the past, in the United States, England, and France.

Throughout his demanding practice, he has maintained an active interest in politics, literature, and reform. He was one of San Francisco's leaders in ending the selection of judges and grand jurors solely by political clout.

Hallinan has paid dearly for his convictions, some of them resulting in actual convictions against him. After defending Harry Bridges in 1952, in the celebrated trial in which Bridges and others were subsequently convicted (the conviction was thereafter reversed in the Supreme Court), Hallinan was convicted for contempt of court and imprisoned for six months. (During that same period, he ran on the Progressive party ticket for President of the United States!)

After his release from jail, Hallinan's troubles with the federal government multiplied. He and several associates were indicted in March 1953 for conspiracy to defraud the government in connection with transfer of certain property. All the defendants were acquitted.

Several months later he and his wife were indicted for income-tax evasion and, while Mrs. Hallinan was acquitted, Vincent was convicted and sentenced to eighteen months in jail. The day after the trial, a dissenting juror was quoted as insisting that "Hallinan was not convicted for income-tax evasion, but for defending Harry Bridges and being the Presidential candidate of the Progressive party." The State Supreme Court appears to have arrived at a similar conclusion and denied the State Bar's motion to disbar him.

In my conversations with Hallinan I was never able to lose sight of the fact that I was dealing with a rare and exceptional man who has refused to be beaten by "the system" that he has fought all of his young and adult years. When he met corruption and payoffs in the very court system in which he was to make his living, he fought it. He has also made money in law and gained a great deal of satisfaction out of his profession.

He has been involved in some of San Francisco's most interesting criminal cases; and throughout California he has taken on the kinds of cases that other lawyers wouldn't touch for fear of their very lives. But Hallinan has never been intimidated by unpopular causes, no matter how serious the threat to his physical safety. In his battles with courts and against the powers that were trying to break him, he found himself time and again defending not only his clients but himself.

Hallinan's philosophy of "There, but for the Grace of God, go I" was captured in this comment: "My notion of all of humanity, including myself, is we're like blind prisoners in the hold of some great ship that's rushing through storm and darkness to its doom. And I feel sorry for everybody, the worst people in there. I think, Well, you poor bastard, you're going to be drowned in a little while anyhow. And if I can do something to make it easier for you, to make it nicer, okay, I'm going to do it."

He was inclined to go along, he said, with H. L. Mencken's notion that "the universe is a great pinwheel revolving at the rate of ten thousand miles a second, and man is a sick fly hanging on the outermost rim of one of the wheels. And religion is the fly's belief that the machine was invented and set in motion to give him a free ride."

Through all his years of productive work, the "rebel" and his family have been subjected to—but not shaken by—the criticism of less adventurous conformists. Hallinan still goes about his job with no less enthusiasm for trial law and with far less concern for his critics: "If I had been a good little Catholic boy and shut my mouth, I could have had any goddamn job in California that I wanted, including U.S. senator. Time and again I have been offered judgeships and more, but I wouldn't do it. If they offered me a judgeship now, I would automatically acquit every drug and sex offender and then I would go to the powers-that-be and say, 'You can't afford to have a judge like me on the bench'—and I would agree to exchange my judgeship for the appointment of a good liberal man who would be a good judge."

The man is by no means a saint. He is simply more outspoken than most and more truthful about his trade. And in no way can it be said that he is any more ethical. He, like many other trial lawyers, will not admit (if he can spar his way around it) that any of his clients is anything less than a darling. The murderess was a little nuts . . . the embezzler was down-and-out . . . the rapist was a drunk. But, to him, they all have one thing in common: They are all decent people.

Hallinan has never been able to tolerate the wrath of authority. The desire of another lawyer to jail one of his clients seems to him incomprehensible—a worse crime, in his book, than the ones he is paid to defend. He will tell you right away that he wants to know the truth about every client. "If anyone is going to make up stories," he tells them, "let me do it; I am a master storyteller."

Although he doesn't exactly say so, he comes as close as any lawyer I have known to admitting that the aim of the trial lawyer is to win, and that the means to be employed are those that he can get away with. "Why, for Christ's sake, Norman, picture yourself defending somebody in Massachusetts back in the witch-trial days. If you told the truth, you were going to be burned at the goddamn stake. Where is the morality? Since the prosecution is so damned stupid, is it any less moral to lie in defense of those charges than to prosecute them in the name of truth?"

And, of course, as with many of the grand masters, a little trickery and deception is surely justified "if the cause is a good one" (and aren't they all?). For example, many years ago Hallinan found himself trying a case against a lawyer with a big reputation and a very short fuse. Hallinan figured it should be easy to unnerve his opponent and get him riled up. At one point during the trial, he walked over and said, "Mr. Jones, I want to tell you something."

Jones, fingering his mustache, looked impatiently at him: "Yes? Yes?" he said. Upon which, Hallinan leaned over and said in his ear, "Jones, why don't you go fuck yourself, you son-of-a-bitch." Jones, as expected, was struck dumb with surprise and outrage.

A few minutes later, Hallinan got up in front of the jury and said, "Tell me, Mr. Jones, in order to facilitate the trial, can't we agree on the date when the complaint was filed?"

Jones, still steaming from what Hallinan had said out of the jury's earshot, thundered, "I will agree on *nothing* with you!"

Hallinan looked plaintively at the jury: Look what a terrible man I have to deal with, read his eyes; why won't he cooperate?

This trial involved a very serious injury to a young girl's leg and took place, incidentally, shortly after World War II. Jones, representing the defendant, called a witness to the stand on his client's behalf and asked: "By the way, were you in the American Army during the recent un-pleasantness?" Hallinan leaped to his feet and objected: "If Your Honor please, that's a very improper question; a lot of us were in the army. He's got no right aggrandizing the man in that fashion."

Later on, during summation, Jones told the jury in impassioned tones that he was very sorry the young girl had been injured, but that her injuries, even if the company were liable, didn't amount to very much.

Then it was Hallinan's turn: "Jones says that the injuries don't amount to anything. Mr. Jones has a stable of five horses, and if he had a horse with that injury to its leg, he would have it shot! But what do you expect from a man who describes the cataclysmic tragedy of the World War as the 'recent unpleasantness'?"

Hallinan has seen and experienced the evils of dishonest juries on which his opponents had planted jurors who would be friendly to them; he has had to deal with fixed judges and paid witnesses. "When you have that," he said, "I would do any damned thing I could, crook-edness for crookedness, perjury for perjury, lie for lie, to overcome the corruption of defrauding people by the methods they were employing, and I didn't have any compunction about it at all."

The honest juror, he maintains, is the best safeguard for the un-derdog—that "poor bastard" whom Hallinan will continue to champion in the hope of making things a little "easier" and "nicer" for him before he finally goes under.

A Gentle Dissenter V.
The City of San Francisco

Much to my delight, Hallinan invited me to come to San Francisco to watch him try the case of *Terence Hallinan* [his son] v. *Michael J. Brady, City and County of San Francisco, and Norbert Gutierrez.*

Terry Hallinan (also nicknamed Kayo because of his college reputation as a boxer) is a lawyer whose practice is largely devoted to representing youngsters who become involved with the police through peace marches, drug raps, and the like.

During one such peace demonstration at the courthouse in San Francisco, young Hallinan, while representing demonstrators, sought to intervene with the police to prevent the arrests of some of the demonstrators. As he waited at the patrol wagon of the city's Police Department Tactical Unit Squad, one of the demonstrators who had already been placed in the police van tried to give Hallinan his name and address so that the latter could contact his relatives.

Young Hallinan stepped on the tailgate of the van and was pulled off by Patrolman Michael J. Brady. He felt at the time that the amount of force used by Brady was unnecessary.

During the next year or so Terry attended other peace demonstrations, usually as counsel but at other times as a concerned citizen and participant. He claimed that on many of those occasions, he saw and was recognized by Officer Brady.

On May 21, 1969, students at San Francisco State University planned a campus demonstration. There had been other such demonstrations and some violence at the university, and student leaders were concerned about the kind of force previously used by the tactical police. They asked Terry Hallinan to represent them at a meeting with other students.

The young attorney earnestly advised his clients to demonstrate peacefully and not to resist arrest when the Tactical Unit Squad arrived. He advised those who did not wish to be arrested to stay out of the squad's reach, and he agreed to stay in the administration building with the student leaders, as they had requested.

As the demonstration mounted that evening, the tactical squad arrived and told Hallinan that if he didn't leave he would be arrested; so he left and stood by a police van into which arrested students and other demonstrators were to be placed.

The tactical police, carrying enormous clubs, proceeded in wedge formation to clear out demonstrators in their path. They waited for nobody, and anyone in their way was either hurled aside or grabbed by back-up policemen and arrested.

During the course of one such sweep, several students were hurled to the ground and clubbed. One in particular, Diane Feeley, was knocked to the ground, allegedly by Officer Norbert Gutierrez, who was at the front of the wedge. Young Hallinan, who saw what was happening, says he rushed toward the spot where the girl lay and began to scream at Gutierrez, begging him to stop the brutality. He claimed that Officer Brady, recognizing him from prior marches, rushed over and clubbed him.

Although the incident was seen by several people, and part of it was filmed by various still photographers and live-television cameramen, the police maintained that the amount of force used was not excessive; that Brady simply went over to help Gutierrez reinforce his part of the wedge; that he acted properly and responsibly; and that he did not know or recognize Hallinan.

Other police officers who had been involved in the prior incidents at the courthouse and the one at San Francisco State corroborated the two officers' testimony.

At any rate, Terry Hallinan was clubbed into a daze. He was a bloody mess that night and required several stitches in his head wounds. As a result, the police lodged criminal charges against Terry, charging him with felonious interference with the police in the discharge of their duties.

Vince Hallinan represented his son in that case, which ended in a hung jury and a five-day jail sentence for Vince for contempt of court.

The contempt conviction was unanimously reversed by the State Supreme Court; and at the second trial, presided over by another judge, young Hallinan was acquitted.

There were several ensuing attempts to disbar the young lawyer, all of which failed. Vince then filed an action against the City of San Francisco and Brady and Gutierrez—"not to get any money for Kayo, but to do something about the police-state mentality" of the San Francisco police, and to make a start at least on putting an end to what both Hallinans were (and still are) convinced is police brutality against concerned citizens.

"How can you represent your own son—" I asked, "—not only in this case where you're seeking damages, but after representing him in a criminal case whose verdict could have affected his whole career?"

"You should know me well enough by now, Norman, to know that I penalize nobody because of accident of birth. My son is entitled to the best lawyer in San Francisco, and now he's got him."

The case came up for trial before the Honorable Francis McCarty in January 1973. At one counsel table sat Hallinan and son, and at the other, two young deputy city attorneys. Sitting behind them and within constant view of the jury were the families of the two police officer defendants.

Hallinan obviously was fully prepared. Both Hallinans were prepared, too, by virtue of testimony that had previously been taken, as well as by their experience in the disbarment proceedings against Terry.

This trial would involve the word of eyewitnesses who had viewed the scene from different vantage points at San Francisco State, and who would tell different stories. Basically, however, it was again the word of the citizen against the police—not just ordinary policemen, but special hand-picked men chosen for the Tactical Unit Squad because of their supposed superior qualifications. They were the best the city had to offer . . . men who daily risked their lives and limbs to protect citizens, men who had to put aside their personal, political, and social views in order to discharge their duties to the community with fairness and selflessness.

Just as they had no stake in the countless dangerous assignments to which they unflinchingly and unquestioningly responded, they had no stake in this university demonstration. They sought law and order; they wanted peace and tranquillity. And where riot supplanted and overcame peaceable assembly, they were specially trained to attempt to restore the status quo as quickly as possible and with as few injuries as possible. They didn't care who the rioters were—left-wingers or right-wingers, hawks or doves, pro-this or anti-that, hardhats, or eggheads.

Vince Hallinan had on his side several disinterested witnesses who had never seen Terry before the incident at San Francisco State and had not seen him again until the various trials at which they were subpoenaed to testify.

One of them, for example, was a colorful and fascinating witness, a student named Byron Lee.

Lee was obviously there to tell it the way it was. And if there was one thing he was clear about, it was that Brady had clubbed young Hallinan on the head.

On cross-examination, one of the deputy city attorneys hammered away at Lee as to whether or not he actually saw the club come down on Terry's head. Lee, a serious young man, kept testifying that while he couldn't honestly say he actually saw the club land on Terry's head, he surely saw it swing back and go forward, and he saw Terry slump to the ground.

Again and again, witnesses were shown the awful club. Lee was even asked to show the jury how it was wielded by Gutierrez when he clubbed Diane Feeley and by Brady when he clubbed Terry Hallinan. Lee asked to be excused. Clearly showing his revulsion for the club, he said he would rather not handle it. Finally, after much prodding, he swung the club with two hands back over his head and came down on a briefcase which had been placed upon a chair and was supposed to represent Terry's head. WHACK!

Vince described the reaction to his wife that evening: "Holy shit! We couldn't believe it. Honey, you could hear the sound of that baton hitting the briefcase all the way to Tokyo. That poor son-of-a-bitch! [referring to the city attorney]. He ought to be on my payroll."

Again and again, Lee was asked if he was absolutely certain that that awful weapon had landed on Terry's head. The elder Hallinan got up and conspicuously held aloft a key chain. He walked toward Lee and said, "Do you see this key chain?"

"Yes. . . ."

Hallinan then let it fall to the floor with a thud. "Did you see it fall?" he asked.

"Yes, sir, I did."

"Did you see it hit the floor?"

"Well, no, not really."

"Is there any doubt in your mind that after that key chain left my hand it hit the floor?"

"No, sir, there isn't."

The examination of Byron Lee and other witnesses called by both sides was exemplary of an observation once made by an eminent English barrister: "The result of most trials depends upon which side perpetrates the most blunders in cross-examination."

In this case, the two deputy assistant attorneys were not only young and relatively inexperienced, but they were in awe of grand master Hallinan. And so they fell victim to (what Max E. Steuer, a fabled American grand master, called) the two greatest dangers that confront a cross-examiner: unnecessary cross-examination and excessive cross-examination.

While the suit involving his son was in progress, Hallinan discovered a motion-picture film of an incident that had occurred in March 1968, and showed Terry on the steps of San Francisco's City Hall representing a group of young people from the Haight-Ashbury district. They called themselves the "Diggers," and, according to Hallinan, they were a nonmilitant group. On that particular day, one of them was reading a poem when members of the Tactical Police Unit appeared with a patrol wagon and arrested a young man who was wearing a shirt patterned in stars and strips.

After the boy was arrested and put into the patrol wagon, Terry stepped onto the vehicle in order to get his name. Officer Brady grabbed young Hallinan by the arm and jerked him violently from the van.

During the course of the trial, Hallinan questioned a sergeant who had been in charge of the "Tac" Squad:

> H.: Now, Sergeant, you've had hundreds of incidents since that time and isn't it possible that you have forgotten this detail and that you are mistaken as to your part and Brady's at that time?
>
> SGT.: Not at all; I remember it perfectly; Mike Brady never laid a hand on him!
>
> H.: Isn't it possible that you escorted him off the step and that after you had turned your back, he got on again and that Brady then took him off?

VINCENT HALLINAN

SGT.: Not a bit of it! I was watching all the time and Mike never touched him!

Subsequently, Brady and several other policemen gave substantially the same answers to the same questions. Only then did Hallinan pull the bombshell out of his briefcase. He showed the court and the jury the motion picture refuting the testimony of Brady, the sergeant, and the other officers.

After the film was shown, Hallinan asked:

H.: Mr. Brady, who is that standing on the patrol-wagon step?
B.: That's Terry Hallinan.
H.: Who is that holding Terry Hallinan's wrist while he is standing on that step?
B.: That's me.
H.: Who is that jerking Terry off the step?
B.: That's me.

Hallinan's production of the film was a devastating piece of evidence. Still, he feared that his basic problem in this case was the tendency of juries to want to believe what their police told them. There were enough holes in the stories of the many eyewitness policemen to drive several freedom trains through. Nevertheless, Hallinan was asking a jury to bring in damages not only against the city but against two policemen individually. And even if the policemen were guilty of having stretched a few points, there they were being represented by two fresh-faced, earnest attorneys, and it was the jury's own City of San Francisco that was being attacked.

Hallinan's summation was typical of his style. As he is a master storyteller, he used this talent with great skill to overcome the negative feelings that he thought the jury would have about convicting policemen.

The summation (which runs to 112 pages in the transcript) is a brilliant statement of Hallinan's personal philosophy of life and may well speak for the philosophies of all the grand masters:

Now, if the court please, and ladies and gentlemen of the jury, you understand that in an argument of this kind where there is a difference between what the lawyer says and what went on in the witness seat, you take what the witness has said. The only purpose of the argument is that a lawyer with probably more experience than the jury in assessing such matters can point out things that may be of use in approaching the case and—to be frank about it—from the position from which he wants the jury to approach it. It's a matter of pointing out things that seem to involve contradictions or support for a particular position.

There are many things that are not involved in the case and that the jury shouldn't take into consideration, and one of them is this: that it's not a case against the police or the police department. We have no quarrel with the police.

Al Nelder was chief of police, and when his daughter and my kids were little they used to play together up at the summer camp of San Francisco, up at Yosemite Valley.

Michael Reardon, who was once chief of police and afterward practiced law for years, was a very good friend of mine. I have two cousins on the police force. This case involves the conduct of two police officers and the veracity of three others. And of the 1805 policemen on the San Francisco force, that's less than one third of one per cent of the personnel of that force.

Now, I have made allusions to my sentiments—and those of a great number of people in San Francisco—that there are two things that have to be overcome: one is a prejudice against the young people who have been demonstrating at schools and other places; another is a prejudice in favor of police officers. They exist; and there is no use denying them because they won't go away. But you have to get rid of prejudice, bigotries, preconceptions. You have to follow the law and you have to follow evidence. If you rely upon these preconceptions and bigotries, then you are throwing out the law. You are making a farce of the court. You are instituting anarchy because one can no longer rely on a jury to establish justice. And you are leading to a police state, which is the last madness of a dying system.

All that the case involves is this: Was a citizen of the City and County of San Francisco illegally struck by a police officer? Was he illegally arrested by two police officers? The fact that the defendants are police officers should not enter into it. Nobody, neither you nor I, nor anybody else, has a right to willfully and unnecessarily injure another person. . . .

The court will instruct you—and this is one of the sections of

VINCENT HALLINAN

the Penal Code of the State of California—Section 149: Every public officer who under color of authority without lawful necessity assaults or beats any person is guilty of a felony. And this entire case depends upon that one phrase—"without lawful necessity." Was there lawful necessity on the part of Brady to strike and injure Terence Hallinan at the time of this incident? It might be a misdemeanor to strike you or me unnecessarily; but with a police officer it's a felony.

We pay these officers $1070 a month. We equip them with helmets, guns, clubs, munitions, tear gas, and we give them prestige and standing. We give them automobiles to move around in, and uniforms. But then we say to them, "Now, this power that we give you is in *our* behalf, not yours. We are the boss; you are the employee. We pay you and you do what we tell you. You follow the laws that we enact, and if you use excessive force, then you are going to pay a bigger penalty than if you were one of us charged with the same thing. . . ."

To what extent can the police officer use force? Can he shoot and kill the person? Can he kill three or four people? Must everybody stand by with his arms folded and say, "Well, after all, he is a policeman. If he wants to kill somebody we shouldn't interfere." And if it does happen, then what do you do?

Now, what happened here? It's rather definite and clear-cut. We say here that the girl was jabbed in the abdomen and went down without any offense on her part, without her having done or said anything. Because she was unable to retreat with the crowd behind her, she was jabbed and went down.

That Terence Hallinan rushed in to prevent the police officer from striking her again or from striking any other person, to say to him, "For God's sake! Cool it. You can't do that." That the officer pushed him away violently out to the curb; and that this other police officer, out of malice and spite, rushed up behind him and struck him two blows upon the head inflicting the injuries that he complained of. And that thereafter to cover this up, they placed him under arrest and charged him with a felony and very maliciously pursued that right up to the present moment.

What is their answer? Gutierrez says, "I jabbed at her, but I didn't hit her." That he heard Terence Hallinan say, "You can't do that." He didn't hear him say the other expletive and he didn't hear him say "You knocked that girl down." He said, "I could easily have gotten rid of him. I could easily have prevented him from holding on to my shoulder and the club and, in fact, I did push him off."

The other man, Brady, says, "I attempted to knock his arm off of Gutierrez's shoulder. . . ."

After reviewing conflicting contentions of eyewitnesses, Hallinan said:

Some years ago I was in another city, and a friend took me to an establishment that he deemed would be interesting. We walked down a curious kind of street with old-fashioned houses on each side and strange-looking, almost artificial-looking trees, and there was no life to it, no traffic along a cobbled street. No birds sang in the trees. There was no sound or sign of life behind the windows. And then we came to one of the houses about a block and a half down, and the door was open and behind it were struts, two-by-fours, holding up the wall.

It wasn't a house at all. It was the façade of a house, a moving-picture set. We were on a Hollywood lot. I didn't have to go back to the other houses to find out that they were façades, too. And you don't have to go back and examine everything that these men said to convince yourself that you can't put a moment's reliance on any single thing that they uttered. They are all capable of committing perjury in front of a jury, of contempt of the jury and contempt of the law that they are paid to uphold; and they are all capable of setting out to destroy a young man whose sole crime was to do a brave and generous act. That's the kind of people they are. . . .

Now, in order to be guilty of an assault, you don't have to touch the person. In fact, then it becomes a battery. Suppose that when Diane Feeley fell down she had injured her back, that she had hit that water-box in the planter area. . . . Then the policeman would be liable for the serious injury civilly as well as criminally.

A few days ago a man died down on Market Street. He was an old newspaper vendor. A seventeen-year-old boy punched him in the face. The punch didn't kill the man, didn't hurt him, but when he fell down, he struck his head on the pavement and he died. And that boy was guilty of manslaughter, because that's one of the things you must anticipate when you make an assault or a battery.

Four or five fraternity boys the other day took some other fellow down and abandoned him in the hills and his dead body was found a few days afterward. They didn't want to hurt him, but they were still guilty of manslaughter. And if this man here struck out at this girl and frightened her into falling down, or if he aroused in the mind the reasonable notion that he intended to inflict some injury upon her, that's an assault.

If a person walks up to you, and even though he doesn't mean a thing, hauls off and takes a punch in your direction and then stops, that's an assault.

Was she about to be injured? Well, everybody in that audience, everybody in that crowd was liable to be pushed by the excesses of Gutierrez and the other police officers. You don't have to wait until you are injured. You can resist and a person can come to your aid before you are injured. It doesn't matter, as I say, whether you are doing it in fun or otherwise. If a person shouts "Fire!" in a crowded theater, he may not intend that anyone be hurt; yet he is liable for any deaths or injuries that result from it. If somebody comes in and fires a blank pistol in front of a man and he jumps out the window—that's manslaughter.

It has been said, "Boys throw rocks at frogs in sport, yet the frogs do not die in sport but in earnest."

These policemen have built up a fictitious case, first to get a conviction of Terry Hallinan, and then to defend themselves.

There seemed to be another conflict in testimony between the police and Hallinan and their respective witnesses. A witness named Stephen Huss testified that he had to yell an order to a photographer, by shouting in his ear, to take a picture of young Hallinan. He also testified, however, that during the same melee he had heard Terry's words from twenty feet away. Here is how Hallinan dealt with these conflicts:

It shows how as you get older your recollections do not improve—even your noticing of things—because there is a young lawyer in the audience who gave me a card calling my attention to something I apparently overlooked.

It says that Huss said he ordered his photographer to take a picture of Terry by shouting the order in his ear. In other words, the noise was so loud that he had to shout in his ear; but from twenty feet away he could tell by the motions of Terry's mouth what he was saying.

These people, ladies and gentlemen, are pretty bad people. They are playing a deadly game here with a young man's future, his career, his liberty, his safety. They have a conspiracy and a plot to destroy him and it's going right on up to this very moment here in this court. But Terry doesn't realize it. He hasn't realized it because he has the kind of faith that youth has—that maybe people are not all bad and that they might have made a mistake here, that they are not really that hostile.

There is a section of this case that bothers me greatly. Terry Hallinan testified that Brady pulled him off the patrol wagon at the Diggers incident. Brady and the sergeant both testified unequivocally that that was false; that Brady hadn't touched him and the sergeant was the one who pulled him off.

Now, when this case is over, what do they intend to do with that? Perjury can be proven by the testimony, and must be proven by the testimony of two witnesses. Terry had nobody to support him in his statement, but they had each other. They built up, my friends, a charge of perjury for which he could be indicted and destroyed, just as they tried to destroy him on the false arrest charge. He had testified to this in the criminal court. Just more malice on their part.

Then this moving picture turns up. Now, it's obvious that we received it just recently, because the danger in the criminal court was so great that if we had had it then, we would have used it, wouldn't we? Obviously, it was much more important to get him acquitted of that false charge than it is to win a verdict in this case. So, they didn't know we had it, and we didn't have it during those proceedings. It hit them like a blockbuster when it was shown this morning. And if we didn't have that picture, Terry would now be in far greater danger than he was at any time through this entire proceeding.

What is another strange thing that happened? You know, the truth is a very difficult thing when it's against you. You stamp it

VINCENT HALLINAN

down here and it pops up there. And you stamp it down there and it's behind you. You kick it out the door and you walk in and it has come in through the window and it's sitting at your fireplace.

James Russell Lowell, a great abolitionist and one of the militant fighters against slavery, said in his poem "The Present Crisis": "Truth forever on the scaffold, Wrong forever on the throne,—/Yet that scaffold sways the future, and, behind the dim unknown,/Standeth God within the shadow, keeping watch above His own." Well, after fifty years or more of trying these cases, one gets a little cynical about God's watchfulness. But every now and then something turns up, like this moving picture, to kill off a fraudulent, illegal, murderous conspiracy.

What about Diane Feeley? We are not under any obligation to defend her or to prove she is this or that or the other. She seems to be a cultured, educated, decent young woman, a teacher in New York. She surprised me with the statements she made that the difficulty out at the San Francisco State College was only that the administration wouldn't listen to the pupils; that they wouldn't talk to them. They wouldn't have a conference. She said, we felt that they should have sat down with us and ironed the thing out themselves and they should not have called in the police. Doesn't that sound like a reasonable solution?

There was a magazine cartoon showing a school principal sitting at a table and four young people are standing before her— two young white men, a young black man, and a young woman. And the principal is saying to them, "I am glad you young people have seen fit to protest nonviolently. It shows you are civilized. Now, get out."

They have got some proof that Diane is some kind of bad person. They have a bag here which they say is hers and which she admits is hers; and I suppose when you look into that bag, which I haven't bothered to do yet, it will contain certain items. Undoubtedly there will be things that will identify it as belonging to Diane Feeley.

They asked her if she carried stones and pool balls in the bag. She says, "No, I wouldn't know a pool ball if I saw one and I have never been able to throw a stone in my life. I don't know how to do it." But the bag was found near her in a demonstration that she was in. Now, it seems kind of incredible that this happened after she had testified in Terry's criminal trial. She would know they were hostile to her and she would know they were looking out for her and yet she carries along and deposits on the ground in sight of these police officers something that would incriminate her with violence! It doesn't sound logical. She didn't look like a fool. But what about the temptation these gentlemen would have to plant a few rocks and a couple of pool balls in the thing? My friends, from my point of view, it would be irresistible. I don't think they could turn it down. I think they let out a whoop when they found the bag. . . . "Let's dump these things in it and see what happens."

* * * *

It may be, however, I must concede, that Diane Feeley may have come prepared following this incident in which she says or imagines or thinks she was jabbed in the abdomen with a club and knocked down and a young man who went to her rescue was clubbed down and charged with a felony. It may be she suffered such revulsion that the next time she came to a demonstration she came armed. That wouldn't be too surprising.

The IWW, the Industrial Workers of the World, long ago had a formula. They said in making a revolutionary there is no pamphlet like a cop's club. Get bolted on the head once, and you form a different opinion as to how policemen act toward citizens. And John F. Kennedy made this statement: he said, "Those who make peaceful change impossible make violent revolution inevitable."

So it may be that Diane Feeley has become a violent person where she wasn't before. . . .

To tell the truth, my friends, I never knew what these young people were standing for out at San Francisco State. I always subscribed to the principle that Voltaire is said to have believed in, and that is, "I disapprove of what you say, but will defend to the death your right to say it."

I have had that attitude all my life. I don't care if it's the police having their convention out on the City Hall steps and ringing the block with several hundred police officers and supporters, or if it's a handful of these poor little Diggers who want to get up there and recite poetry with an American-flag shirt on. They have

VINCENT HALLINAN

the right to do it, and the police have the same right as everybody else. The police, however, don't seem to feel that way; they feel they have the right, but we have not. To them, these youngsters are "rattlesnakes, dissenters destroying our way of life. . . ."

What did the students want? What was their criminal activity? And what necessitated the pounding and the beating and the slander? Well, their own witness, Huss, was the one who stated—and I didn't ask, wasn't interested, but he did say—one, that they wanted to get rid of the ROTC on the campus; two, they wanted to employ black teachers; three, they wanted to retain a Chicano professor who was in danger of being fired; and four, they wanted to admit more minority students, and they wanted to lower the admission requirements so that the people who were disenfranchised and people who didn't have the opportunities could come into this school and get an opportunity that would fit them for something to do.

All the arrestees were white. The pictures there show it. There wasn't a black face among them. They weren't asking anying for themselves. They weren't saying, "Give us something." They were saying, "Give the other fellow—who hasn't the advantages that we have—something."

And why the sit-in? Only to be heard, only to be heard.

*   *   *   *

Now, about these dissidents who are trying to change our way of life. . . . What is so sacred about our way of life? War, poverty and its offspring, pride, racial and ethnic discrimination—they are the great problems confronting the world.

In my life, starting with the Spanish-American War, the world has gone through five major wars and scores of interventions, punitive expeditions, landing forces in aid of friendly countries, usually military autocracies. I have seen them go in the Philippines, Mexico, Haiti, Santo Domingo, the Soviet Union, China, up and down Central and South America, and even Lebanon.

We have just seen the signing of a document that ends a war in which it has been estimated a million six hundred thousand people lost their lives.

In the Second World War, ten per cent of the population of the globe was killed and another twenty per cent was left to mourn their loss and try to repair their shattered properties and their dismal fortunes.

Poverty, war, racial injustice, and the next war that these people don't want to foment and don't want to be a part of—whether it's to be the high fliers or any other part of the ROTC going to exterminate all life on the globe. . . .

Racial discrimination . . . We who live in this country, my friends, are living on top of a volcano that's going to explode. No people are going to long endure insult and degradation. No people are going to endure taking shabby jobs, being treated as second-rate and inferior people when they are just as good as everybody else. All through this country in the past few years we have had racial riots. We have young men coming back from Vietnam taught how to use deadly weapons. We tell them they can't get a job and they can't get an education and they can't do anything because of their color. And they [pointing to Gutierrez and Brady] expect that some day those boys are going to try to use those guns right here in San Francisco! You have never had an incident of it because these young people went out and forced the Palace Hotel and restaurants and so forth to employ black people in washing cars, washing dishes, and other jobs.

Dissenters . . . If dissenting from things of this kind makes criminals, then what a host of magnificent criminals the U.S. history has produced!

Officer Epting and his associates would have burned heretics at the stake. They would have marched with the British at Lexington and Bunker Hill to kill off the dissidents who weren't going to stand for being enslaved by English businessmen any longer. They would have pummeled the abolitionists and the men who were willing to lay their own lives and their own safety on the line, just as these young people have, for the emancipation of men.

When Ralph Waldo Emerson, one of the greatest minds this continent has produced, walked up the stairs of the Supreme Court and burned a copy of the Fugitive Act saying, "I will not obey this filthy law," and hundreds of people applauded him—they would have been there to jab them out of the way. They would have stood by and watched William Lloyd Garrison, the

VINCENT HALLINAN

abolitionist, dragged—not through the streets of Charleston, South Carolina, but through the streets of *Boston*—with a rope around his neck and a mob intent on lynching him. They would have turned away when William Lovejoy was murdered and his printing shop destroyed—not in Louisiana, but in Illinois. They would have slammed down the union labor organizers as the ILWU was slammed down in the waterfront of San Francisco back in 1939. And they would have broken up John L. Lewis's sit-ins, which were devised as one way to starve out the employers instead of allowing the employers to starve them out. They would have force fed Carrie Chapman Catt and Elizabeth Stanton and the other women suffragists who, after undergoing all kinds of humiliation and embarrassment, being stoned and having objects thrown at them, were force fed in jails for trying to get votes for women—for trying to do the things that you ladies on the jury are now permitted to do and to dissent from restrictions imposed upon them for literally thousands of years.

They would have arrested Rosa Parks, a strange and gallant figure who had the courage, when she sat down in a front seat of a streetcar in Birmingham, Alabama, and the conductor said, "Go back to the back seat where the colored people are supposed to be," she had the courage to say, "I won't." When she was arrested, my friends, that started the whole civil-rights movement in the United States. It was followed up by people like Martin Luther King and other heroes.

They [pointing] would have looked away when two fine kids from New York—[James] Goodman and [Michael] Schwerner, and [James] Chaney, with Terry Hallinan along—went down into Mississippi for what? To enforce the federal laws and to require the state to allow black people to register and vote in the elections. And those three kids were murdered by a crowd of deputy sheriffs.

Mr. Epting and his friends wouldn't have done this because of the job they have. They would have done it from a sense of rectitude. "We are right. This is our way of life and we are not going to allow these scoundrels to change it, these rattlesnakes, these dissenters, these importers of a new strain of gonococcus."

Dissenters . . . You look back. The only people who are worth anything were the dissenters. It has been said, the conservative now is the man who wants to hang on to what the radicals got for him.

Copernicus, refusing to concede as had been established for centuries that the sun revolves around the earth. . . . Columbus discovering America because he dissented from the conviction that the world was flat, not round.

We have wonderful dissenters. Do you know who is the biggest dissenter, the most important dissenter, in the world at the moment? It is the United States Supreme Court, which, just a short while ago, came down and, ignoring Congress, legislators, biblical invocations, and religious groups, outlawed antiabortion laws. "A woman," it said, "is the master of her own body and if at least for the first three months of pregnancy she doesn't want to have a child, that's up to her and her doctor and no state and no nation has the right to restrict her in it." That, my friends, is a dissent from a policy that has existed for over four thousand years.

*   *   *   *

Now, about these dissenters who are trying to change our way of life, what about them? When the police decide to change our way of life, what about it? When they don't like the laws enacted by the board of supervisors or the state legislature or whatever— well, they come out and hold a demonstration on the Polk Street stairs of the City Hall (in the same spot where the Diggers were, but filling up the entire structure). And they march around the four blocks of the City Hall about two-deep so that they have enough people to circle the whole thing. They are picketing the Hall of Justice. They are keeping people from going in to ask for justice.

I don't quarrel with them on that. If they think they are not being properly treated, then they have every right to go out there and make these objections. But they have no right to say: "We are entitled to do this, but you are not." I don't know what demands they were making any more than I know what the Diggers wanted or what the kids out at San Francisco State wanted, but I do know this: that nobody risks imprisonment, humiliation,

VINCENT HALLINAN

beating, being kicked out of school, reprimanded by a police superior, unless he thinks he is right. . . .

Hallinan's argument, which had begun at two o'clock, ended for the afternoon recess. He continued the next morning:

Of course, it must have occurred to you ladies and gentlemen of the jury that there is much more involved in this matter than an injury unlawfully inflicted upon the plaintiff, or even the vexation, annoyance, humiliation, and so forth, that he suffered. It's a much more principled and important issue than that, and that is, can a young man, a young lawyer, launch a crusade—whether he is right or wrong in it—launch a crusade against police brutality without having his life, his career, his health, his safety endangered in retaliation? That is what it amounts to.

That he has launched such a career, a crusade of that kind, is evident from the evidence that has been introduced here, and it isn't the first of such crusades. In this country, with its rough and frontier beginning, I suppose police brutality has been a significant problem that governments have had to face. One of the early ones within our time was back in 1931, when President Hoover organized the Wickersham Committee to investigate that particular thing. It went all over the country and made examinations and held hearings on it; and quoting here, from the *United States Supreme Court Reporter*, they mention this:

"In 1931, President Hoover's Wickersham Committee found extensive evidence of police lawlessness, including unjustified violence.

"Sixteen years later another Presidential committee, this one appointed by President Truman, concluded that police brutality, especially against the unpopular, the weak, and the defenseless, was a distressing problem. And now in 1961 this commission must report that police brutality is still a serious problem throughout the United States."

The report continues with this, the court says: "The commission is particularly impressed by the fact that most police officers never resort to brutal practices. Because of this fact, instances of brutality or discrimination in law enforcement stand out in bold relief. It is hoped that by focusing the attention of the President, the Congress, and the public on these remaining incongruities, this report may contribute to their correction."

Hallinan then read a series of other articles concerning police brutality and police corruption appearing in various newspapers throughout the United States.

I don't want to hammer this to death, but we have seen in the paper recently where police have stolen heroin out of the evidence lockers in various departments and sold them to narcotic sellers in the streets of the cities. The temptation is rather great. The number of persons involved in it, I am sure, is minimal. But to say that a policeman is automatically entitled to some special status when he takes the witness stand, or when he is included in an offense, is to just lie in the face of reality and to ignore what everybody should know. . . .

In our case, we ask this: Can a young lawyer crusade against police brutality *legally* in the *courts* without danger to his safety, his health, his career, his life? Can a retaliatory squad of five or six men, including one axeman, Brady, can they retaliate against him by forging documents for the State Bar to prevent him from being admitted? Can he be manhandled on the street when he gets up on the police wagon to get a name? Can he be smashed down violently in front of a large group of people? Can they file false felony charges against him which they know are false? Can they commit perjury to procure a conviction and follow along relentlessly to do so?

When Terry was out there that night he should have known what he was up against. When he went out there that night he was a marked man. . . .

The trouble with Terry when he was out there, the trouble with him all his life up to the present is, he is an innocent. He thinks that you can go down into Mississippi and try to enforce the federal laws and people are going to be responsive and, especially, the authorities are going to protect you. He retains this attitude, this somewhat childish naïveté after three of the people who are party to this are murdered by deputy sheriffs while he is down there. He comes back up here, and when he investigates

VINCENT HALLINAN

and condemns and tries to prevent police brutality and is jerked off the patrol wagon by Brady, he says "What is that for?"

And the reason for his question is, my friends, that there is nothing malignant about him; and people who are not malignant themselves don't suspect malignancy in other people. They think everybody has the same attitude.

So what is to be done in a case of this kind? When it is brought by the district attorney, the district attorney stands in with the police. He becomes part of the police procedure. He shouldn't be, but he is. Now, the district attorney goes along and calmly proceeds with the prosecution instituted by the police, although they know and must know that Terry is entirely innocent of the charges. We come up into the civil court, and what do we have?—city officials defending the police, not saying the city isn't liable or we will settle our end of it or something of that kind, but vigorously defending their right to do this.

So our only recourse is to a jury. A jury is part of the law-enforcement agencies of the state. When all else fails, you can come before a jury to assess damages; and if damages are assessed against police for brutality, then the supervisors have to take a look at it and they say, "Well, push that fellow into some desk job so he hasn't any excuse to go out and slam somebody." We will stand for police officers possibly brutalizing people, but not if the city has to pay for it. And this is the only way that we have of curing this situation.

Well, if the jury says, verdict for the defendant, then that ratifies what the police say. That says to the police, "We are not interested. Go ahead. If some idealistic fool wants to go in and fool around in these things, why, we are not interested. That's *his* trouble. He was out there waving the banner of idealism, which you have when you are young and someplace along the line you lose." Somebody wrote, "There are gains for all our losses, there is balm for all our pain, but when youth a dream departs it takes something from our hearts and it never comes again."

So, he is preserved and he has kept the idealism and the flame of youth. Now, do we give the police carte blanche to be brutal? Do we tell the police, "all right, go out, shoot people, beat people up, we are not interested"?

As far as this thing here is concerned, we have done our part.

Terence Hallinan started out in the crusade against police brutality. Do I expect that we will get a verdict? I do. Maybe I am an innocent, too. Maybe I haven't lost the thing that he has. I assure you when I was around his age I launched on crusades that cost me bitterly. But I hope he keeps it up. I hope he isn't discouraged by it. I hope he stands up to things he believes to be right, and I think that this jury should and will go along with that.

You don't lose faith in human nature. He hasn't and I haven't, despite long periods of disappointment and frustration. You have faith in people if you have faith in yourself; and just as I feel that people who are not malignant don't suspect others of malignancy, so do I feel that people who have some belief in the justice of things feel that other people have the same belief. I say that there is throughout human beings a universal sense of justice and equity. That they want to see people get a square deal. That they don't want to see people oppressed or beaten or destroyed for trying to do what they consider to be good. That this is something in all of us which Addison back in the 1700s thought, too, when he wrote: "This sense of equity, this sense of justice is the one thing that our first parents were permitted to take with them when driven from the Garden. They looked back with tear-filled eyes to hear across the flaming swords of the Guarding Angels the dying music of paradise."

Thank you.

The jury returned a verdict in favor of Terence Hallinan against the city in the sum of $10,000 and $300 exemplary damages against Brady personally.

By no means was it the most important case ever tried by Vince Hallinan, but I think he is as proud of it as any of the others he has tried. For one thing, one of his sons was involved. For another, it gave him an opportunity to express in his favorite forum his fervent beliefs concerning justice and the need for change and the dependency of us all on the dissenter.

THE CASE OF THE
UNCONSCIOUS KILLER

The spectacular case of the *People* v. *Irene Mansfeldt* came up for trial in the San Francisco Superior Court in the winter of 1945. Irene Mansfeldt was the wealthy wife of an established San Francisco physician and the mother of their three children. Mrs. Mansfeldt convinced herself, with little evidence to solidify her suspicions, that her husband was having an affair with a nurse in one of the hospitals at which he was a staff member.

The distraught woman telephoned her supposed rival and made an appointment to meet her in front of the latter's apartment. She invited the nurse into her car to discuss the matter and, after a very brief conversation, Hallinan's soon-to-be client withdrew the pistol she had concealed in her purse-muff, shot her victim through the heart and, in a state of hysteria, drove the dead woman to a hospital. There, she gave complete and voluntary statements to police officers, newspaper reporters, and hospital attendants.

By the time Hallinan was retained, it all looked rather hopeless and a plea of "not guilty by reason of insanity" was formally entered—even though his client, up to the day of the shooting, had been engaged in her many normal activities, including amateur acting.

Before the matter came to trial, Dr. Mansfeldt died from an overdose of sleeping pills, taken either by accident or with suicidal intent. As Hallinan said: "This put us in a situation somewhat analogous to that expressed in the apothegm: 'Nothing is more useful than a dead partner.' We proceeded on the defense that her husband had prescribed sleeping pills and other narcotics for her over a long period of time; that he had given her an especially heavy dose the night before the

89

tragedy, and that this, supplementing the injury done by previous dosages, had caused such actual physical injury to the nerves of the brain as to bring her within the legal meaning of the word 'unconscious.' "

The Mansfeldt trial got under way two months after the shooting. It was an extremely dramatic trial and received daily front-page coverage in all the local newspapers. The state called in Dr. Harvey Dittstein as its neurological expert to refute Hallinan's contention that his client was "unconscious" within the meaning of the law at the time she shot the nurse. As the facts surrounding the homicide were established beyond cavil, Dr. Dittstein's testimony took on crucial importance.

Unconscious—while she engaged in her normal day-to-day activities? Unconscious—when she phoned her victim and met her as planned? Unconscious—with a gun concealed in her purse? Unconscious—when she shot her victim, then drove her to a hospital? The "unconscious" theory became most incredible, perhaps in the light of reports made by at least two newspapermen. They had interviewed the defendant shortly after the homicide, they said, and they testified that while the woman was undoubtedly upset or even hysterical, she certainly never gave the impression that she thought she had been unconscious.

When Dr. Dittstein took the stand, he recited his considerable experience in the United States and in Europe as a specialist in "diseases of the nervous system." He was assistant clinical professor of neurology at the University of California Medical School.

The prosecutor asked him a hypothetical question, based mostly upon incredibly damaging testimony already in evidence. The testimony indicated that Mrs. Mansfeldt, prior to and while committing the crime, knew exactly what she was doing, although she indeed may have been overwrought and may have been administered some pills and alcohol by her husband the previous evening. (The question, in transcript, consumed over forty-eight pages.) In response, the doctor told the court and the jury:

> My impression . . . would lead me to state that from the salient and important facts in the hypothetical question . . . there is nothing that leads me to believe that Mrs. Mansfeldt was in an unconscious or amnesic condition at the time of the shooting.

He explained his reasons:

VINCENT HALLINAN

. . . there was no interruption in the flow of consciousness and activity from the morning of October 4 [the day before the shooting], when we first picked up our information of Mrs. Mansfeldt's activities—that is, she was giving her daughter a violin lesson. All through that day and into the next, when she continued to tell her story—to the people at the Central Emergency Hospital, to Inspector Corrasa and his associates in the car, the people who interviewed her in the county jail, including, I think, two reporters that day and one the following day—there was a continuous, consecutive flow of ideas and activity without any break. And when I say "without any break," I mean gross break. I don't mean momentary drifting away, taking a mental rest, as it were, for a few seconds; I mean a complete break in the flow of consciousness, so one set of ideas left off and a new set of ideas came in, completely obliterating the incidents that occurred inbetween. . . .

At the time of the trial, some two months after the shooting, we find the first statement of any interruption in consciousness, in which she says that the first thing she remembers is finding herself on the floor of the car. That is the earliest point where she mentions a change in her state of consciousness.

Then I also find her statement while in court that on or about the eighteenth she first told Mr. Hallinan that she didn't remember what had happened on that day. If she told anybody anything to that effect before that time, there is nothing in this record. I also note from the record that she at no time expresses any sudden appreciation of the fact that there has been a blank period in her life. . . . An individual who passes from a state of amnesia into a state of consciousness, in my experience, invariably shows bewilderment and surprise and says, "Where am I? How did I get here? What has happened? What has been going on?" But no place in this record is there any evidence that Mrs. Mansfeldt passed through such a phase. I find nothing suggesting there has been a blank period in her life during this time, except these two incidents I described: the one in the car and her statement to Mr. Hallinan on the eighteenth, as related in court.

Now, I would like to take up the incident in the car. . . . There is nothing to indicate that the people who were with her at the time—the inspector, the stenographer, and the other person [whose name he didn't know or had forgotten]—made any comment that all of a sudden her condition changed, that she manifested surprise, and said, "Where am I? How did I get here?"

I can't conceive of a transition from amnesia to full consciousness, or even partial consciousness, which would not involve the recognition of the fact that something unusual has happened.

Long before the trial, Hallinan, knowing that the state would produce a doctor to debunk his unconsciousness theory, had for weeks immersed himself in medical textbooks, treatises, and journals. He had studied the brain and the nervous system to the point where he knew he was as familiar with the brain's anatomy and the professional medical words for it as anybody but a professor of anatomy might be. It was essential to his strategy that he give this impression to the jury in his cross-examination of the prosecution's expert. It was equally important to Hallinan that he commit all this recently learned technical information to memory, since he did not want to use any notes during his cross-examination.

His questioning of Dr. Dittstein was a tour de force, a masterful show of his own unique brain power. For hours and without any notes, Hallinan asked the expert countless questions about the brain, its various parts, and the specific functions of each part. In the beginning, the doctor, who was not as familiar as Hallinan was with all the nitty-gritty nomenclature of the brain, confined himself to fairly lay language; he was trying not to be "too technical," he said. Hallinan asked him not to do that and told him he wanted him to use technical terms.

He then had the witness draw a diagram of the brain and its various parts. One look, and Hallinan began to pick the diagram apart, pointing out that it really wasn't accurate. Finally, dismissing the doctor's drawing in disgust, he himself drew a diagram of the brain. He worked swiftly and casually, as though any lawyer, let alone any doctor, should be able to make such an immediate and accurate sketch. He didn't stint much on details, either—frontal lobe and temporal lobe, the Sylvian fissure, the Rolandic fissure, the gyrus, and the just-you-name-its, down to the last intricate detail.

As the hours went by, Dr. Dittstein offered and kept offering to save his interrogator time by freely admitting he was not a "neurosurgeon," but, rather, a neurologist.

Hallinan, however, chose to ignore the offer and with growing sarcasm began to refer to his own diagram, asking the doctor where various parts of the brain "lived":

H.: Now, if you cut through the brain along the mid-line and look at the same hemisphere from the other side, from the inside, you will find a structure that resembles that in some respect, isn't that correct?
DR.: Yes, that is correct.
H.: At least it will be as close as the little cartoon you drew this morning, isn't that right? (Forlornly, the doctor agreed.)

Again and again, Hallinan feigned surprise at the so-called expert's inability to name structures in the brain or to pinpoint precisely where they belonged—on either the doctor's "cartoon" or the lawyer's "more accurate" diagram. As the siege went on, Hallinan grew even more facile and at home with the subject, while the doctor's answers seemed to border on the realm of amnesia:

H.: As a matter of fact, the fissure does cut through, otherwise it wouldn't be called a fissure?
DR.: My recollection isn't that that particular fissure goes through. It may be, but it isn't my recollection.
H.: Fissure of Rolando; there is a large sulcus that runs about in the fashion I have indicated; do you know the name of the sulcus?
DR.: I don't remember.
H.: That is the cingulum, do you recognize that?
DR.: Vaguely.
H.: What do you call the gyrus underneath?
DR.: It is the—er—ah—
H.: It is called cingulate gyrus; do you recognize that?
DR.: Well, I have forgotten that.
H.: What would you say is the name of the portion above that?
DR.: I am trying to remember it. It slipped my mind. I thought I had it.
H.: Would you call that the sagittal, or something like that?
DR.: Maybe; I have forgotten.

The grand master wasn't about to relax his grip. . . . Besides, he had no intention of wasting a moment of all those weeks of cramming for the big test that was taking place now. He continued:

H.: Underneath that is the inferior temporal sulcus; in other words, the same one we saw here which does penetrate in part so that this lower structure is the inferior temporal gyrus.

Dr.: It does not penetrate; there is no point at which it penetrates.

H.: You say that this is the calcarine fissure?

Dr.: Yes.

H.: Are you sure of that?

Dr.: Yes.

H.: Are you sure it is not called the collateral fissure?

Dr.: No, I don't think so.

H.: Do you know what the gyrus above it is called?

Dr.: No.

H.: It is called the hippocampus.

Dr.: I know the front part of it. I thought possibly the back part of it was something else.

H.: Well, it is not. Do you know what the gyrus underneath is called?

Dr.: No.

Tireless and unrelenting, Hallinan continued to hammer away with one formidable question after another. And more and more, the doctor's responses grew weaker and vaguer. . . . "I don't know," or "I don't remember," or "Maybe; I have forgotten."

Finally, it seems, he'd had enough:

Dr.: I am not interested in this thing at all. I told you, Mr. Hallinan, a long time ago, that I wasn't qualifying as a neuroanatomist, and you keep going on and on and I am frankly—oh, I am not a neuroanatomist.

H.: Well, if a man gets up here and claims to be an automobile expert and he doesn't know a carburetor from a filling stem, some doubts might be cast on his qualifications.

Here, the prosecutor jumped in and asked the court to strike that statement of Hallinan's. The jury was instructed to disregard it. And, of course, as in all jury trials, although the statement was stricken from the record, it stayed in the jurors' minds.

Shortly after, Hallinan looked at the withered witness and said in a voice weary with exasperation, "Well, I am not going to ask you any more questions." (You could almost hear, "How utterly useless for a man like me who knows so much about the brain to question the state's so-called expert who knows so little.")

The prosecutor then attempted to rehabilitate the witness by pointing out that to be an expert on the brain and the nervous system, one did not have to be a neurosurgeon or a neuroanatomist.

By the time Hallinan rose to recross-examine, Dr. Dittstein looked as though he were sorry he hadn't studied dentistry instead. The examination was short and devastating:

H.: You now tell us you specialize in neurology and psychiatry, is that right?

Dr.: Right.

H.: When you first gave your qualifications you said you were a specialist in diseases of the nervous system, didn't you?

Dr.: Well, I am perfectly willing to qualify it—

H.: I asked you, did you say that?

Dr.: I did. Now, I am going to explain that. That is where I have been trying to anticipate you. I didn't mean to say that I specialized in every condition of the nervous system. I specialize in certain conditions of the nervous system.

H.: But you did give as your qualification when called here as a witness that you were a specialist in diseases of the nervous system, is that right?

Dr.: That is a general statement.

H.: The principal part of the nervous system is the brain, isn't it?

Dr.: True.

H.: Now, however, its having been demonstrated that your acquaintance with the anatomy of the brain is, shall we say with charity, a little sketchy, you state you are an expert in neurology and psychiatry, is that right?

DR.: Right.

H.: Of course, these things like psychiatry, where a man expresses his opinion as to what a person will do under given circumstances, are impossible to pin down so that a person is definitely committed to any fact that can be demonstrated, isn't it?

DR.: Perfectly true.

H.: But in the matter of the anatomy, if that can be demonstrated by books of anatomy and a person's qualifications would be fixed definitely by having him identify the parts of the very instrument he professes to be expert in—

DR.: *I didn't intend to present the opinion I was an expert on the structure of the brain.*

No further questions. As in so many trials, even those lasting weeks or months, trial lawyers know that everything they may hope for may come in a single sentence by a witness; one admission, a wrong date, a faulty observation, a seemingly innocent mistake may turn the tide. Less seasoned lawyers make the mistake of showing their glee or attempting to emphasize or re-emphasize a point, thereby giving an unsuspecting witness or inattentive adversary the opportunity to correct the record.

When Hallinan seduced the doctor into "admitting" that he wasn't an expert on the structure of the brain, this grand master knew enough to quit, to tuck that admission away for its crucial use later in summation. After all, the state's chief witness, who claimed Mrs. Mansfeldt wasn't unconscious, didn't seem to *know* too much about the brain. On the other hand, it surely appeared that Hallinan knew *all* there was to know about it.

Finally, when Vincent Hallinan summed up to the jury and told them that the poor unfortunate woman he represented was unconscious when she shot the nurse, they believed him. Mrs. Mansfeldt was not criminally insane under any theory of the law; yet if she was unconscious when she shot her victim, there could be no willfulness or premeditation, and she could only be convicted of manslaughter.

And so said the jury.

VINCENT HALLINAN

REVENGE IN PURGATORY

Those of us who have read Hallinan's book, *A Lion in Court*,* are familiar with the long struggle he had with the Market Street Railway Co., owner of the San Francisco Street Railway system. According to Hallinan, this company stacked the trial jury panels with friends and relatives of its officials, employees of public-liability insurance companies, and others who could be reasonably counted upon to vote against plaintiffs in actions brought against the company.

Among his antagonists was David Supple, a real-estate broker, who, Hallinan says, drew a salary from the City and County of San Francisco as a "grand jury expert."

Supple was a devout Roman Catholic and had been Grand Knight of the Knights of Columbus. One of his duties, it was charged, was to tip off Roman Catholics on the grand jury that Hallinan was a renegade Roman Catholic, to dispel any sympathy they might develop for Hallinan or any of his clients. The "disclosure" was also designed to counteract Hallinan's popularity in the Irish-Catholic community, as, in his youth, Hallinan had captained the football team of the small Catholic club that had won the Pacific Coast Club Championship.

Concerning his own beliefs as to Catholic dogma and traditions, which had dominated most of his life, Hallinan says, "I publicly denounced them as such with the energy and indignation of a sincere believer who suddenly realizes that he has been taken."

Hallinan was able to enlist other lawyers to join in the public fight against Supple and the jury commissioner; but the system continued to

* New York: Putnam, 1963.

prevail. Hallinan promised himself that one day he would pay David Supple for his treachery. "I did, too, even though he was dead before I had an opportunity to do so. But then it was an epic vengeance: I kept him out of heaven for seven years."

When Supple died, he left an estate of approximately $200,000. In his will, he left the bulk of his estate to be divided among twenty-eight agencies of the Roman Catholic Church. Supple's grandnephew consulted Hallinan in the hope of contesting and upsetting the will. As Hallinan explains it:

"The grandnephew was himself a Roman Catholic and I suspected that the Church, when the going got rough, would pull him off. A simple substitution of attorneys would leave me all dressed up and no place to go. However, in addition to his catholicity, he was impecunious; and for two hundred dollars, I purchased a half-interest in his claim for one of my sons, and then filed a contest of the will on behalf of both. It was direct and unequivocal. It was based upon the statutory grounds that the will had been procured by fraud."

The charges filed by Hallinan in this case struck at the very roots of Catholicism. They stated that, from childhood, David Supple had been a devout member of the Roman Catholic Church; and that all during his life, until the time of his death, he had been continuously taught, educated, and instructed by agencies of the Catholic Church that the following facts were true:

That in every human being there exists an entity called a "soul"; that the said soul is immortal; that it survives after the death of the body of the person to whom it pertains and continues to survive thereafter forever;

That the said soul, even after the death of the person to whom it pertains, can experience both pleasure and pain; and that each person's soul remains personal and identifiable with him;

That there exist in the universe three regions called, respectively, heaven, purgatory, and hell; that heaven is a place of complete and eternal bliss; that hell is a place of complete and eternal torment; and that purgatory is a place of temporary torment;

That immediately upon the death of a human being, his soul departs from his body and is forthwith consigned to one of those three regions; that if it is consigned to heaven, it remains in said region forever after enjoying consummate happiness and delight; that if it is consigned to hell, it remains there forever suffering excruciating pain and torment; that if it is consigned to purgatory, it will, during the term of its confinement, suffer excruciating torments but that sooner or later it will be released therefrom and permitted to enter heaven, where it will thereafter enjoy the same delights and benefits of those originally consigned thereto;

That the consignment of the soul to one or other of the said three regions depends upon the degree to which the person to whom it pertains, during his lifetime, observes and practices certain rules, regulations, and commands . . . proscribed by God who had created and ordained the situation hereinabove described; that God had designated and appointed the Roman Catholic Church as the depository, interpreter, and promulgator of each and all of the said rules [et cetera]; that the Roman Catholic Church is, in fact, the vicar and representative of God on earth and that its rules and regulations are actually those which have been made and ordered by God Himself;

That in order that the soul may enter directly into heaven upon death, it is necessary that the decedent shall have faithfully practiced and obeyed each and all the said rules, regulations, and commands; that if he has died while willfully guilty of the violation of any important such rule [et cetera], his soul will forthwith go to hell; that if he is guilty of lesser derelictions of such rules [et cetera], his said soul will be sent to purgatory where it will remain until such time as the offenses of which the decedent was guilty have been expiated, upon which it will be transmitted to heaven;

That in order for his soul to enter heaven, in addition to a certain disposition of the mind called "Faith," he must have performed certain good works. Included and important among such good works is that of bestowing gifts, legacies, and devices upon the said Church and upon its divisions and agents; that as a reward, the priests and agents of said Church will recite prayers and perform ceremonials which will have the effect of facilitating the consignment of his soul to heaven; and that the same may be employed to shorten the period which his soul, or that of any other person whom he may designate, may be required to spend in purgatory before being released into heaven.

It was further alleged that Supple firmly believed in all the representations and that all of them were untrue. Hallinan maintained that there was no such thing as a "soul"; that there was no part of the human being which, after his death, continues to carry on an independent existence; that there was no such place as heaven, hell, or purgatory; and that the procurement of bequests to the Church based upon such misrepresentation was fraudulent.

Hallinan, in part, relied upon a California statute that defined fraud as follows:

"(1) The suggestion, as a fact, of that which is not true, by one who does not believe it to be true;

"(2) The positive assertion, in a manner not warranted by the information of the person making it, of that which is not true, though he believes it to be true."

He argued:

> We are in an age which describes itself as scientific and professes the right to subject every concept and circumstance to a skeptical inquiry. . . . What we claim is that they cannot lawfully be employed to coerce the transfer of property or the execution of a will.
>
> . . . inquiry into the tenets of a religion and their operation has always been permitted where their observance violates a criminal statute, where they contravene personal or property rights, or even where they run counter to general government policies.

Hallinan then ticked off some of the religions in point:

> The United States government used military force against the Mormons in Utah when they refused to relinquish a basic tenet of their faith, the practice of polygamy.
>
> Close inquiry has been made into the religious tenets of Quakers, Jehovah's Witnesses, and other churches in numerous prosecutions for alleged draft evasion; and many adherents of those faiths have been sentenced to long terms in federal penitentiaries, often upon very narrow construction of their religious belief.

VINCENT HALLINAN

Next, the Seventh Day Adventists:

Forcible inoculation, blood transfusion, and other therapies have been imposed upon [them] in frank violation of their conscientious objections to them and the energetic protest of the individuals involved. Their long-established religious doctrines forbids such treatment. Sunday-closing laws have similarly been used against them.

Sincere and religious Dukhobors [a Russian religious sect separated from the Orthodox Church in 1785] have undergone conviction and imprisonment under indecent exposure statutes for standing naked before the Lord in public places.

For the courts to conduct themselves toward these relatively small fry while not daring to touch the leviathan Roman Catholic Church is to violate that other constitutional doctrine which guarantees equal protection to all.

Hallinan also argued emphatically that in this proceeding, plaintiffs' counsel was not engaging in any general attack upon any religion or denomination:

Fanticism in religious belief has written some of the darkest pages in history, but sanguinary massacres have also originated in unreasoning attachment to one's birthplace, a political party, an abstract principle, or even the colors worn by the participants in a chariot race. We regard human foibles with tolerance and, under appropriate circumstances, would courteously participate in ceremonials honoring Jehovah or his rivals described in 1 Kings 11: Ashtoreth, the Goddess of the Phoenicians, Chemosh, the God of the Moabites, and Milcom, a God of the Children of Ammon.

This does not mean that the various hierarchs of those devotional systems should have carte blanche to possess themselves of the properties of believers by imposing on their credulity. In the present instance, are the agents of the Church permitted to invent a fictitious region of eternal torment, con credulous people like David Supple into accepting the fact of its existence, terrify him with the prospect of eternal imprisonment in it, proffer their good offices to rescue him from it, and take over his estate as compensation for their efforts?

To ask this question, we repeat, is not to assail any religious belief or system. But religion is only incidentally involved in the takeover of David Supple's estate. From the most primitive times, man has sought some answer to the enormous mystery of existence which everywhere and forever surrounds him. Restricted by the limitations of his senses and intellect, he has accepted fantasy and illusion rather than uncertainty. In the same way that he evades those aspects of reality which he cannot endure by the several escapist devices open to him, so he evades the insoluble enigma by the device of religious faith. His right to do so and the particular forms of his faith are protected by law.

How far does this go? We have stood before the palace of the Archbishop of Manila, surrounded as it is, by the miserable hovels of that city's countless paupers, and discussed that cleric's ownership of banks and insurance companies. Those particular financial institutions are, in practice, exempt from legal interference.

In Italy, the principal political party is controlled by the Vatican. There, as in Spain, the Church and the State become merged and the Church controls the State, just as, in the United States, the Mormon Church controls the State of Utah.

As church property is exempt from taxation in California, it is impossible to obtain an appraisal of its value, but it certainly constitutes a fantastic acquisition. Are the courts powerless to prevent its expansion by fraud because the deceit involved includes some asserted theological doctrine?

Hallinan's fantastic notion that the proceeding instituted by him was of the same significance as the Scopes trial was coolly received. And although he denies that he felt he would win, his description of how he felt arguing against six opponents is interesting:

There seemed something curiously unreal in these proceedings. I knew these six lawyers, either personally or by reputation. For the most part, they were able, intelligent, and sophisticated. Yet they appeared not to recognize the incongruity of men of that description vigorously protecting processes and beliefs which be-

VINCENT HALLINAN

longed back in the Middle Ages. I felt, like Mark Twain's American Yankee in King Arthur's court, puzzled about how to raise a question as to the validity of a belief in minds which were closed to any inquiry.

The matter was in the courts seven years before the Supreme Court turned down Hallinan's request to be heard. As Hallinan viewed the case:

All of this took seven years and meanwhile the Church was deprived of the use of the money while it was held by the special administrators. I believed it likely that, although the possibility of losing the bequest existed, the Church would not hand over from its "savings account" the indulgences that would permit David Supple's soul to enter heaven. I felt I had squared my grievances against him by holding him for so long a period in purgatory.

Meanwhile, as there was no such thing as David Supple's soul, heaven, hell, or purgatory, I had this small satisfaction without injuring him or anybody else

BARNABAS F. SEARS

Barnabas Sears, a robust little gray-haired man, is a grand master who has received appreciation and acclaim countrywide. He is in every way the complete trial lawyer.

Like Vincent Hallinan and Edward Williams, Barney Sears is also a teacher and student of the art and history of advocacy. His thinking and conversation reflect the influence of some of the greatest legal minds to be found in literature. Sears has "studied" with Sir William Blackstone, Lord William Mansfield, Oliver Wendell Holmes, Louis Brandeis, Felix Frankfurter, Benjamin Cardozo, Paul Stryker, John W. Davis, Max Steuer, and many others. He thinks of his illustrious idols as teachers and prophets and believes that a knowledge of their ideas and skill is absolutely indispensable to the trial lawyer. His chief criticism of lawyers in general, and trial lawyers in particular, is that they have forgotten what he regards as the signal importance of the history of the law, of judges, and trial lawyers.

In discussing the requisite qualities for a trial lawyer, Sears usually goes back to history: "I've always had an abiding interest in history, particularly in legal history. I haven't read as much of it in the last ten years as I used to because I really haven't had the time. Hell, I'm practically in and out of court most of the time; but I've got in my library Lord John Campbell's *Lives of the Lord Chancellors* and the *Lives of the Chief Justices*, and I've got biographies of all the great English trial lawyers as well as the Irish bar, and they produce some great ones, too. I'm sure I learned something from studying their methods. But a lawyer—and this is not an original statement—a lawyer without a knowledge of history, without a smattering of the classical culture, is a mechanic.

"To be a trial lawyer, you've got to have a working knowledge of human nature as much as possible; you've got to have a pretty fair knowledge of history; you have got to have a pretty good knowledge of the life of the trial lawyers who have preceded you and what their experience has been; you've got to study some of their methods. That's not to say that you should try to copy them—because you can't copy them. I've said this, I don't know how many times—and I say it again: there are as many ways to try a lawsuit as there are good lawyers to try them."

Interviews with Sears involve captivating excursions into the past history of English and American law and advocacy. Jurors, spectators, and lawyers listening to his summations are a rapt audience of his lectures on what the great legal scholars would have to say if they were alive and able to add their genius to the matter on trial. (Invariably, the great scholars would have said that Sears's clients were right and his opponents wrong.)

His father, who had begun his law practice in the territory of the Dakotas in 1888, died when Sears was eight years old. Young Barney had always been impressed with his mother's stories of his father's accomplishments as a trial lawyer, and it seemed only natural that in time he, too, should turn to law. Typical of the grand masters whom he was to join, Sears was a performer at an early age. He appeared in high school plays and was always interested in dramatics and debating.

After graduating from high school, Sears attended St. Thomas Military Academy and College in St. Paul. Then he spent a year at Notre Dame Law School, and continued his postgraduate work at Georgetown University Law School. Sears was on the debating teams at St. Thomas, at Notre Dame, and at Georgetown, and one of his most prized possessions is a silver loving cup received by him in 1926 at his law-school graduation, for being the prize debater.

Sears began practicing law in Jacksonville, Illinois, for a member of that state's General Assembly. His wife, Alice, was one of his clients.

Although Sears had been offered jobs with several prestigious law firms in Chicago, he declined them all in favor of striking out on his own in Jacksonville. ("Hell, I didn't even know where it was!") Sears wanted trial experience and decided he could get more of it as a country lawyer, trying forty-dollar claims, than he could working in a large Chicago firm writing briefs and memoranda.

The country boy (now in his mid-seventies, married, with twelve grandchildren) came, as they say, a long way. . . . He has managed to amass a rich professional profile: past president of the Illinois State Bar Association; past chairman of the American Bar Association, House of Delegates; past president of the American College of Trial Lawyers; and, in 1971, he was named Chicagoan of the Year by the Junior Association of Commerce and Industry.

Like most trial lawyers and many grand masters, Sears fears young lawyers the most. "If they show real aptitude as trial lawyers, they can butcher a veteran." As usual, he has stories to illustrate his point. Once, he was trying a case against Ed Burke, one of the most famous trial lawyers in Springfield, Illinois. Burke's case was so overwhelming, Sears says, and his so weak, that out of a sense of desperation he appealed to the jury for help. He pleaded with them that as much as he believed in the righteousness of his case, he was unable to plead it properly in the presence of one of the state's greatest trial lawyers. His entire summation consisted of nothing but accolades for Burke's skill and apologies for his own ineptitude. After Sears had won the case, Burke approached him and said, "Barney, you have a great future. . . . I've had a hell of a lot of lawyers try to curse me out of court, but you're the first one who ever kissed me out."

Sears then tells about William T. Wilson, another well-known lawyer in Morgan County in the 1930s. "He never had an unrighteous case in his life, never in his life. I tried cases against him for four years. Good cases. I never won a one." In one case, Sears represented an insurance company whose client was the Great Atlantic & Pacific Tea Company, whose truck made runs between Springfield and Jacksonville, Illinois. On one trip, a bridge overpass, maintained by the Burlington Railroad (Wilson's client), collapsed. Sears says that Wilson made one of the finest opening speeches he ever heard before a jury. "He had that goddamned A & P Company truck *attacking* the Burlington Railroad's bridge. You knew that something was going to happen with that Great A & P truck lumbering down the highway approaching that poor damn bridge."

Sears was finally able to win the case by complaining that he had tried a great number of cases against Wilson and had never won one. He asked the jury, "Could it be that here again, as in the cases in the past, Mr. Wilson represents all the honest, God-fearing, law-abiding citizens of the community and I represent all the liars, fools, and crooks?" Again, Sears was able to triumph over a far more skilled advocate by appealing to the jury's sympathy and sense of fairness.

And then, as has happened so often in interviews with other grand masters, Sears proceeded to illustrate his point by telling a story that refuted it:

"I tried a case once in a little town called Yorkville, over in Kenneth County. I represented an insurance company and the case was against Stillman's Celebrated Freckle Cream. It seems the wife of the promotional manager of Fred Waring's orchestra walked into a hotel drugstore in Detroit, and bought a jar of Stillman's Celebrated Freckle Cream, which she applied around her shoulders, her bosom, and so forth, and she sustained a burn, which she claimed was caused by excess mercurial content in that cream. Now, they did an assay up in Detroit which was an incorrect assay. Actually, she was allergic to the cream.

She was one of the most gorgeous-looking creatures, about thirty-five years of age, that you'd want to look at. We tried that case before eight Kenneth County housewives and four men, one of whom was the cashier of a local bank. And God, these guys on the other side [opposing counsel] were so glad to get those women! Well, when those eight ordinary-looking Kenneth County hausfraus saw that plaintiff, they thought to themselves, What the hell does she need money for? Anyone as beautiful and gorgeous as this, what does she need money for?

"And how was the case decided? Eight-to-four. Eight women against the plaintiff, four men for the defendant. I talked to the bank cashier afterward. He said, 'That's the goddamnedest case I was ever in. The four of us, we were all for the plaintiff, but hell,' he said, 'we couldn't move one of those women at all.'"

Among the portraits hanging in Sears's office is one of Lord Erskine, a great English advocate and later judge. Pointing to it, Sears said:

"There's [Lord John] Erskine. Now, it's no mere coincidence that those two pictures [the other of Lord Mansfield] happen to be there. I've got those two pictures there to remind me of the independence and rights of trial lawyers. Lord Erskine was trying a case before Lord

Mansfield, who was a very austere Englishman. And he said something to Lord Mansfield that met with his displeasure and Mansfield rebuked him with: 'Young man, I hope you are mindful of your duties towards this court.' And Erskine replied, 'I am, your Lordship, and I trust your Lordship is equally mindful of his duties towards the bar.' Well, Christ, nobody had ever spoken to Mansfield that way! But a good trial lawyer takes no guff from a judge."

I would venture to say that a Barney Sears, independent and mindful of his rights as a trial lawyer, would have spoken to Lord Mansfield that way.

Sears's name and fame have gone all the way to the top—to the White House. In April 1973 the Chief Justice recommended that a special prosecutor be appointed in the Watergate matter. Attorney General Richard G. Kleindienst met with President Nixon to discuss it. The President wanted to know if Kleindienst had anyone special in mind for the post.

A section of the Presidential tapes that were delivered to the Judiciary Committee discloses the following remarks by Kleindienst: "The one person that everybody kind of comes together on is a guy by the name of Barnabas Sears in Chicago. He is the attorney that was appointed to prosecute the killing of those blacks by the police—you know the thing in Chicago? . . . Barney Sears is a past president of the House of Delegates of the American Bar Association, a 'distinguished' lawyer and, you know, has all those credentials. He's a very, very independent person."

Sears was never offered the post. Asked if he would have accepted it, he said he didn't think so.

In May 1975, at the twenty-fifth annual meeting in Chicago of the Bar Association of the Seventh Federal Circuit (Illinois, Indiana, and Wisconsin), Mr. Justice Harry A. Blackmun of the U.S. Supreme Court addressed several hundred federal judges and lawyers. In speaking about the "inside workings of a strange institution," he explained that Mr. Justice Thurgood Marshall had a habit of stating a view in the middle of a lawyer's argument and then asking, "Am I right or wrong?" "The lawyers always say, 'You're right,'" said Justice Blackmun. "But I'm waiting for the day when someone like Barnabas Sears will say, 'You're wrong.'"

CONSPIRACY IN BLUE

In early 1960 Chicago and the entire country were stunned by shenanigans alleged to have taken place within the Summerdale District of the Chicago Police Department. In January of that year, police and representatives of the State's Attorney's Office in Cook County entered the homes of some police officers and discovered a boodle of stolen valuables that had been pilfered during the course of several burglaries in the Chicago area during 1958 and 1959.

The case broke after the arrest of Richard Morrison, a twenty-five-year-old experienced thief and burglar. At the time several unrelated criminal charges were pending against Morrison. He confessed to the burglaries and said they had been accomplished with the assistance of two companions and members of the Chicago Police Department. And he named several police officers in whose homes a considerable quantity of the stolen property could be found.

In March 1960 a Cook County grand jury returned indictments against seven police officers, all of whom had been working in the Summerdale District. Each defendant was charged with conspiracy to commit burglary and receiving stolen property. The indictments further named Morrison and his two accomplices as co-conspirators.

The indictments charged that in June 1958 some of the defendant police officers had met with Morrison and assured him they would give him protection while he committed burglaries in their district, provided they received a portion of the proceeds of the burglaries. During the trial Morrison testified at great length and with great particularity concerning the various burglaries committed by him in conspiracy with the defendants.

Barney Sears and another Chicago lawyer, Charles M. Rush, were appointed as special prosecutors. Sears achieved a great deal of fame in Illinois and throughout the country as a result of this case. His summation to the all-female jury in the prosecution of these defendants has been recognized as a masterpiece. The defendants were represented by some of Illinois' most outstanding trial lawyers. Traditionally, it has been difficult to find juries willing to convict policemen. Whatever their transgressions, officers of the law are always successfully portrayed by defense attorneys as brave men whose courage and willingness to sacrifice their lives stand between all of us and chaos. Here is Sears in his closing argument:

May it please Your Honor, distinguished counsel for the defense, and ladies of the jury: This is the third day of the eleventh week of this trial. I am certain it is evident, without a great deal of extended observation, that His Honor and you ladies of the jury have devoted yourselves to the cause of justice. If I may be permitted the personal reference, as that seems to be the custom of counsel in this case, I want to say that in the more than thirty-five years that I have practiced at the bar of this state I have never felt more that I was in a courtroom and that I was addressing a judge and a jury more devoted to their task.

I have listened for better than six hours to the stirring, the eloquent, and the able arguments of counsel who represent these defendants. I heard about Socrates, Plato, Learned Hand, Judas, Ponzi, Krueger, Perry Mason, ghosts, Fagin, Little Nell, Napoleon, corporation lawyers, insurance-company lawyers, hoaxes, the Prudential Building, the greatest wrecking crew, pie plates, lead balloons, Tennyson, Shakespeare, and finally, the navy.

It has been my experience that long before the lawyers ever begin to address a jury, the jury has fairly well considered the case. There is a reason for that, and that is, only the jury knows what the facts of the case are.

It is one thing for a lawyer to stand up and read to the jury questions and answers, which the jury has heard, ignoring completely the conduct and demeanor of the person on the stand when the question was asked and the answer given.

I want to say to you that I don't believe there is much I can do in this closing argument to the jury to assist you insofar as the facts are concerned, because I believe that each and every one of you knows more about the facts of this case than I or any other lawyer in this courtroom. You know what we lawyers do. . . . We write down the questions and answers that we want to write down—unwittingly, if you please—and we write them down out of context. And then we presume, in an argument to the jury, on the faith of our personal assertion, that such-and-such were the facts of the case. Well, you can't do two things. You can't ask questions and get answers and take notes and know what is going on in a courtroom.

Now, you heard the evidence, and you heard it from the mouths of the witnesses, and you heard perhaps as stirring a series of arguments to a jury that I have ever heard in any case.

He then began to complain to the jury about the tactics used by defense counsel throughout the trial and in their summations. Defense counsel had remarked upon the fact that neither Sears nor Rush was a criminal lawyer. Sears told the jury that there was "no 'mystery' about the practice of criminal law"; that although the defense attorneys were criminal lawyers, this did not mean that they "breathed life into the Constitution, as one of them suggested." Referring to one of the defense counsel, he said, "It can truly be said of him, as was once said of that Montana judge, he may be in error but he is never in doubt."

He proceeded to give illustrations of how the defense commented on some of the evidence without even mentioning far more damaging evidence. Sears then spoke solemnly about the jury system, in which he has an abiding faith:

I give you those two illustrations solely for the purpose of proving my deep conviction that only the jury knows what the facts are. And that is why you are here. The story of why you are here is an interesting, romantic one. Our law has never been able to devise a better method of determining the truth in any given case except by a jury of twelve. It goes back, your duty, your awesome, awful duty—and one can never stand in front of a jury without a feeling of awe at the responsibility that the law has rightfully entrusted to the jury—it goes back to the fifteenth century. You are the judge of the whole case. The law, you get from the court. You take that law and you apply it to the facts of the case, or you apply the facts to the law of the case. And you don't have to give any reasons for your answer. Your answer is yes or no.

Something has been said of the fact that this is a jury of women. I want to say something about that, too, because I lived at a time and practiced at a time when the jury was a male jury and when the administration of criminal justice was left solely in the hands of men. The judges were men, the jurors were men.

I think it was twenty, maybe twenty-five years ago, that our legislature, in its wisdom, passed an act that permitted women to serve on juries (after it had declared unconstitutional a previous act of the legislature putting forth the same purpose).

And this is not flattery. I don't seek to flatter you ladies. I seek to assist you, if I can, in some small measure in arriving at a correct result.

I seem to feel that from the time that women were permitted to serve on juries, a more moral tone was infused into that collective jury than had existed before. And there is a reason for that. This is kind of a tough old world. There are many things done in this world that shouldn't be done, and men are exposed to those things much more than women.

It has, in truth, been said that a woman is the anchor of society around which our whole social order of necessity revolves.

Now, ladies, the law also says that you don't have to act any differently as jurors than you act as women. Because you are sitting in that jury box you don't have to apply to your judgment in the matter any different standards than you would apply in a matter of ordinary affairs. And that is the genius of the jury system. Its positive genius is the collective common sense that it has infused into the law. So much for that.

This is a courtroom, and a very distinguished one, and you are parties to the administration of criminal justice. That is what this case is about. And although I may be ill-fitted by experience to participate as a prosecutor in this case, it being my first appearance as counsel for the state, I will try to do honorably and fairly the best I can in assisting you to arrive at a correct result.

This indictment charges that these defendants, together with Morrison and Wilde [another accomplice], combined, conspired, confederated, and agreed with each other—not that they only "agreed," as Mr. Bellows [one of the defense counsel] says. And His Honor will instruct you as to what a conspiracy is.

Now, this is not the case of Morrison versus these defendants. There was a time in the history of English law when criminal prosecutions were private. That private prosecutor would not be Morrison himself, one of the thieves; he would be the gentleman who owned the property that was taken. It was found that it disturbed the public peace to permit private prosecutions in criminal cases; and so the people of the state, in their sovereign capacity, took over the prosecution of criminal cases.

You ladies of this jury could not be on a more important mission in your life, because the very basic fabric of society, the legal order upon which all of the social interests of the state depend, is a proper and true administration of the criminal law.

Here, Sears dipped into his awesome reservoir of legal history for a few words from Mr. Justice Donovan, the distinguished English judge who presided in the Brighton conspiracy case:

". . . one of the most serious cases that has been tried in this or any other criminal court for a long time. The ordinary criminal is problem enough for society; but if those who are paid to protect us against him instead join forces with him, a much more deadly enemy appears upon the scene. So far as these guardians-turned-criminals are concerned, the community's defenses are for the moment down, and until the difficult tasks of detection and conviction are accomplished, much more may be done. Because he [meaning the police officer] is not only familiar with the devices of the crook but by the very nature of his office he will not readily be suspected."

That, ladies of the jury, is the posture of this case. That is the case we are trying here. We are trying here the People of the State of Illinois against seven police officers, and we are trying them for conspiracy. They acted and combined together to commit burglaries and to receive stolen property.

"O, conspiracy, / Shamest thou to show thy dangerous brow by night, / When evils are most free? / O, then, by day / Where wilt thou find a cavern dark enough / To mask thy monstrous visage? / Seek none, conspiracy; / Hide it in smiles and affability." That is

BARNABAS F. SEARS

to say, if you please, affability of counsel; or, as Marc Antony later remarked, "So are they all, honorable men."

Now, a conspiracy case, as the books expound, is normally a difficult case to prove, because usually it has to be proved by circumstantial evidence in which the devious windings of the conspirators must be followed, due to their natural tendency to avoid detection.

Is that right? Does that make sense? Were these not committed in the dark of the night, when peaceable and law-abiding citizens were asleep in their beds and had the right to presume that they, their spouses, their children, and, yea, even their property, were secured by the hands of these gentlemen in blue? For who is the law at the corner of Wilson and Broadway; who is the law at Lawrence and Sheridan; and who is the law at Western and Bryn Mawr, or Devon? Who is the law? Is it the man in the blue uniform with the star? If it isn't he, who is it? That's what this case is about.

Sears then dealt with the traditional problem of a prosecutor who has decided to grant immunity to a participant in a crime. Morrison, the burglar, without whose testimony the state probably could never have proven its case, had received such immunity. Of course, the defense lawyers had capitalized on this fact and on the equally important fact present in almost all criminal prosecutions—that the state's case rested largely upon the testimony of unsavory characters. After pointing out that immunity had been granted by prosecutors throughout the years, Sears told the jury:

And His Honor will instruct you that that act of granting immunity was the sole and exclusive right of the prosecution, and that the question of immunity may be considered by you only for the purpose of determining the credibility of the accomplices. I am as confident as I am standing here addressing you ladies that you are going to follow that instruction to the letter, notwithstanding the impassioned appeals that have been made to you on that question and on that issue.

Elsewhere it was said, "Of course, the accomplices were very bad men. Accomplices in murder always are. But it is almost a truism in the criminal law that if the testimony of bad men were absolutely rejected, many murderers would escape the punishment which they deserve." Now, does that make sense?

You know, we have had a son brought into the case, we have had a daughter brought into the case. I'd like to bring in my dear old Irish grandmother. She used to say a few things, uneducated and unlettered as she was, that she got from the wisdom of the ages, from the folklore of our culture, and one of them was, "It takes a thief to catch a thief." Another was, "Birds of a feather flock together." And another of them was, "Take a look at them. Take a look at them."

And Sears indeed took a long good look at the defendants—a look so compelling that the jurors found themselves glaring right along with him. His attitude was one of disgust for the defendants and sadness for the people he represented. Then he walked over to the counsel table, near which most of the exhibits, including the alleged stolen goods, were stored. Pointing to those exhibits, he again addressed the jury:

Now, we get to the facts in this case. How many times did they object to these exhibits? May I ask what is wrong with these exhibits? You ladies know what is wrong with them.

"For there is no good tree that bears bad fruit." Nobody has quoted from this book before. "Nor is there a bad tree that bears good fruit. Every tree is known by its fruit, for from thorns men do not gather figs, neither from a bramble do they harvest grapes. A good man out of the good treasure of his heart bringeth forth good things, and an evil man out of the evil treasure bringeth forth evil things. For out of the abundance of the heart the mouth speaketh." Is that true? "By their fruits ye shall know them."

What are these the fruits of—the good tree or the bad tree? Each and every one of them, all some twenty-seven of them are illicit, are stolen, are ill-gotten. They are, ladies of this jury, the fruits of the crime. No wonder they object to what they call a parade. Don't be influenced by this "parade." We will come to what they had to say about those articles a little later.

As I understand the defense in this case, Morrison is all of the things they said about him; and being all of the things they said about him, you are to ignore what they themselves are.

BARNABAS F. SEARS

Now, I don't rise above the level of my acquaintances, so long as I keep their company and consort with them, because a pupil doesn't rise above his teacher any more than a river rises above its source.

Item by item, Sears reviewed the evidence that had been presented against each of the defendants during the ten-week trial. He reminded the jury of the inconsistencies between what the state's chief witness said and what the police officers said. And, again and again, he reminded them that every time an exhibit—such as a stolen article found in one of the defendant's homes—was sought to be introduced into evidence, the lawyers quickly objected:

And isn't it odd that five of them are the recipients of these exhibits, which you shouldn't see? I'll tell you why you shouldn't see these exhibits. They can't cross-examine those exhibits. They can't ask those exhibits any questions and, with the art that is justly their pride and their privilege, corner or confuse those exhibits. They are mute, incontrovertible evidence of what transpired in this case. . . .

The defense attorneys had constantly referred to the "hoax" that Morrison had perpetrated on the defendant policemen. Sears now addressed himself to that:

Oh, but this is all a big hoax. Morrison fooled the state's attorney, fooled the chief of police, fooled us, the wrecking crew, fooled everybody. One big hoax. The master swindler, the modern Ponzi and modern Krueger, took in each and every one of these poor, unsuspecting defendants.

Was this master swindler hoaxing all of these gentlemen trained in the detection of crime who are supposed to know a confidence man when they see one, and who were being paid by the people of Chicago to enforce criminal justice?

One of the defendants' contentions was that all the burglaries alleged by the state were independent of each other and not the product of conspiracy or confederation among the defendants. Sears reminded the jury of that contention and asked:

Where have I been for ten long weeks through this hot, humid summer? Where have you been, ladies of the jury, with the sacrifice that you are making, with your personal matters put aside? Where has His Honor been, with the heavy black robes he so adorns? Where have we been? Not a conspiracy? What else could it be? What else could it be?

A chair, alleged to have been stolen, was found in a policeman's home. One of the defense counsel, in his summation, referred to it as a "lousy chair" and asked the jury if they were prepared to send a man to the penitentiary over the theft of a "lousy chair."

Sears dealt with that argument with emotion:

And that is the "lousy chair" his counsel speaks about, and all he can see in that chair is a lousy chair. He can't see in that chair a stained blue uniform, he can't see in that chair an oath forsworn. He can't see in that chair a public trust violated.

What do you ladies see in that chair? I think I know what you see in that chair.

Relentlessly, Sears went over and over the evidence, pointing out the inconsistencies between what the defendants said and what they did. He was understanding, touchingly so, about the difficult position of the wives of the defendants in whose homes the stolen property was found. He benignly excused the absence of the wives who failed to corroborate their husband's testimony, as well as those who chose to honor their marital vows above their obligations to testify truthfully.

Finally, and patiently, he again reminded the jury of the importance of their function and of the fateful importance of their deliberation in this trial:

Now, what do we do in a case of this character? What do we do? You have been brought into a case by destiny, a case that is writing an indelible chapter in the history of this city. And no one will ever write the story of the City of Chicago without writing the story of the Summerdale trial. I don't, heaven knows, by any manner mean to say to you that, therefore, you should convict these defendants, and each one of them. I don't want to have it upon my professional career that I suggested that to a jury. But I do want to have it upon my professional career that I reminded the jury of the interest of the people of the community—not that I think it is necessary, but because it is my duty to write the record that way.

You are the organ of this community. That's why we have juries, so that the level of the community, good or bad, will never rise above or fall below its true level. The indignation, the virtue, or the vice of a community is represented in the verdicts of its juries, because its juries, not His Honor, enforce the criminal law. His Honor is but the organ of the law, and you ladies are the organ of the community. It is an awesome responsibility; but you have never had a finer hour. You will never again in your life ascend to the heights of civic duty and civic responsibility and civic power that you now possess.

I will speak but briefly on the matter of punishment. If you believe beyond a reasonable doubt that all or any one or more of these defendants are guilty of the crime of conspiracy as charged in the indictment and as laid down by His Honor, I say to you that regardless of what these gentlemen say about the penitentiary, it is the only proper verdict that can be entered. The law has always frowned upon conspiracy and the law has always looked with extreme disfavor upon breaches of the public trust. Mr. Bellows [opposing counsel] himself said that you should send to the penitentiary men dangerous to the community.

I remind you again what Justice Donovan said: "Who could possibly be more dangerous to a community than policemen who have forsworn their oaths?" Is it not true, as he said, that the defenses of society are down if the men we pay to track down and apprehend criminals themselves consort and commit crimes with them?

I want to read you those words that are inscribed upon the walls of Judge La Buy's old courtroom. I will never forget them: "It is the duty of every intelligent juryman to consider that the functions with which he is invested by the state are limited by the extent of his commission, and he must remember that not merely power has been delegated to him, but trust reposed in him. He ought ever to consider not his own wishes but the obligation which the law and his oath impose." And may I say to you that duty performed or duty violated will be with you all the days of your life.

How difficult it is for us to perform our duty with the feelings of compassion and sympathy that are in every human breast. It is not criticism of anyone to say that on occasion we shirk our duty. We all do. We are but of the flesh. But here is a case where your duty indeed must be an onerous one. Your proper natural sympathies, your feelings must necessarily be with the defendants at this bar. It isn't a pleasant thing to find that people have engaged in conduct beyond the pale of the law. But as theirs was, so is yours a duty of public trust. And may I say to you in conclusion that I have every confidence that you will discharge that duty in the finest tradition of any jury that ever sat in this or any other court.

Mine is now over. I didn't ask for this job any more than you did. As I told you before, in over thirty-five years at the bar, this is the first time I ever prosecuted anybody for a crime. I am ill-fitted by disposition to perform this task, but I do it for the forces of civil society, for the republic that His Honor so eloquently describes, the faith, the hope of our ancestors in this form of government that we have (man's first enduring victory over tyranny since the days of republican Rome) for the liberty of the individual, for the liberty of the state; and for those countless thousands of people in the City of Chicago who have a legal right to sleep peaceably in their beds.

After you have performed the duty, the onerous duty that I feel you are about to perform, you will have the consolation of having preserved your personal dignity, your personal integrity. And thank God a dedicated group such as you are going to pass upon the facts of the case. Thank you.

Each of the defendants was found guilty as charged and sentenced to prison. All the convictions were subsequently affirmed by the Illinois Supreme Court.

BARNABAS F. SEARS

Sears V. The State's Attorney,
The City of Chicago, Public Apathy,
AND *Judicial Ineptitude*

During the career of almost every grand master, he is subjected to at least one skirmish with the law, in which he, rather than his client, becomes the focus of attention.

Too often, the authority of the government and those who serve it (such as prosecutors and judges) and the political climate during the trial of some celebrated cases combine to make fair trials impossible. Perhaps it is the prosecutor seeking to pad his reputation, or a biased judge too willing to destroy a reputation, or perhaps certain civic-minded organizations or the free press intent on espousing their own viewpoints—any one of these "perhapses" can pollute the impartial atmosphere requisite for a fair trial. Sometimes the resultant pollution tips the scales of justice so preposterously that even the wizardry of a grand master cannot restore an equitable balance.

Almost all these pollutant factors came into play in the bizarre Black Panther case in Chicago, a case that was dragged and banged about the courtrooms for almost three years. This particular case constitutes one of the most disgusting and frustrating sagas of official hypocrisy, judicial ineptitude (if not downright dishonesty), and public indifference ever experienced in the United States—or, for that matter, Chicago, where, to the powerful, "justice" means favors and folderol more often than not.

In the early morning hours of December 4, 1969, fourteen police officers assigned to the State's Attorney's Office converged on an apartment that was thought to be a Black Panthers' headquarters. They had a warrant to search for illegal weapons allegedly maintained in the apartment. According to the police, who were armed with a sub-machine gun and five shotguns, among other things, they announced themselves with all peaceful intentions and were met with "a thunder of gunfire." After a total of 130 rounds of ammunition had been fired, two of the apartment's occupants, Fred Hampton (age twenty-one) and Mark Clark (age twenty-two), lay dead and seven surviving Panthers were arrested.

Shortly after the raid, the state's attorney, Edward V. Hanrahan, gave an exclusive interview to the Chicago *Tribune* in which he "conclusively" proved that the Panthers opened the battle by firing a shotgun blast through the door. The following day, Hanrahan's office staged an alleged re-enactment of the raid for a local television station.

The Panthers claimed that not a single shot had been fired from their apartment and that the raid was a simple case of an assassination by the police of two of its members and the deliberate wounding of four others.

One thing became increasingly clear: were it not for the unfunny fact that two human beings had been killed, Hanrahan's bush-league police assault resembled a Mack Sennett comedy or a scene from a Three Stooges movie far more than a serious attempt by a sophisticated police force to uncover arms allegedly stashed away by black militants. Strangely enough, it was not until December 17 that the Cook County Coroner ordered the Black Panthers' apartment sealed, so that for almost two weeks the "scene of the crime" had been trampled over by literally thousands of curiosity-seekers. Stranger still, nobody was able to come up with Panther bullets proven to be from Panther guns, although many, many police bullets were found in the apartment. Critics of Hanrahan's raid pointed out the absurdity of contentions by the police and others as to how many bullets supposedly fired by the Panthers were fired through open doors and windows in a small slum apartment, while so many bullets fired by the police seemed to be accounted for in floors, ceilings, walls, and closed doors.

Irrespective of what had actually happened in the Panther apartment on that day, the police so badly bungled its own investigation of what took place, so much evidence seemed to disappear, that even the most conservative and right-wing Chicago newspaper, along with a number of civic agencies, demanded either a federal investigation or the appointment of a special prosecutor.

BARNABAS F. SEARS

A whitewash by the Chicago Police Internal Investigations Division on December 19, and the twelve-day "investigation" by a coroner's jury ending in a verdict of justified homicide were considered totally inadequate, and a federal grand jury was convened. After five months of deliberations, the grand jury report failed to indict anybody; but it concluded that the police raid, consisting of fourteen plain-clothes men with insufficient equipment for a night raid and "no plan for dealing with potential resistance, seems ill-conceived." It pointed out that although the Panthers had been accused of firing ten shots, the FBI had been able to ascribe positively only *one* of the 82-to-99 shots fired to a weapon confiscated from the apartment. (The firearms expert who made the initial police report subsequently testified that he was told he would lose his job if he did not sign the report, even though he had not considered all the evidence available.) The grand jury concluded that the Internal Investigations Division's procedure "was so seriously deficient that it suggested purposeful malfeasance."

Petitions were filed by eighty-four individuals and organizations, including the Chicago Bar Association, the American Civil Liberties Union, and the Chicago Council of Lawyers. Finally, Criminal Court Chief Justice Joseph A. Power appointed Barnabas Sears to replace Hanrahan as prosecutor for the inquiry into the Panther raid. Having been thus "drafted," Sears once again found himself pitted against the police.

Sears's appointment was heralded by civic leaders, but it was greeted with less than enthusiasm by many leaders of the black community, including the leadership of Illinois Panthers, who were perhaps justifiably concerned with a few incontrovertible facts: Sears was white, an Establishment lawyer, and had been appointed by one of Mayor Richard Daley's protégés, Judge Power. Indeed, Power had been a former law partner of Daley's and was a personal friend.

Joseph A. Power became Chief Justice Power in 1954, at the age of thirty-eight, largely on the say-so of Daley, who was then chairman of the Cook County Democratic Organization. Without Daley's approval, neither dogcatchers nor judges retained office. Power's reputation as a hard-working and able chief justice of the Criminal Court was secure enough; but those familiar with Chicago justice would probably say that when push comes to shove, Judge Power was not beyond saving his political neck by doing what was politically necessary.

Thus Sears found himself in the hapless, if not hopeless, position of trying to be an independent and fearless prosecutor investigating the state's attorney (another Daley ally), while having to deal with a judge whose impartiality was questionable, at best.

Small wonder that Sears proceeded with his prosecution slowly. Although appointed in June, it was not until December that he convened a grand jury consisting of twenty-three jurors. During the ensuing months those jurors heard more than fifty witnesses and reviewed over a hundred and fifty exhibits. By April 1971 it became apparent that the grand jury was getting ready to act.

On April 22 Judge Power held a closed session with the grand jury— in the rumor-ridden climate of imminent indictment of Hanrahan by the jury. Just like that, he decided to charge the jury with respect to their duties and the duty of Sears. Sears objected to Judge Power's holding this closed session. He made it clear that in his view the judge had "gone beyond his power in law." The grand jury was an independent body, Sears insisted, and their vitality depended upon its independence from judicial interference.

Mike Royko, a political columnist for the Chicago *Daily News* and a biographer of Richard Daley, reported what next took place a few days later on Monday, April 26, when Sears appeared before Judge Power:

> But on Monday the time came for Judge Power to pay his dues, so to speak, for having been provided by the Machine with so smooth a road to a prized judgeship.
>
> When he walked into his courtroom and sat down, the hottest political potato in modern Chicago history plopped into his lap, right on his black robes. Standing before him was Barnabas Sears, the unflappable old star lawyer who is conducting the special grand jury investigation of the Black Panther case.
>
> To his right were the twenty-three ordinary citizens who make up the special grand jury, a body that has enormous legal powers. And in the rest of the seats were more reporters than Power has ever seen gathered in his courtroom.
>
> Power was grim. Hours earlier, a court worker in the hallway had said: "He just went by me, and somebody is going to get it today. I don't even want to be around."
>
> In his nasal tenor voice, Power went straight to the cause of his anger, demanding to know if Sears had said the things he had been reading on the front pages of the newspapers.

The columnist went on to describe the judge's reading of the quotes (his voice rising as he read), all of them having to do with Sears's criticism of him for calling in the grand jury and ordering it to go back and hear witnesses who, according to Sears, were not needed. Power was "surprised and shocked" at what he felt was a "deliberate attempt to embarrass the courts and me personally." To go back to Royko's account:

Power didn't say it, and he didn't have to. The impact of the stories, to be blunt, was that the fix was in. In Chicago, even when it is untrue and unjust, the suspicion is so often unavoidable. Where else do you find a political system that results in the almost fiction-like drama that existed in Judge Power's courtroom, to wit:

A friend and former law partner of the mayor is deeply and controversially involved in a case that could bring ruin to one of the mayor's political protégés, serious embarrassment to the mayor's police chief, whose father was a close friend of the mayor, legal troubles for another top police official whose father-in-law is a close friend of the mayor? A case that could still be causing embarrassing headlines at the time of next year's elections?

It's difficult for anyone familiar with Chicago politics not to have the fleeting thought that blood is thicker than lawbooks. . . .

"Did you," he [Power] finally asked Sears, "say that Judge Power improperly interfered with the conduct of a special grand jury?"

Sears spoke for the first time. But in his raspy voice, he calmly asked a question of his own: "Of what do I stand accused?" Power stammered, as if surprised by the question: "Contempt of court."

Sears knew that, of course, because only four hours earlier Power had told him over the phone that if he didn't come to court and do as he was told, Sears would be held in contempt. But Sears wanted it said for the court stenographer's transcript, because this is a case that will go up and up, probably to the Supreme Court, before it is resolved.

"All I did," Sears said, "was to state [to the press] what the law was." Then he attempted to recite for Judge Power those laws that pertain to grand juries. But Power didn't want to leave the matter of the news stories and his sullied reputation.

"Did you make a remark that prompted the newspaper to headline: 'Panther Prober Rips Judge'?"

Smiling, Sears told the judge that he had no control over the headlines newspapers write. Once again he returned to the question of who tells a grand jury what to do.

At this point, the layman can do little more than follow the broad legal arguments. Simply stated, Judge Power says he has the authority to call in a grand jury, as he did, and to tell it to go back and hear more witnesses.

Sears says that under the grand jury system, dating back to ancient England, Judge Power exceeded his authority. The grand jury decides when it has heard enough, and if it wants a judge's advice, it will ask for it.

A third point of view might be that of the nonlegal cynic who can't help but note that the grand jury was reported to have finished its work, and was about to threaten some well-known necks with indictments, when the judge summoned it for a closed-door meeting he later described as "routine." Some lawyers say it is so routine they have never heard of it being done before.

Power said that the special county grand jury must hear all the witnesses who testified at an earlier federal grand jury investigation. No, says Sears. He doesn't need all of that testimony, presumably because he is pursuing different breaches in the law than was the federal grand jury.

During the long recital of precedents, reading from the record and legal fencing, Power's edgy temper finally surfaced, and he snapped:

"The position of this court is that you invite all witnesses. I want a full and complete investigation and—" at this point he broke into a shout, pointed his finger and looked like a tough desk sergeant "—and you are not doing it."

The outburst startled several members of the grand jury. A woman looked at the juror next to her, shook her head, and glared at the judge. She and the others have been hearing testimony for months. They may have grown used to the grandfatherly figure of Barnabas Sears, his considerable charm, his dignified manner. Now the grandfatherly Sears was being bawled

BARNABAS F. SEARS

out in their presence. It's only a guess, but Judge Power could not have helped the cause of those being investigated.

He may have sensed this, because a few moments later he smiled woodenly and made a point of saying that he was talking loud only because he wanted everyone in the courtroom to be able to hear him.

Sears showed no reaction to the rebuke. He could have been taking part in a routine probate matter. Larding his calm statements with the traditional courtesies—"with deference to Your Honor . . . with respect for Your Honor"—he stayed with his legal arguments. Finally he put down his sheaf of documents and said, almost casually: "That is all I have to say upon the subject."

Both men knew what their next lines would be.

Power: "I ask you once more, are you going to comply with the order of this court?"

Sears: "I would be violating my oath. . . ."

Power: "The court finds you to be in contempt and fines you $50 an hour. . . ."

Several reporters started for the door to phone in bulletins, but Power called out, "Mr. Bailiff, anybody moving, have them arrested." The reporters came back and sat down.

One of Sears's associates asked Power if the $50-an-hour fine was for the traditional workday or what?

Power glanced at the clock. "It starts now and will continue running until he obeys the order of the court."

Sears raised his brow and smiled. But the grand jurors were turning and looking at each other, shaking their heads. If any of them were good at mental arithmetic, they were adding it up: $1200 a day, $8400 a week, $436,800 a year.

Sears started to say something, his first sentence beginning: "Your Honor, I have a reputation for . . ."

The rest was lost as Power cut in: "My reputation is as good as yours."

And he went on to describe, defiantly and resentfully, how he had stood for re-election as a judge, and had been appraised by the bar associations, and the voters and the lawyers had been satisfied that his reputation was good.

All of which is true. But Sears's reputation has been built through many years in the private practice of law. Unfortunately for Judge Power, his reputation was made possible by the Cook County Democratic Central Committee, which is why he is now acquiring those political battle scars.

The charges and fines that had been leveled against Sears, and Judge Power's insistence that he had the authority to meet with the grand jury in closed session and instruct its members—these somehow had become the paramount issues in the case. The vital investigation into the killing of two men and into the integrity of an elected official had ground to a halt.

Was Sears guilty of contempt? The judge had said so. Was he, as special prosecutor, mishandling his public trust? The judge had said so. Were Hanrahan and other prospective defendants being railroaded into an indictment by the underhanded tactics of an overzealous prosecutor? A judge had implied so. Such charges, whether they are true or not, stuck in the minds of the public, which was guilt-ridden about the length of time it was taking its system to work. The public outcry for justice obviously becomes muted when an investigator (Hanrahan) becomes the investigated, and the second investigator (Sears) also becomes the investigated.

The Hanrahan defense (and, of course, Mayor Daley) could not have been more delighted with the new turn of events, which took the heat off Hanrahan and made him the victim in the eyes of some citizens. Many people now thought that perhaps the police were right after all and Hanrahan was being thrown to the dogs by a politically ambitious special prosecutor bent on self-aggrandizement.

While political writers and courtroom buffs may have had a good idea of what was going on, the public in general did not. Americans take very seriously what their leaders in authority say. When a judge said that Sears was in contempt, that he was not doing his job right, and that the grand jury was only hearing some of the evidence, these are things to be taken seriously. And so, the deaths of the two young blacks receded in importance, dwarfed by the more immediate issue of the *People of the State of Illinois* v. *Barnabas F. Sears*.

In May 1971 the Supreme Court of Illinois heard argument on an application for appropriate relief by Sears and the Chicago Bar Association, the American Civil Liberties Union, the Lawyers' Committee for Civil Rights under Law, and the Chicago Council for Lawyers. It asked that Judge Power be directed to refrain from interfering in the opera-

tion of the grand jury that had already been empaneled and from interviewing grand jurors individually (a practice he had already engaged in
with two grand jurors). It sought further to vacate the contempt cita-
tions issued against Sears.

The appellate court also had before it an application by John Meade,
a prospective defendant, complaining about Sears's alleged tactics and
the alleged massive, unfair pretrial publicity which "so grossly
breached the security of this grand jury and so irreparably tainted its
proceedings as to make further deliberations meaningless and a violation of your petitioner's constitutional rights."

On June 23 the Supreme Court of Illinois pointed out that Sears had
presented a "scholarly review of the history of the grand jury from its
genesis in 1176" and found that authorities cited in his brief supported
"his contentions that the circuit court cannot limit the scope of the
grand jury's investigation and that the grand jury may make present-
ments of its own knowledge without instructions or authority of the
court." The appellate court found that Judge Power did not have a sufficient basis for holding Sears in contempt for refusing to call witnesses
whom the judge wanted called. A second contempt citation, for displaying a "contemptuous attitude" toward Power, was reversed because Sears was entitled to a hearing on the charges Power made
against him.

The Supreme Court, while finding that the grand jury was to some
extent subject to the authority of the court and not to the whim of a
prosecutor, nevertheless found that the judge had exceeded his authority in meeting with individual grand jurors and in directing Sears to call
witnesses. It held, however, that the judge could hold interviews with
the entire jury if "so requested by it."

The Supreme Court's findings, of course, did not go unnoticed by
the Chicago press. An editorial in the Chicago *Daily News*, headlined
"For Strong Grand Juries," clearly states the political undertones that
underlay the then-pending inquiry into Sears's conduct:

Since Britain scrapped the grand jury for all but exceptional
cases nearly 40 years ago, it has survived mainly as an American
institution. Though the grand jury in this country has some obvious faults, these are heavily outweighed by its potential for independent action on the public's behalf.

The Illinois public should therefore welcome legislation in-

troduced in the General Assembly to strengthen the independence of the grand jury by limiting a judge's authority to direct
what evidence it should hear. . . . The [proposed] bill would
prohibit the presiding judge from excluding evidence the jury
wanted to hear or forcing it to hear evidence it did not wish to listen to.

So-called runaway grand juries have long exercised broad
rights in dealing with prosecutors the jury looked upon as lazy,
incompetent or even corrupt. More often than not such juries
have performed an indispensable public service by digging into
political scandals that otherwise might never have seen light
because of official coverups. The American system of criminal justice is largely under the jurisdiction of politically chosen judges
and prosecutors, unlike the British system in which appointments
are made on the basis of merit without regard to politics. The
British could afford to dispense with the grand jury, but the
course of criminal justice in the United States can best be served
by bolstering the grand jury's powers. . . .

No matter what the outcome of the appeals, the legislation to
give grand juries a freer hand should be adopted by the Assembly, even though certain of its members as politicians may be
reluctant to strenthen a system that might be turned against
them or their cronies on the bench or in state's attorney's offices.

It was hoped that the appellate court's ruling would finally permit
the special grand jury to get on with its business and return the indictment against Hanrahan and others which had effectively been blocked
by Power. On June 30, however, Judge Power refused to accept the
grand jury's report. It was as though the appellate court's ruling meant
nothing. Power's action was met with jubilation by the prospective defendants and with utter disgust by those anxious to inquire into the
guilt or innocence of Hanrahan and others who participated in the
Black Panther raid. Sears, the public, and the law were about to be led
on another merry chase. Power had been presented with petitions
from potential defendants claiming that Sears's own conduct may have
prejudiced and tainted the grand jury. Power, refusing to accept the
indictment, set a hearing for August 5.

On that date Sears was informed that Power had appointed Mitchell
Ware as an *amicus curiae* ("friend of the court"?) to determine whether

BARNABAS F. SEARS

or not the grand jury had in fact been tainted by Sears and his associates. The judge disclosed "that somehow no stenographic transcript had been taken of grand jury proceedings on April 20, 21, and 22" (the days immediately preceding the grand jury's decision to indict Hanrahan and the others). He expressed his concern about what Sears and the jury were up to on those days. But Sears and the press were more concerned with what Power was up to. Sears had informed the judge that no witnesses were heard before the grand jury on those days, and Power knew full well that it was not customary for stenographers to record grand jury deliberations during those periods in which witnesses are not testifying.

Although Ware is a black and a Republican, his appointment to investigate Sears, at a time when the grand jury was ready to indict after months of deliberations of evidence presented by the special prosecutor, was more than strange: it was outrageous. If defendants in criminal cases could delay their trials by hurling accusations of misconduct toward grand juries that were indicting them or toward a prosecutor whose job was to present evidence against them, the speedy resolution of criminal trials could be delayed almost endlessly. However, the "nicety" of a speedy resolution of an investigation into the death of two blacks hardly seemed to weigh on Judge Power's conscience.

The August 5 charade was duly reported next day in the Chicago *Sun-Times* in a story by Tom Fitzpatrick, titled "Barney Badgered All the Way":

It's certainly a grand and good thing that Barney Sears likes to run obstacle courses. Barney, the white-haired special prosecutor in charge of the grand jury investigating the Black Panther raid, seems to run into one every time he enters the courtroom of Criminal Court Chief Judge Joseph A. Power.

Wednesday's meeting with Judge Power proved no exception. Barney strode erectly into the court wih a bulging briefcase in his right hand. He had a smile and shake of the hand for many of the reporters seated in the front of the room.

"Barney," one of them told him, "the word is out that there'll be no move made to either suppress or publish the indictments today."

Barney looked surprised.

"The word is they're going to appoint an *amicus curiae*."

"What the hell is that?" asked another reporter not so versed in legal terms.

The experienced court reporter looked around at his younger colleague in disgust. "It means 'friend of the court,' " he said. "In this case, it means the investigation goes on and on. We have now reached the stage where the investigators are investigating the investigator."

"I get it," said the younger reporter. "I studied drama in college. What you really mean is that the show goes on."

"That's right," said his older colleague. "In Chicago criminal circles it has a relevant application: 'Time is a great healer. . . .' "

As this newspaper story went, the judge got right to the issue and explained to Sears that he had appointed Ware to hold a special investigation to determine whether or not Barney had indeed used coercion to obtain the still-sealed indictments.

"I appointed you to this position of trust," Judge Power said in the tones of a father betrayed. "Now you have been accused of improper conduct. That is why I must appoint Mr. Ware, a man who commands great respect in the legal profession, to see if these charges are true."

Barney glared up at the bench and put one hand on the microphone in front of him. "Well, in all respect," he began, "I'd like to be heard on whether it's necessary to bring in a friend of the court. Mr. Ware is head of the Illinois Bureau of Investigation. Don't you think there would be a conflict of interest? He's in the same position as those men who might very well be the subject of the sealed indictment you're now holding."

Judge Power appeared pained. He removed his glasses. "Mr. Ware has agreed to take a leave of absence from that post while he conducts his hearings," Judge Power replied.

Ware remained standing at the side of the bench, rolling his tongue over his front teeth. His two hands were clasped behind his back. He looked like a man waiting for the gong to sound the opening bell.

"And what about the ruling of the Illinois Supreme Court?"

Barney asked. "They ruled on this matter and they didn't say anything about holding a hearing."

Judge Power smiled down at Barney the way that people glance at small children who have not yet fully learned the rules of the adult world.

"The Supreme Court also did not say that such a hearing can't be held," Judge Power replied, suppressing a yawn. "Just how do you propose we proceed? . . ."

"I propose that we proceed according to the law," retorted Barney. "I propose we open the indictments."

This suggestion did not meet with any positive response and so a little later Barney grabbed the microphone again. "I just want to say that we are here representing the people in this matter," he said, his voice rasping now under the strain, "and we are doing it under the most adverse circumstances in an attempt to see that justice is done."

"I too represent all of the people of this state," Judge Power said. "That is why I want this to be fair and impartial."

The judge's remark, in a battle that lasted more than an hour, drew the one and only laugh from the crowd that day. The laughter came from the three solid rows of white Black Panther supporters.

Columnist Mike Royko, too, pulled no punches in his August 6 coverage in the Chicago *Daily News*:

In more than a century in Cook County, thousands, maybe hundreds of thousands of criminal indictments have been sent out by grand juries. But all of a sudden, Judge Power has imposed a stunning array of legal safeguards, standards, moats, and fences to protect the person being indicted. As he himself said in yesterday's hearing: "I'm playing this by ear. This is a new proceeding in Illinois, you know."

New, yet old.

It is new because Judge Power produces something new at every hearing. It wouldn't surprise anyone if he next asked old Barnabas Sears, the special prosecutor, to chin himself 100 times before the secret indictments can be opened.

But the spirit behind it is as old as the earliest wink and nod from one politician to another.

Because of the envelope, Sears, who has long been rated one of the city's finest lawyers, is fast becoming a bumbler. Nothing he does pleases Judge Power. If Sears makes a motion, the words are hardly out of his mouth before Power is denying it. Yesterday, Sears repeatedly pleaded with Power to stop interrupting him so he could finish a sentence. . . .

As of yesterday, Sears had somehow become the villain in the case. A headline screamed: "Panther Jury Files Missing," and the idea seemed to be that it was Sears who filched them.

These "missing" records, which Power wanted from Sears, never existed in the first place, for good reason. In grand jury proceedings, a court reporter takes down all testimony and evidence. But the court reporter does not take down the discussions between the prosecutor and the grand jury about the case. Hanrahan's office itself concedes that this is never done. So Sears simply followed the standard procedure of Hanrahan's office.

Sears's transformation from special prosecutor to chief villain in the case became complete yesterday when Judge Power brought in somebody to investigate Sears.

Judge Power picked Mitchell Ware to seek evidence that Sears somehow bullied or stampeded the grand jury into sending forth that terrible envelope. If evidence of this kind is found, the judge will be within his authority in ordering the envelope forever to remain glued tight.

Undoubtedly, there is somebody among those 13 grand jurors who is ready to say he or she was hypnotized or something by Sears. And I imagine that it won't take much more than that to convince Judge Power, not that he has developed such a deep concern for the rights of those who have been indicted.

This same newspaper, in an editorial, pointed out:

The Black Panther grand jury case grows curiouser and curiouser, and it becomes increasingly difficult for the people of Chicago to keep their eye on the ball.

But remembering the central issue is increasingly important, as the suspicion grows that Mayor Daley's political establishment is building a Maginot Line to protect one of its functionaries, State's Atty. Edward V. Hanrahan.

BARNABAS F. SEARS

Even the Chicago *Tribune* referred to the August 5 hearing as a "continuing spectacle." And in a Chicago *Sun-Times* editorial called "The Fox and the Chickens," the more than obvious was put this way: "Criminal Court Chief Judge Joseph A. Power's handling of the grand jury weighing the Black Panther case is fast becoming a parody of the American concept of swift justice and due process."

Other articles in other newspapers blasted the appointment of Ware, and Judge Power's actions were characterized as "judicial tyranny" by an August 13 editorial in *Chicago Today*.

On August 14 the chief justice of the Illinois Supreme Court stayed the hearing then scheduled in the Black Panther case, which had degenerated into an investigation of Sears.

Shortly thereafter, the high court directed Judge Power to open the suppressed indictment and he was directed to rescind his appointment of Mr. Ware. Lo and behold, when the indictment was opened, Hanrahan, one of his assistants, and twelve policemen were indicted for conspiracy to obstruct justice! Immediately thereafter, State's Attorney Hanrahan said, "I have done absolutely nothing wrong. I welcome the conclusion of these proceedings as quickly as possible so that the public can have that demonstrated to them as quickly as possible."

It would be neither useful nor instructive to further chronicle all the travails and obstacles encountered by Sears in prosecuting Hanrahan and the other defendants. Judge Power stepped down after ordering his own investigation into Sears's conduct. The case was assigned to Judge Philip Romiti, who refused to disturb Power's ruling that the defendants could interview grand jurors. The Illinois Supreme Court upset that ruling, too. The Chicago Council of Lawyers, the American Civil Liberties Union, and businessmen demanded in the public's interest that Judge Romiti withdraw in favor of another judge outside of Cook County. Romiti retained the case.

Four special grand jurors submitted affidavits accusing Sears of having used improper influence in obtaining the indictments.

By October 1971 Sears had spent $7000 out-of-pocket to finance the case he had never asked to be brought into. Judge Power had refused to authorize pay vouchers totaling more than $100,000 due Sears and his staff since April 1971 for legal fees and expenses. Sears had been working for $50 an hour, a sum which had been expressly approved by the Chicago Bar Association and by Power himself.

Finally, in December 1971, the Illinois Supreme Court blocked the last attempts to hold the hearing into Sears's conduct. In February 1972 Judge Romiti finally held that State's Attorney Edward V. Hanrahan and thirteen codefendants must stand trial for their alleged conspiracy to obstruct justice. That same month Judge Power finally approved payment to Sears of over $100,000 in legal fees and expenses from April through August 1971. And he dismissed a defense motion to hold up payment on the grounds that the indictments against Hanrahan and his codefendants were improperly returned.

During his desire to "get all the facts out" and for "speedy" vindication, Hanrahan appealed the Illinois Supreme Court's latest decision to the United States Supreme Court, which, of course, further delayed the trial. When the Supreme Court declined to hear the case, Hanrahan called that decision "disappointing and unjust."

In July 1972—two and a half years after the deaths of Hampton and Clark—Hanrahan and his codefendants were brought to trial.

But in the middle of the trial, Sears's assistant prosecutor, Weyland B. Cedarquist, while researching and preparing the Black Panther case, discovered new evidence in the files of the Illinois Defense Project at Northwestern University. Among this evidence were four previously unrevealed (and unknown to Sears) statements by Black Panther party members who were present at the raid on December 4, 1969. Until that time, in all the accounts of the raid, the Panthers had maintained that only one shot had been fired by them. The new evidence indicated that at least two other Panthers actually fired shots, that another had a gun in his hand, and still another was attempting to fire a gun.

Sears declared that his oath as a prosecutor was far more important to him than his winning or losing the case. "I'm not going to wind up my career doing something like that. To hell with it." He turned the new material over to the trial judge and the defense. Sears maintained that the new evidence did not affect most of the counts in the indictment; but he also knew that his chances of conviction were seriously impaired, if not totally obliterated. As the Chicago *Tribune* put it: "For a prosecutor to put justice and personal rights ahead of a minimum chance of securing conviction sets a good example for us all, and especially for other prosecutors, including Mr. Hanrahan."

When the fourteen-week trial was over, Hanrahan and his thirteen codefendants were acquitted by Judge Romiti. Barney Sears had lost. He sat during several days of summations in which it seemed it was he who was the defendant and the defendants the prosecutors.

After a fair reading of the trial transcript, it could not be said that Sears proved his case, particularly in light of the evidence that he and his assistant turned over to the defense. But no one could gainsay that he fought all the way in the highest tradition of the law against a system in which the law was represented at its worst. Sears was tired. Perhaps he was not as effective as he would have been had he not been forced to spend two and a half years fighting against obstacles and dirty tricks which not even he could overcome.

The truth of what happened the night of December 4, 1969, will never be known. The system by which such truth was supposed to be uncovered and rectified was so contaminated, so foul, that neither the Panthers nor Hanrahan and his codefendants were ever really convicted or vindicated. The cost of the unsuccessful prosecution was estimated to be $800,000. As one editorial said, "The acquittal does not make their man into a hero, nor does it erase a bad blot on Chicago's record."

And how did Sears feel about it? "There is a certain amount of victory in defeat," he said. "It is no great loss to be defeated, if you did your best." Nobody could deny that Barnabas Sears had done his best.

ALFRED JULIEN

Perhaps the most denigrated, unappreciated, and least understood practitioners of the trial bar are the personal-injury specialists, or (as they hate being called) "negligence lawyers." These specialists, like those of the criminal trial bar, have attracted a great deal of criticism, much of it unwarranted.

Some of our greatest trial lawyers—Williams, Hallinan, and many other grand masters—began their trial careers in the specialty; Belli earned his reputation as the "King of Torts." Many just-beginning young lawyers gravitate to that practice for obvious reasons: first, because there is such a large volume of negligence cases (automobile, malpractice, slippery sidewalks, burst water mains, and so on); and second, because those cases are usually taken on a contingent basis, with the lawyer collecting a percentage of the ultimate verdicts.

Many of the claims in the negligence field rely upon exaggerated or perjurious testimony and this tends to tarnish the reputations of the negligence bar in general. Nevertheless, some of the most important litigation is to be found in this field, and many lawyers have justifiably earned towering reputations and small fortunes in trying personal-injury cases.

Among the best in this important specialty is Alfred Julien. In his mid-sixties, this nattily dressed, diminutive dynamo represents the ultimate in personal-injury advocacy. His successes have been astounding and his contribution in the teaching and practice of this specialized work have won him a national reputation.

As do most personal-injury lawyers, Julien resents the label. He regards himself as a *trial* lawyer, able to try any kind of case anywhere. Although his successes have been mostly in his specialty, he believes that the reason he is not known or appreciated in loftier fields of civil litigation is that he is trapped by his reputation as a negligence lawyer. That may well be: Julien's law office, like most personal-injury firms, is not geared to the researching or processing of complex civil litigation. Then, too, his trial schedule is so heavily weighted with major negligence cases, which only he can try, that it is doubtful if he has the capability of becoming another Williams or Sears.

While Julien may try thirty or forty negligence cases during the course of a year, Williams or Nizer try only a fraction of that number of civil cases in that time. Julien's clients, who pay him out of the large recoveries of damages he gets for them in court, are quite willing to wait their turn on his busy roster. Not so the commercial client who pays six-figure legal fees in advance. That kind of gambling money buys priority.

As we shall see, whenever he can, Julien will try any kind of case. He claims he felt just as comfortable trying his first murder case or any of his civil cases as he does any personal-injury matter.

Many students of the trial bar, as well as some of the great trial lawyers mentioned in this book, would scoff at the inclusion of Julien as a grand master. But the scores of clients whose "impossible" cases he has won would heartily agree that he is indeed a grand kind of master of his trade. Having seen him work his magic on so many occasions, and having seen him teach his art, I have little doubt that, however limited his range, his excellence in trying personal-injury cases is unsurpassed, in fact rarely equaled.

Julien was born and grew up in the Bronx in New York City. From boyhood, he knew he wanted to be a lawyer, and again, like so many lawyers-to-be, he was a "performer" long before he went to Brooklyn Law School. He was a professional musician (saxophone and clarinet) at the age of fifteen. He saved and used his earnings to put himself through law school, and though often he played in various nightclubs in Greenwich Village until three o'clock in the morning, he was indefatigable. He studied law all day, worked at night, and still graduated with honors.

Julien's first job was working for a politician in the Bronx at $15 per week. His first client was his father, for whom he remembers trying and losing the case. The first Big One came early. The parents of a fifteen-year-old boy from the East Bronx were referred to Julien by a Legal Aid panel, which in those days referred indigent clients to young volunteer lawyers. The boy had tried to crash his way into a Bronx movie theater. An unidentified man threw the youngster out with such force that his skull was fractured and he died.

The theater operators claimed they had no idea who the boy's assailant was and obviously could not be held responsible for intentional assaults committed by their patrons. The theater was represented by Isidore Halpern, who was then and still is a well-known trial lawyer in New York City. Although the case had been turned down by several law firms, young Julien decided to take it. It was a difficult case: and to try and prove damages on behalf of a vagrant adolescent was equally difficult. And the thought of opposing Halpern, even in the best of cases, was a forbidding one.

Julien, aided by his then-secretary/fiancée, now-wife, embarked on a heroic and tireless search of the East Bronx neighborhood. Their perseverance finally paid off; miracle of miracles, they came up with the man who had ejected the young theater-crasher! They also learned that he actually had been employed by the theater as a bouncer, although he did not appear on their payroll.

Julien won his case. And having "knocked off" Isidore Halpern, he began getting work from other lawyers who had heard about it. Within a surprisingly short time, his practice proliferated and he became one of New York's best-known personal injury lawyers.

Julien, like Belli in San Francisco, has given an enormous amount of thought to how a case should be tried, and for many years has given countrywide courses to aspiring young lawyers. He feels that his early training as a musician and vaudevillian was invaluable, and that study in the theater is great basic training for the trial lawyer. According to him, the trial lawyer has to become a different person in every case, because no two cases, judges, juries, clients, or opponents are alike.

Most important, he maintains, the trial lawyer must passionately believe in his cause. Julien thinks of himself as someone else's surrogate, the proverbial "knight in shining armor," to use his words. As is true of so many grand masters, he clings rigidly to the notion that he's "no damn good" in a case he doesn't believe in. And again, as with the others I interviewed, when I produced the names of some of the blackguards he's represented, he almost childishly and petulantly claimed that he "never knew" or "never had the slightest idea" about any of those bad things when he was representing them. As is typical of the trial lawyer, once the case is over and he is engaged in other cases, he forgets how he psyched himself into believing in his client.

There seems to be no way to convince Julien—or Nizer or any of the great trial lawyers (except Hallinan)—that their notion of steadfast belief in their clients often rings false. The *Finian's Rainbow* refrain, "When I'm not near the one I love, I love the one I'm near," may be generally descriptive of the philosophy of most grand masters. Once they like the case, the fee, the notoriety, the intrigue, and the challenge—they seem to love the client behind it.

ALFRED JULIEN

THE $50,000 LUNCH

Julien was once called upon to represent a young woman who fell from a golf cart while her husband was driving it in Palm Springs, California. As a result of the accident, she suffered extensive brain damage which left her in an almost vegetablelike state.

Although the extent of her damages and injuries was incontrovertible, it would be very difficult for her to prove or even allege carelessness or any liability on the part of either the golf-cart manufacturer or the club whose course she had been playing at the time. The defendants saw no reason to make any offer of settlement and refused even to discuss it.

However, when they heard that Julien was entering the case, they decided to offer the woman $25,000. They didn't really believe, "deepdown," that this New York lawyer would come all the way to California to try such a rotten case. But on the off-chance that he just might, they opted to offer the plaintiff this appeasement sum in the hope of aborting the action (and Julien's trip as well).

No go. Julien arrived on schedule and headed right for the courthouse, along with the lawyer who had referred the case to him; and that same day, the offer went to $75,000. It was made, in fact, on the courthouse steps as counsel converged to go inside: "Mr. Julien, I tell you frankly, we are only offering this much money because you are in the case. There is not a single piece of evidence that connects our clients with any wrongdoing."

"Mr. Smith," said Julien, "I don't want to appear immodest, but I am a very busy man. Now let's face it, you know it and I know it: the big gun is here from New York. And if you think I came all the way out here for that kind of money, you've very much mistaken. I told my young associate here that he would hear a jury foreman render a verdict for over a million dollars. He has never heard that kind of sum before in a courtroom and I am going to keep my promise."

Just then, as though it were planned, a young lawyer appeared and reminded Julien that he had been one of his students at a seminar on trial practice. He and several other lawyers had heard that Julien was going to try the case in Los Angeles and they all wanted to watch. All four defense attorneys blanched and withdrew immediately to confer. A few minutes later, they returned with an offer of $100,000. Julien appeared to be enraged: "Look, I am a trial lawyer," he said. "If you wanted to settle this case, you should have thought of that a long time ago. I am here to try this case. Let's go."

(Julien's opponents were unaware, of course, of the warning he had issued to his client's husband and to the family lawyer: "This case stinks. I am very sorry, but I have to tell you the truth. I haven't the slightest doubt that I will get you and your wife a verdict of over a million dollars; but that's because the jury is going to be sympathetic and their reason is going to be stampeded. But it will be the obligation of this court to set aside the verdict because there isn't any liability. Now, you have your choice of having the pleasure of hearing that you have been awarded a million dollars and then losing it, or of letting me try and settle this case for a reasonable figure."

A reasonable figure, he told them, would be $200,000. The client agreed.)

Leading the way to the courtroom assigned to his case, Julien announced to the judge that he was ready for trial. He saw no possible way to settle it, he said, and asked and was given permission to begin selecting a jury later in the day.

At this point, one of the defense lawyers poked his head nervously into the conference room being used by the plaintiff's side, and he asked Julien if he would step outside again. It seemed that the defense attorneys had been authorized to go to $125,000. Julien smiled at his four opponents and for the first time appeared friendly. "Well, at least you're offering some money," he said. "Not nearly enough, but something. Now if you can get me another one hundred thousand dollars, I can make an afternoon plane out of here." The chief defense counsel protested that he had gone as far as he could. Julien said he would be ill-disposed to settle the case after lunch and recommended that an-

ALFRED JULIEN

other call be made to the insurance company, and added, "This time, use a little pressure."

Defense counsel withdrew once again, and Julien announced that he was going to disappear for about half an hour. As everybody reminded him, they were all waiting eagerly for the results of the telephone call being made at that moment—presumably to the insurance company. Julien said he didn't want to appear to give much of a damn.

When the defense lawyers reappeared, Julien had disappeared, and they were repeatedly told he would be back in a few minutes.

About forty-five minutes later he came back and immediately began to discuss the architecture of the courtrooms, as though he had no idea that everybody there was waiting to find out whether or not the case was settled. Finally one of the defense lawyers said, "Well, we can go to a hundred and fifty thousand dollars, but that's it. That's just it, Mr. Julien, we can't go any further."

"I'll take it," he said. His client's husband's jaws slackened and his associate counsel almost fainted. "There is just one condition," he said.

"No more money, Mr. Julien," quavered the defense lawyer. "We have no more money."

"No, not money. No, the condition is that you gentlemen, all four counsel, join me and my client for lunch. She's up in a hotel room and I want you to see who it is that you won't give the money to. Now, I can't promise you will have a very pleasant lunch. As a matter of fact, you may not eat lunch for another month; but I just want you to see the tragic condition of this woman. Of course, if you want to add another fifty thousand dollars, you don't have to have lunch with us at all."

After a hurried conference, the defendants agreed to pay $200,000 and the court was so informed. The presiding judge remarked that he was very glad the case had been settled because he realized that the woman needed the money; and yet, from what he had heard in a preliminary conference concerning the case, he would have had to dismiss it. Julien made his afternoon plane back to New York.

THE OPERATION WAS A SUCCESS,
BUT THE PATIENT IS NOW DEAF

We had been preparing our case for well over a year and the big day had finally come—our "day in court," the Supreme Court of New York County. When the clerk called our case, *Harry Coleman* * v. *Carpenter, et al.*, my heart did a flip-flop and sank. Everybody but Julien, my co-counsel, was there. My client-plaintiff, who four years earlier had been admitted to hospital for a gall-bladder operation and had emerged four months later totally deaf, was there with his wife and family. The six defendant doctors were there, along with counsel—four veteran and talented members of the trial bar.

And, most formidable of all, the Honorable Emilio Nunez, a highly respected no-nonsense judge was there, with gavel poised:

> JUDGE: Is the plaintiff ready?
>
> S.(mumbling): Not quite, Your Honor. Mr. Julien will be coming down from the Bronx very shortly. He had to argue a motion there.
>
> JUDGE: I set apart this day to begin this trial and Mr. Julien was so informed. Pick a jury.
>
> S.: Who—*me*, Your Honor?
>
> JUDGE: That's right. You are the attorney of record. This case is going to move forward. Pick a jury.

How I had the nerve, I don't know, but mustering as much naïveté as I could in my face and voice, I looked up at the judge and asked, "Tell me, sir, where does the jury sit?"

---

* The names of the litigants have been changed in this case.

146

My opponents began to smile and salivate in contemplation of a rare carte-blanche chance to pick a defense-minded jury. Fortunately, however, even this was a little much for Judge Nunez, who laughed and said he would give me one hour in which to produce Julien—or *somebody* who did know where the jury sat.

Well, at least I had managed to buy some time; and all I could do with it was wonder why the hell I had ever talked my client into hiring Julien.

At the time I took on this case, I was a young attorney with five years of general practice under my belt and was just starting out on my own. I had tried many cases by that time, but never one for medical malpractice, and certainly never one involving so much money, against so many lawyers, and experienced talent at that. The Coleman case was an interesting one, all right, but I wondered if I hadn't bitten off more than I could chew.

In 1958 Mr. Coleman was in his late fifties, a rather unsuccessful salesman, married, with two children to whom he had been a devoted father. His medical history had been comparatively uneventful. In May of that year, he appeared jaundiced and his family doctor referred him to a surgeon. Tests indicated that he required gall-bladder surgery, and he was admitted to Mt. Sinai Hospital, in New York, on May 28. Surgery was performed on June 6, and late in September, Coleman was discharged, relieved of his initial complaints, but totally deaf.

During the course of his treatment, Coleman and his family knew only this: that he had apparently developed a staphylococcus infection while in the hospital and somehow it had resulted in his losing his hearing. The Colemans had consulted several personal-injury lawyers and were told that what had happened was unfortunate, but that it was unavoidable, and that the doctors were not responsible.

This was hardly surprising as medical malpractice cases are somewhat difficult to prove in court, experts are difficult to find, and juries are reluctant to find negligence against doctors. It is even more difficult, if not impossible, to prove negligence on the part of a hospital or any doctor just because a patient becomes disabled, or even dies, as a result of a staph infection. Those infections are present in every hospital, and staphylococci in a variety of strains inhabit even normal bodies. In a hospital ward, for instance, four patients may contract staph infections from four different carriers, including hospital personnel and visitors, bedding, linens—you name it.

On looking into the case, the first thing that aroused my suspicion was the hospital's failure to release the medical records to me, despite my repeated requests. It took a motion in court, finally, to get the hospital to send them to me. I did not understand the records when I read them. All I knew was that I was dealing with the sad case of a man who had become deaf after contracting an infection in a hospital, and whose only hope was proving that the hospital and/or doctors were somehow responsible.

Perhaps I could dig up something at the library. At the Academy of Medicine, I looked up infectious diseases and the names of prominent doctors who wrote about them. Among them was a Dr. Peter Dineen, surgeon and associate professor at New York Hospital.

When I telephoned him, Dr. Dineen told me he did not like medical malpractice suits, but he also did not approve of doctors who tried to cover up things. If I would send him the medical records, he said, he would render an honest opinion as to what happened to my client. Some weeks later he informed me that a review of the records indicated that Mr. Coleman had not lost his hearing because of a staph infection but because of the overadministration of a drug.

After several visits to this doctor, I became convinced of several things: first, Coleman had been the victim of extremely poor medical practice; second, the case was bewilderingly complicated; third, the defense that the doctors would make—that they had to risk the overadministration of a drug and its attendant side effects in order to save my client's life—was plausible, but probably untrue; fourth, the various doctors and the hospital would be defended by top defense attorneys; and, finally—I was ill-equipped to try the case.

Around that time I had attended a lecture group of fairly famous trial lawyers and had been most impressed with Alfred Julien. I was convinced that the Coleman case required a lawyer with far more experience and expertise than I had, and Julien was going to be it—if I was lucky.

I was. In the half-hour we spent together, I was amazed at his ability to zero in on relevant facts, his comments on what he thought I had done right (or wrong) in the preparation of the case, and his reasons for what he thought ought still to be done. He refused all calls, convinced me that we couldn't lose the case, charmed me out of my shoes, and became my partner.

Our client signed a suitable retainer, I rolled up my sleeves to begin work—and Julien disappeared. Even when I was able to get him on the telephone, he never seemed to know what I was talking about.

As the case approached trial, I decided to call Julien and fire him. Naturally, he wasn't available, so I fired him through his secretary. That evening he called me at home and invited me to his office the next day.

The charmer went into action again: "Look, Norm, how many cases do you think I can carry around in my hat at one time? I am on a trial every day. I try every case as though my life depended on it. When your case comes up, it will be the only case I give a shit about. If you want me to be honest, right now I don't know who Mr. Coleman is or what happened to him—except that he is deaf, and that I told you we had a great case. I can't win cases and hold the hands of neurotic lawyers." He asked me to trust him, and I did. Once the Coleman case began, Julien promised, he would be closeted exclusively with me, our client, and our witnesses. He also pointed out that when that time came, the twenty-five other lawyers who had referred cases to him for trial would be pulling their hair out just as I had, wondering where the hell he was.

Well, the Coleman case was on trial right now, and where was Julien? As I left the courtroom, suddenly there he was—looking as happy and confident as I was sullen and dejected. The clerk ushered him into the judge's chambers and his apology was immediately accepted. Judge Nunez asked how long the trial would take. "Three days," said Julien. The judge replied, "Mr. Julien, it takes that long for you to clear your throat." We were instructed to pick a jury.

(At that time, juries in New York were chosen outside of the judge's hearing; and if the lawyers got into a squabble over whether or not a juror could be excluded or if other questions of law arose, the matter was taken to the judge for determination.)

We arrived in the room where the jurors were waiting, and as soon as twelve prospective jurors had been seated, Julien announced that he thought Mr. Coleman was entitled to twenty-four peremptory challenges (the right to exclude twenty-four jurors), inasmuch as the four different lawyers for the defendants were entitled to that many (six each). I was surprised. Surely Julien must know that his position was legally unsound and contrary to New York law. But he insisted he was right and that we go to the judge for a ruling.

As we walked along the corridor toward the judge's chambers, Julien whistled contentedly while I told him I thought he was wrong. He looked at me patiently and said, "Whenever you try a case, make yourself the underdog. I know I'm wrong, but after the judge overrules me, we can make some points with the jury."

Julien spoke eloquently to the judge about the disadvantage he was operating under with his side's having only six challenges and his opponents twenty-four. It was time the law in New York was changed, he said, and the court ought to rule in his favor as a matter of justice. Judge Nunez said he was not a legislator and he applied the law as it was; our position was quickly overruled.

My first lesson from a grand master in trial strategy began when Julien addressed the panel of prospective jurors:

Now, ladies and gentlemen of the jury, from time to time all of my opponents and I may leave this room in order to get rulings from the court. It would be unfair for you to draw any inferences about why we are asking some rulings on questions of law. For example, I just told the judge I didn't think it was right that just because the plaintiff has one lawyer and not four, like the defendants, we should have the right to exclude only six jurors, while they have the right to exclude twenty-four. It is bad enough for one lawyer to have a try a case against four distinguished opponents without having an additional handicap. But the judge ruled against us and we will, of course, abide by his ruling.

So there we were, the underdogs. Julien then told the jurors something about the case:

I represent a man who could not hear my voice if he were present and listening to us. The case involves a suit by a sixty-one-year-old deaf man, Harry Coleman, whose hearing was unimpaired before he entered Mt. Sinai Hospital for a gall-bladder operation. During the course of the trial, we [and various witness-

ALFRED JULIEN

es] will tell you much more about what happened to Mr. Coleman. . . . But, briefly, we claim that as a result of improper treatment by the doctors who treated our client, and as a result of improper treatment received in the hospital, my client lost his hearing.

You, ladies and gentlemen, must understand how important it is to the administration of justice that we select jurors who believe they can listen to all the evidence and render a verdict that is fair and not based upon prejudice or sympathy. You may think it strange that I represent a man who has sustained the type of injury that my client has sustained and that I tell you we don't want sympathy. Mr. Coleman has had the sympathy of his family, his friends, and others. He wants from you only justice. . . .

As I listened to Julien eschewing sympathy, I marveled at how he, at the same time, was subtly asking for it in large globs. I was as transfixed as the jurors at his sincerity.

In the selection of the jury, Julien had to make sure there was no hint of the doctors being charged with criminal negligence, that in no way was this an attempt to smear all doctors. He would turn to each prospective juror and say, in effect:

Now you understand, sir [or madam], that this is not a criminal case, and we are not charging any doctor with intentionally doing any harm. We are not trying anybody's reputation here. But if you find that any of these defendants has been guilty of wrongdoing, as the judge defines that wrongdoing, are you prepared to find for Mr. Colemen? Do you understand how terribly unfair it would be to Mr. Coleman if you were to find that any one of these doctors was not responsible simply out of sympathy for any one of them, or solely because you were worried about his reputation?

Did you notice, as I did, coming into this courthouse, the figure of Justice? Did you notice that she was blindfolded? Do you see how important it is that Justice not know or care about who is before her? She doesn't care whether the defendant is a man or a woman, a doctor or a lawyer or a judge. Do you see how important that is in this case? Will you be able to be impartial, as she is? Can you do it? *Will* you do it?

As Julien continued, he made repeated references to those popular TV heroes of the day, Dr. Kildare and Dr. Casey, and warned against drawing any comparison between them and the defendants. He questioned each prospective juror about his background. One was a nurse, but that would not prejudice her in any way, she said. Julien, hoarding his six peremptory challenges, worked on her to get her to admit she *would* be prejudiced, so that he would not have to waste a precious challenge.

Under his deft questioning, the admissions came gradually. Yes, many of her friends were doctors and nurses. Yes, she thought she would be able to be fair in calling the shots exactly as she saw them, despite her close association with the medical fraternity. Wasn't it just possible she wouldn't be able to be fair? She really didn't know, but would like to think she was impartial.

Julien then established that she had been a nurse for over fifteen years. "And in your dedication to medicine, would not some of your enthusiasm perhaps color your thinking? If it were a close question, wouldn't there be a natural tendency to say, 'I'll give my brothers and sisters a break.' Wouldn't you do that?" Well, yes, she thought she would.

Julien looked benignly at opposing counsel. "Don't you think, gentlemen, that we can spare this woman the difficulty of having to sit in a case like this, and can't we agree to excuse her?" Reluctantly, they agreed and Julien retained his challenges.

Coincidentally, among the prospective jurors, one was hard of hearing, and another wore a hearing aid. During luncheon recess, Julien walked along Foley Square and introduced himself to several handicapped people, asking their advice as to whether or not a handicapped person would be a good juror in a case such as the one he was about to try. Their responses were almost identical: No, because nobody ever gave them any money for their handicaps and they didn't think they would be sympathetic to somebody who wanted money for his. When Julien returned to court, he excused those two prospective jurors.

Next, he began questioning a young woman whose father was a judge and brother a lawyer. She practically pleaded for the opportunity to sit on the jury. Julien disliked her. "This lady is a real takeover artist," he whispered to me. "She would try and run the jury and tell them what to do." She was excused.

As the defense lawyers began questioning jurors, their propaganda began to surface:

You understand, ladies and gentlemen, that medicine is not a science. It is an art. You will see that these doctors are men and not gods, and they must be judged as men and not gods. Can you do that? Sometimes physicians have to make the most terrible choices. Should they risk giving a drug which is very dangerous to give, or should they make a desperate attempt to save their patient's life even though the patient may suffer serious side effects? And if a doctor is criticized simply for errors of judgment, if it is just second-guessed or judged by hindsight by doctors and lawyers who were never there, then you can see how difficult it would be to get doctors to try to do their best for a patient. They would just play it safe. Do you see that?

Julien jumped to his feet, and peered at the lawyer who had just spoken: "Oh, that's unfair!" he cried, looking wounded. "How unfair that is! And you *know* it, too. What a terrible thing to do!" Then he bellowed, "Don't do it again, or we'll be before the judge."

As he sat down, shaken with disappointment over his fellow lawyer's conduct, I leaned over and asked him what was so terrible. "Nothing, really, but the jury thinks he did something bad, and so does he."

The jury was finally selected toward the end of the afternoon and the trial was to begin next day.

Julien and I went to his office, and the day's work began.

This was going to be a rough one. Both sides had logic and substance going for them. Based on the opinions of our experts and our review of the facts and many months' worth of research, we maintained that Coleman had been the victim of medical malpractice.

These were our contentions: our client entered the hospital for a relatively simple gall-bladder operation. Six days after surgery and during a period when his fever was rising, the patient's wound "dehisced"— that is, came apart. Surely the rupture of the wound should have alerted the treating physicians that the patient was suffering from an infection. We would claim, in view of his fever, that cultures of the wound should have been taken and sent to the laboratory to find out what the infecting organism was, so that appropriate drugs could be administered.

During the course of Coleman's treatment with general antibiotic therapy, his condition became worse and worse; his temperature and white blood count climbed alarmingly higher. It should have been even more obvious then that these nonspecific antibiotics were ineffective, and that specific drugs to treat the specific infecting organisms should be ordered on the basis of laboratory testings. No cultures were taken from June 6, the date of Coleman's first operation, through June 12, after his second.

Finally, on that day, cultures were taken and it was indeed discovered that he was suffering from a particularly virulent form of staph infection. The laboratory reported that that particular bug could be combated by three drugs, one of which was Neomycin. That drug was manufactured at the time by the Upjohn Company and it was distributed with a brochure warning against its toxic effects. The pamphlet specifically stated that a patient's hearing should be tested by a device known as an audiometer not only before administering the drug but regularly during its administration. As the brochure further warned, the drug was particularly toxic after ten days of intake.

The defense had conceded that the drug was administered to Coleman in excess of twenty days; that no audiometric tests were taken; and that he suffered irreversible and total deafness because of the drug's toxicity.

According to our experts, Coleman developed a subhepatic abscess during or after his gall-bladder operation. This pocket of pus and bacteria around his liver caused and explained many, if not all, of his symptoms—all of which were ignored by the attending physicians.

In our experts' opinions, as a matter of practical medicine, Neomycin should have been discontinued much earlier than it was because it was proving to be almost totally ineffective or, perhaps, it should never have been used because of its potential destructiveness to Coleman's hearing. Surely, they maintained, his hearing at least should have been regularly monitored with a portable audiometer.

The defendants' defense was emotional and logical: It's one thing to look at a hospital record after the event, but quite another to be there and watch your patient's life slowly ebb away. These doctors were trying to save a man's life. They would have done anything to save it, even if it meant risking his hearing. They contended that it was good

154   ALFRED JULIEN

and acceptable medical practice to treat an infection in its early stages with wide-spectrum antibiotics—those which are effective (and less toxic) against a wider variety of bacteria. Normally that is sufficient. In the case of Coleman, when it became obvious on June 16 that those less dangerous drugs were ineffective, they called in Dr. Nelson, a well-known antibiotics specialist, who from that point on carefully supervised the administration of all drugs to his patient.

According to the defendants, Dr. Nelson's towering reputation and his skills carried a lot more weight than the words of some unknown author of a drug manufacturer's brochure. Drugs that are effective in a laboratory may not be effective on the patient and vice versa. It was not up to a lawyer (Julien), or some professor (Dr. Dineen) who never saw the patient, to now say that Coleman's hearing and not his life should have been of primary concern.

Audiometric tests were not given, said the defendants, because their results would not have influenced the treatment given this patient. As long as his life was in danger, they still would have elected to continue his treatment, regardless of its effect upon his hearing.

The lines of battle were drawn.

In Julien's office that night before the trial, I was greatly impressed as I watched the man in action. This lawyer, who only a week before knew virtually nothing about the case, now knew more about it than I did. He began poring over hospital records and making appointments to interview witnesses.

He asked if I had subpoenaed the two pharmacists he wanted in court. I had, and they would be there. But why did he want them? One had never been at Mt. Sinai Hospital, and the other had been employed there after Coleman was discharged. As I reasoned it—and explained to Julien—one of the most essential elements of this lawsuit was that the doctors administered Neomycin for twenty-two days instead of ten, without regard to the loss-of-hearing hazards and in defiance of the warning on the accompanying brochure. So I couldn't see why the brochure should be introduced through two pharmacists who knew nothing about it.

Julien winked as he said, "This is really too good for me to tell you about. Just have them there."

I began asking him dozens of questions on which I had been making notes for months. To my surprise, he became totally absorbed in them. As I would remind him of one telling piece of evidence after another, he would say, "Forget it, stinks, no good, what else?" Then, "Great! Wonderful!" He took out one of his fifteen-cent composition books that he uses for trial notations in each case, and soon all my elaborately spelled-out points were reduced to two- and three-word jottings: June 12, second operation—or—June 7, patient out of bed—why no tests?

Julien complimented me on the amount of homework I had done. For every day that the patient was in hospital, I had prepared a complete diary giving his condition, temperature, white blood count, what the doctor said, what the nurse said, and so forth. "It's a wonderful thing for me," Julien said, "but as long as you overprepare like this, you'll never make a good trial lawyer. You have to remain flexible. You can't fall in love with a position. If you become used to writing everything down, you will become panicky when new situations develop. We don't know what's going to happen tomorrow or the next day or the next. You have to wait, and you have to be able to respond. We know goddamn well that Coleman shouldn't be deaf. We just don't know how we are going to prove it—yet; but we know we're going to prove it."

I asked Julien why he had subpoenaed each of the defendant doctors, and why he proposed to put them on as his first witnesses.

"The jury will never be as receptive as they'll be tomorrow. This is a new experience for them. They will be alert; their first impressions are the most important. These doctors have to lie. We're going to put them on just long enough to make the jury dislike them. That's going to be their first impression."

I was amazed and delighted with Julien's total absorption in the case. He hadn't taken another call; he even refused to talk to his associates. And when I left him, he went home to work.

The following day, Julien opened to the jury. In a very slow and emotional manner he told them how difficult his job was in representing a man who could not even hear his voice. It would not be easy for a deaf man and his lawyer to uncover all the various things that had befallen the plaintiff. Doctors have their own way of covering things, and it was easy for a doctor to say, "We're very sorry about what happened to this man, but we did our best."

After pointing out that much of the evidence to come concerning Coleman would come from hostile witnesses, he told the jury:

Figuratively, you and I are going to go into that institution. You and I are going to reconstruct what actually took place there, not always by the acceptance of what somebody says took place, but by testing what they *say* with what was *recorded* at the time.

You can easily see that where a patient is involved, getting information may sometimes prove difficult. Therefore, it has to be tested. *We* will do that here. *We* will be asking questions of doctors and of people working at the hospital, and these we will match up with what was written, and in that way *we* will try to get at the truth.

Already, Julien was part of the jury, and he and they were off on an investigation together.

Then he began to explain his basic criticism of the doctors who treated our client. With all the diagnostic machinery available at Mt. Sinai, why hadn't they used it to try and determine what was causing Coleman's infection and fever, which were immediately noticeable from June 9 through June 16 (the first critical period in this case)? The theme so frequently used throughout the trial was begun—a large hospital, vast laboratory facilities, yet a man's life and his hearing were allowed to hinge upon guesswork. What awful irony that the simple use of those laboratory facilities could have pinpointed the culprit germ and answered so many mysterious questions: "What is the focal point of the infection? Where is it coming from? What is the nature of it? Which bug is it?—there can be so many. And once having found the bug, which is the best medication that can be employed to treat that particular bug? And each of those steps is no longer dependent upon the guessing of a physician."

Julien went on to other standard laboratory tests that were available but denied to Coleman. He explained the mechanics of cultures—for blood, for sputum, and, most important in this case, for infectious matter draining from a surgical wound. Next, he dealt with the sensitivity test, in which the offending organism is exposed to various medicines to determine which has the greatest effect on it. Then came "the earlier-you-do-it-all" benefits, which added up to "the greater likelihood of curing and stopping the spread and preventing it from getting throughout the man's body instead of its being a localized thing."

Gradually and meticulously, Julien stressed what we would prove. His knowledge of the dates, the drugs, and the events was complete.

On and on, at times softly, at times almost in tears, he recited how his client lay there in a hospital bed with a virulent infection coursing through his body, while the doctors did nothing to find out the nature of the invading organism.

"Mr. Taylor here [singled out with a reproving look], who represents this hospital and has the hospital records, knows that there was not a single sensitivity test taken up to June 16 to find out which of all the medications the doctors have in their armamentarium, which one will fit this case."

On June 16, he pointed out, an antibiotics specialist was called in and *finally* he ordered sensitivity tests. Here, Dr. Nelson's lawyers were subjected to a look of sheer disgust (duly noted by the jury) as Julien continued his sad saga. After those sensitivity tests, he noted, the antibiotics man took "all the medication Coleman was receiving and threw it in the wastebasket; he says it is ineffective. It isn't what the patient needs, because the tests showed that the bug had spread throughout his body—in the bloodstream, in the stool, and in the pus from the wound."

And, to Julien's obvious incredulity and horror, the tests also showed that there were indeed other drugs that would have been—at least might have been—effective against the bug circulating throughout the plaintiff's system.

Julien then outlined the second stage of his case.

We would show, he said, that Neomycin is a highly toxic drug when injected into the musculature (and not so when given by mouth or other means). It can affect two things . . . it says so on every bottle: "Highly toxic. Can affect hearing. Can affect the kidneys. Don't use it for more than ten days intramuscularly." We would also show that every bottle came with a little pamphlet wrapped around it telling doctors to test the patient's hearing before giving the drug and *while* giving it, and again, not to use the drug for more than ten days.

At this time in the sequence of events, Julien pointed out, we have three doctors in the case: antibiotics specialist Nelson, surgeon Carpenter, and family doctor Morton. These doctors finally instituted the use of this drug on June 18 and continued it through June 25—eight days of continuous Neomycin therapy.

But it was the equivalent of considerably more, since, prior to that, the patient had been given Streptomycin, a drug of the same family.

ALFRED JULIEN

Neomycin is not only highly toxic, it is *additive*, so that if you have already given a closely related drug, the Neomycin time has to be appropriately reduced to prevent damage to hearing.

Now, the second prong of Julien's attack began:

Well, you would think they were testing his hearing during all this time, seeing that everything was going fine. The audiometer, the thing you use to test hearing, is portable, or it can be. You can take it to a man's bedside.

Here, his voice boomed and the "never" would echo through the courtroom as he said:

We will prove to you that NEVER—never—not once, did they test this man's hearing, before, during the interval when they stopped for two or three days, or during the fifteen days that they continued, most of which time Dr. Nelson was away on vacation. *Never once.*

It has been said to you already, "We did it deliberately. We made this choice to save this man's life."

We will show you, there were several choices that could have been made; that there was a period when this man's recovery was such that you could have stopped [the drug] if you were testing and if you knew, and if somebody was caring or watching, and that none of this was done.

We will show you that other drugs could have been substituted. And we will prove to you that if a drug like Neomycin is not accomplishing its results within the ten-day period, there is no use continuing it, because you slide downhill and your body builds up resistance and immunity to the drug itself, and that this was carelessness.

By the time of the trial, of course, Julien was well aware of the defendants' position: that they administered Neomycin, knowing it might cause the patient's deafness, and they did it deliberately because the choice they had was simply between life or death. Under those circumstances, the loss of a patient's hearing could hardly affect their judgment. *But* the defendants' argument had at least one serious flaw—a note a nurse had made in the hospital record on July 12.

Anticipating the defendants' life-or-death theory, Julien told the jury:

> July 12 becomes an important date. It is the twenty-second day
> of the administration of Neomycin plus its additive, Strep-
> tomycin. Watch what happens on that day, because if you knew
> and if you were prepared to use Neomycin because that is what
> the man needed—even if it caused deafness—then when
> deafness appeared, that would not alarm you. You would con-
> tinue to use it, isn't that so? That is not what happened here.
>
> On that day when the nurse (none of the doctors, but a *nurse*)
> noticed and wrote in the hospital record that the patient was now
> deaf, the doctors discontinued the drug at once . . . these same
> doctors who now say they had to use it and would have used it
> whether it caused deafness or not. See what happened when they
> found out, to their horror and surprise, because they had not
> watched, that this was causing deafness. Like *that*, it stopped
> [slamming his hand down on the counsel table]—and other drugs
> were substituted.

It was time now to give the jury a before-and-after look at our client,
which Julien proceeded to do in quiet and very moving tones. He
would prove, he said, the effect all this had had on Coleman—a man
who had been active, had had many friends, and whose work had involved a great deal of commingling and talking.

> You will see what it does to a man to be suddenly cut off in this
> fashion . . . how it affects him from a psychiatric, as well as a
> neurological, standpoint. In addition to the cutting off of his hear-
> ing, there are the roaring head noises which go on almost con-
> stantly. And, more than anything else, this is a cause of such dis-
> comfort, such inability to live with himself—well, perhaps
> he—and he cannot hear a word I am saying, by the way—but
> perhaps he, in his inarticulate way, will be able to give you some
> idea.

At the conclusion of his address, Julien was virtually in tears. And so
were several members of the jury.

James Treanor, of the prestigious firm of Barry, Treanor, Shandell,

& Brophy, arose to address the jury. He represented Drs. Carpenter and Nelson. Bristling with indignation, he dramatically denied any wrongdoing on the part of his clients and the other doctors, whom he described as heroes. These doctors were dealing with a man suffering from a ravaging disease; appropriate tests were made when symptoms indicated they should be made; and when it became necessary to use Neomycin, it was used as a desperate measure to save a human life. He claimed that this was a deliberate choice, potential kidney or hearing damage notwithstanding. It was a decision made by all the doctor defendants and concurred in not only by leading specialists called in by them but by the patient's wife to whom the risks had been carefully explained.

Treanor attacked Julien's accusations concerning the drug's accompanying brochure. The decisions of the expert doctors who use these drugs, he said, are not based on some kind of advertising brochure, but on their own clinical experience and knowledge of the action of the drug. In short, he claimed, the tragic loss of Coleman's hearing was the "inevitable consequence of the heroic efforts made by all the doctors who treated this man" to save his life. This case was a "cliff-hanger" with a patient who "was hanging on to life from minute to minute."

One after another, the attorneys for the other defendants rose and made similar addresses, each one claiming that the doctors and the hospital collectively were not responsible, but that even if any one of them was, it surely was not *his* client. The parade of defense lawyers ended with counsel for the hospital.

Julien then called one of the two pharmacists as his first witness. I was as puzzled as everyone else; and when the witness said he had not been employed at the hospital during any of the period of Coleman's hospitalization, puzzlement turned to astonishment. What the hell was Julien doing? He proudly displayed an Upjohn Company brochure and, after asking a series of inconsequential questions, requested it be marked for identification. He then asked the witness, in a serious and dramatic voice (suggesting that this was the most vital question of them all), if he recognized the brochure as being the same as the one that had accompanied the drug Neomycin in 1958.

All four defense lawyers leapt out of their chairs with the alacrity of Belmont's best. Each of them objected, and Julien fought for the introduction of the brochure (waving it in the air) as though his entire case depended on it. During this struggle over admissibility, Julien asked the court's indulgence for a moment and strode over to me. Cupping the brochure over his mouth, he whispered, "Look at the jury, look at the goddamn jury. Do they want to see this brochure or don't they?"

With Julien protesting all the way, the court properly sustained the defense's objections and Julien and "his" jury shared their first disappointment together. As much as the jury wanted to see that brochure, as much as Julien wanted them to see it, it appeared that the court and "the other" lawyers had successfully conspired to keep the document away from them. Our defeated attorney, looking downcast and frustrated, carefully placed the brochure on the counsel table (in tantalizing sight of the jury).

Then Julien, with a just-in-the-nick-of-time brilliant "afterthought," "suddenly remembered" that before the trial had even started, a notice to admit the authenticity of the brochure had gone unanswered by the hospital, and under the law, the fact that the brochure accompanied Neomycin was admitted as far as Mt. Sinai was concerned. After further argument, the judge permitted the introduction of the brochure only against Mt. Sinai, and Julien was finally permitted to read it to the jury. He had found a way to share the secret of the brochure with them! Thanks to his persistence, the silent document was at last given voice. (Subsequently, through expert testimony, he was able to introduce the brochure against each of the defendants. Throughout the trial, it remained on the counsel table as a constant reminder of how hard the defendants fought to keep it away from the jury, and how ferociously Julien fought to share it with them.)

Morton, the family doctor, then took the stand. Julien had told me he wanted to make the most of this elderly practitioner whose association with the other doctors was not particularly close. Morton had neither their knowledge nor confidence and seemed somewhat out of his depth. In the course of pretrial examinations, it had become apparent that Morton had really not read the hospital charts as meticulously as he should have, or, if he had, he was not able to retain the information.

Julien got right to the point and asked him about his knowledge of the hospital records. Morton said he had read them, as well as the surgeon's operative report. Had he read the surgeon's report within two weeks following the operation? "Oh, yes. I think I could describe that without reading it further. I knew what was found because I did read it, but just when I read it I can't recall." He recalled, did he not, reading the operative report before Coleman left the hospital? Yes, he did.

Poor Morton had given the wily Julien just what he wanted. Julien coolly pointed out that although the operative report was dated June 1958, it had not been transcribed until April 1959—ten months later, and almost seven months after Coleman had been discharged! Julien bore down on the doctor. He waved the report close to the doctor's face and thundered: "Where is the operative report that was in this hospital record before your patient left the hospital in September 1958?"

The doctor's reply was devastating: "I don't know."

He attempted to recover by suddenly recalling that he hadn't read the report while the patient was in hospital, but that he had read it later. He had been mistaken, he said; he had been "careless." (Just what Julien was trying to prove!)

Julien proceeded to introduce all of the hospital records relating to his client, and to bring out that this doctor, who had regularly visited and charged his patient for almost daily visits, knew very little about Neomycin or its toxicity. Julien apparently knew much more about the hospital records than this doctor did. Although he had not been familiar with Neomycin, Morton conceded he had found out that Neomycin and Streptomycin were additives; and he agreed with Julien that had he wanted to find out more about the drug and its hazards, he need only have looked at the brochure (lying virtuously on counsel's table).

Julien pointed out that on June 29, the antibiotics specialist, Nelson, after placing an order in the hospital record that Neomycin was to be restarted, left for a vacation leaving Morton alone with other nondrug specialists. The implication was plain. Morton thought Julien was accusing him of being in charge of the case after the specialist left. He would have none of it and fell for the trap that Julien had sprung:

M.: I don't know just when Dr. Nelson went on vacation. He didn't tell me. . . . He didn't report to me that he was going on vacation. I would not be the one he would report to.

Julien looked stunned as he glanced at the jury, then at Morton, then back to the jury.

J. (almost inaudibly, but very distinctly): Are you telling the members of the jury that one of you three doctors went away on vacation and you, one of the other doctors, did not even know about it?

M.: That's right. I wasn't aware of it. He didn't report to me that he was going.

(As though reeling from this disclosure, which Julien knew about long before the trial, he asked the witness if he had ever ordered an audiometric test of Coleman's hearing. Silence.)

J. (bellowing): Did you?

M. (barely whispering): I never ordered an audiometric test.

J. (bellowing even louder): And you knew from looking at the record that no one else had ordered it either. Is that right?

M. (sheepishly): That's right.

J.: And you are acquainted with portable audiometric testing equipment?

M.: I have never seen an audiometer machine, I am ashamed to say.

(Only moments before he had confessed carelessness, and now, shame.)

Julien stared at Morton, as if at a loss for words with which to dismiss such a travesty of a witness. And then he simply sat down.

It was now Mr. Treanor's turn to examine and try and repair the damage to his "hero" client. Under kindly questioning, Dr. Morton told of a conversation he had with Mrs. Coleman, in which she was told of the hazards of Neomycin and of her husband's desperate condition. Morton, we were given to understand, had not held himself out to be a specialist and, in fact, had called in specialists, including Mt. Sinai's surgical director and other eminent physicians.

Treanor was through and Julien sprang to his feet. He demanded to know whether or not, when Morton spoke to Mrs. Coleman, the patient was "critical." Morton "thought so."

The next question was tinged with sarcasm:

J.: Well, having thought so, did you write in the hospital chart that day, "patient is critical"?

M.: No, I did not.

J. (even more sarcastically): The day before, you wrote: "General appearance better." Is that right?

M.: Right.

J.: June 29, when *you* say this patient was now in critical condition, and it had occurred overnight, what was written in the hospital chart by Dr. Nelson?

M.: I didn't say he was out of danger by any means.

(Again, Julien pressed for an answer about what Nelson had written.)

M.: I wrote, "Patient improving slowly. Less distended. Better orientation."

J.: That means his mental processes are better, isn't that so?

M.: That's right.

No one, as Julien brought out, had charted Coleman's condition as "critical" on June 29—only that he was improving slowly.

The first day of the trial was over and the jury retired for the evening to consider the case. Surely, as of that moment, Julien's accusations had at least been supported by the defendants themselves. We, with Coleman in tow, returned to the office and worked late into the evening.

For the first time, Julien interviewed our client in depth. He had twice seen him very briefly; now he spent over two hours with him. They liked each other, and Julien obviously wanted to know everything he could about the man. They talked about the old days and life on the Bronx streets. Julien spoke so slowly and so distinctly that Coleman had little difficulty reading his lips.

Julien was a sympathetic listener and Coleman soon gave vent to all his frustrations. He talked about the roaring in his ears (a condition known as tinnitis) and how difficult it was to communicate with his friends and family. He was beginning to think that various people were plotting against him (a common condition among the deaf). During all this conversation, Julien kept scribbling words into his little trial book.

By the time Coleman left, Julien was visibly upset. What a terrible tragedy had befallen the poor soul, how unnecessary, how unfair it was! He was whipping himself into a state of frenzy and passionate belief in this man who required his assistance.

I asked about the list of words he had scribbled down. "These are words that Coleman can't read on my lips. Wait till tomorrow." He rambled on at length about how much Coleman needed him, how much he wanted to help him.

When Julien opened the next day, he put the other pharmacist on the stand and questioned him about the use of Neomycin and its distribution throughout New York City, The defendants' thunderous objections were sustained—to the amusement and delight of Julien, who, together with the jury, kept staring at that brochure on the table. It had been admitted against only one defendant, and it was still a silent reminder of its own importance and the other lawyers' obstinate refusal to allow it into evidence against *all* the defendants.

Julien then called Dr. Carpenter as his own witness. If anybody was going to be responsible, it would have to be he. He was the surgeon. He was in on the case from the very beginning and it was his patient who'd lost his hearing. The attack began with the question of the hospital record and the fact that Carpenter's operative report was not dictated until many months after Coleman's discharge.

J.: When you perform an operation, Doctor, at this or any other hospital, you do an operative record after the operation, is that right?

C.: Yes, that's right.

J.: And that is something which is dictated and signed by you at or shortly after the operation, is that right?

C.: No, sir, that is not right.

(Now, Judge Nunez intervened, determined to clarify this point.)

N.: How many operations do you do, say, a week?

C.: Two or three.

N.: And when do you get around to dictating those operations?

C.: Well, maybe in one particular day I would dictate a whole batch that had gone on before.

N.: Tell me—yes, or no, Doctor—is there a rule in the hospital about dictating operation reports by the surgeon?

C.: There is a rule now, sir.

ALFRED JULIEN

N.: There is a rule in practically every hospital that you know of, isn't there, Doctor?

C.: Yes, a rule that it should be dictated.

N.: But now how soon after?

C.: They would like you to do it within forty-eight hours.

N.: Within how long?

C.: Forty-eight hours—if possible.

N.: It is your custom to wait as long as nine or ten months?

C.: No, sir.

(The no-nonsense judge had confirmed his reputation, all right, and Julien was going to ride in his wake.)

J.: Was there an operative report in the record while your patient was still in the hospital for the other doctors to look at?

C.: No, never.

(Finally, after a rough go-around, Carpenter was forced to concede that only after the hospital informed him that I was requesting the records had he gone over those records; that he told the hospital officials, or else was told by them, that there was a possible malpractice suit involved in this case—long before our suit had been instituted.)

J.: And then you went over the record again, didn't you, Doctor? . . . Wasn't it then you dictated these two operative charts?

C.: No, I don't think it was then, but earlier.

J.: Before January 1959?

C.: Yes.

J.: And it took more than four months for it to be transcribed?

C.: Yes. . . .

(Again, this was too much for Judge Nunez.)

N.: Are you telling us that it is usual to take four months to transcribe the report of an operation that a surgeon dictates into a dictaphone?

Carpenter's answer left something to be desired:

C.: It usually takes at least one month.

Julien was almost enjoying himself by now. His next questions were designed to bring simple but devastating answers. When Carpenter dictated his report long after Coleman's discharge, was he depending upon his memory to describe that four-hour operative procedure? That's right. Was he again depending on his memory between the time of those two operations (the gall bladder and subsequent sewing up of the broken wound)? That's correct. And there had been many operations in between? Correct. . . . Was this Carpenter's general practice? Yes, it was.

But Julien had worse in store. In reviewing the hospital record, he had noticed that Carpenter almost always skipped a line between his entries. Yet among the doctors' notes for June 12 (the day Coleman's wound had broken open and he was again taken to surgery) Carpenter had made an entry without skipping the usual line. And that entry, Julien insinuated, had been put in the hospital record after our suit had begun.

Carpenter, of course, denied having made any belated insertions in the record at the time he reviewed it. His June 12 entry, though squeezed in and overlapping, was made and signed by him on *that* date—even though in subsequent entries, he reverted to his line-skipping practice.

The chase went on; and each time Carpenter was cornered, Julien got him to concede another point: that in the ten postoperative days, when his patient's fever and blood count clearly indicated infection, he never ordered a culture or a sensitivity test; that cultures *are* a means of trying to identify the invading organism; and that the sensitivity test *is* a well-known diagnostic means of ascertaining what medicine will combat the germ.

Julien knew that this witness was all-important. He also knew that the witness would be less prepared today than he would later, because with every day that witnesses can observe you during a trial, they become better prepared to withstand your cross-examination.

He continued his attack:

J.: Didn't you know about Neomycin and its toxic propensities and about the instructions provided by the drug's manufacturer? And what about the audiometric equipment, both portable and

ALFRED JULIEN

stationary? Is it available at the hospital?

C.: I don't know.

J. (incredulously): You *never* inquired?

C.: I have *since* inquired. But, no—never at that time.

J.: At no time during the total period of the administration of Neomycin to *your* patient did you ever inquire of the ear service in *your* hospital whether they had a portable audiometer which could be taken to the patient's bedside?

(With Carpenter's "No," Julien—looking helplessly at the jury—repeated the question, as though to make sure he, and his jurors, had heard the answer right the first time. They had.)

J.: Knowing, as you have told us, of the potential hazard this drug is to the eighth cranial nerve, and that the manufacturer recommended that hearing tests be given, did you at any time inscribe on the hospital record at any place, for yourself, for your medical associates, the residents, the doctors, the interns, the nurses, "Watch this patient's hearing"?

C.: No.

(With *this* "No," Julien had another eye-message for the jury: What we are hearing is just too painful to bear!)

The onslaught contined. Was Carpenter depending upon the nurses, interns, and residents to inform him of the state of his patient's hearing? No, he was depending on himself—and the other doctors. Yes, the hospital residents visited the patient regularly; and yes, Carpenter would be interested in their observations. Did the nurses see his patient very often? Yes, but not as often as he did. They did converse with the patient about food, bowel complaints, et cetera, and yes, their observations with respect to Coleman's hearing would be of critical importance to this doctor.

Carpenter was looking hard-pressed by now. Julien studied him for a moment, walked over to the counsel table and leaned over to whisper to me that the witness had gotten a haircut since yesterday. He walked away, then came back and said, "I think he looked a lot better yesterday."

The doctor, certain we were discussing further strategy, braced himself as Julien resumed the attack. Now he established that in the hospital record there were order sheets designed for the doctor in charge to communicate with all personnel who would be treating his patient. "And you could have written in that order sheet, 'Watch this patient's hearing. Make notes and report'?" Yes, he could have, but he didn't; nor did any other doctor connected with the case.

Julien then forced another painful admission: that after twenty-two days of Neomycin plus three of Streptomycin, when a nurse reported that Coleman couldn't hear any more, the drug was stopped that day; and that the hearing damage was by then irreversible.

Up until that fateful day, had he ever asked an ear man to look at his patient? No, but he'd spoken to them. Carpenter then testified about a whisper test he had given Coleman. Why, Julien wanted to know, wasn't this put down in the hospital record, and why do you give such a test when there are so many other ways to determine hearing loss? Why should *you* give it rather than an ear specialist, and why give it at all if the real purpose of the drug you were giving was to save the man's life regardless of its effect upon his hearing?

With the dismissal of this witness, the jury was again told (as they would be throughout the trial and again in summation) that the truth here would be determined ultimately by what the doctors had—or had not—put down in the hospital records, and not by what they tell you from the witness stand.

One by one, the doctors were paraded before the jury, and one by one they steadfastly maintained their own innocence. Yet they were unable to explain why the operative report was either missing or dictated so many months after Coleman's operation, and why it wasn't transcribed until many months after that. Again and again, Julien hammered home all the points he had established with Drs. Morton and Carpenter.

Dr. Nelson then took the stand and he had even fewer places to hide than had the others. He was *the* specialist. He, more so than any of them, knew what precautions should have been taken. Julien made a big point of the fact that this doctor had gone on vacation, leaving inexperienced doctors in charge of a desperately sick man. And on the very day he left, Neomycin had been restarted at his instructions.

J.: Did you leave instructions with anybody as to when it should be stopped?
N.: No, I didn't.

ALFRED JULIEN

J.: And knowing what you knew about its possible effect upon hearing, did you at any time note in the doctor's order sheet that the hospital's personnel should watch and report any changes in the patient's hearing?

N.: No, we don't put down all negative findings . . . it's impossible to put them all down.

J. (getting testy now): I'm not talking about your negatives. I am talking about your doctor's orders. . . .

(Again, he asked the doctor if he had left orders for someone, *any*one— the nurses, interns, residents—to check Coleman's hearing.)

N.: No, I did it myself.

J.: Before you left for a week's vacation, did you write in the chart that someone was to watch and report?

N.: No, I didn't. . . . Yes, I stopped the medication on July 12 when the nurse reported the patient was deaf.

J.: Did you make any note about testing the patient's hearing on July *11*?

N.: No, because I didn't find any hearing loss. . . . No, I didn't do a test with a tuning fork.

J.: How about the whisper test?

N.: I used other tests. I don't know whether I used the whisper test. I don't believe I did.

J.: Whatever you used for the sake of the record, so that the other doctors could see it, so that we could see it here, did you ever write any of your findings down until the day after the nurse found that there was hearing loss?

N.: No, because they were negative.

J.: Even negative, Doctor, when you are dealing with a toxic drug like this, and you were going to go away for a period, didn't you write in the record, "I have tested the hearing. It's all right, but continue to watch it while I am away"?

N.: No (with helpless resignation), I didn't.

Finally it was time for the plaintiff himself to take the stand. Julien began by reading from the hospital and otological consultation report, issued just prior to Coleman's discharge from the hospital. The report clearly stated that the patient was irreversibly deaf due to Neomycin toxicity.

Julien, approaching his client with great tenderness, spoke as distinctly as he could. He asked him his age, what kind of work he did, and what salary he earned. Occasionally he would insert one of the words he had learned Coleman could not lip-read. In that exaggeratedly loud voice characteristic of the deaf, Coleman would ask him to repeat the question. Julien usually took out the offending word the second time, but now and then he kept it in, and try as Coleman might, he could not understand or respond.

As the examination continued, Julien inserted more and more of those words, and the mounting frustration of this poor man, who so desperately wanted to communicate with the court and the jury but couldn't, became painfully apparent.

At one point, Julien turned his back on the witness and the jury, and asked Coleman to stand. He remained seated. Julien turned and fixed him with an inquiring look, and Coleman said, "I hear sounds but I don't know what you're saying."

J.: Did you hear the sound of my voice when I had my back to you?

C.: Not the voice; just sounds in general.

J.: When you have this hearing aid on, can you make out what I am saying without reading my lips?

C.: Never, definitely not. If I were to close my eyes I wouldn't know what you are saying; but I notice what you are saying when I watch you and you talk carefully, as you did.

J.: What does the hearing aid do for you?

C.: What?

J.: What does the hearing aid help you to do?

(Coleman, with years of misery, panic, and anxiety welling up, began to ramble disjointedly, just as Julien had expected.)

C.: Well, sometimes, in a small room when we are gathered, I can detect the lips a little better than without it. I mean I am under the impression I may be hearing something. Actually I'm not. It's just sounds. I am at all times reading the lips, because without it or with it, it doesn't make any difference. If you're not facing me, I'm done. I don't know what's going on.

I can hear a honk of a horn. I can hear a fire alarm, a plane, all from the distance. I can't hear it close. Sometimes I'll hear a knock, a bang, or maybe a knock of a gavel or something like that. I may hear the reaction of it, but without it I can't hear nothing.

I at one time drove a car. I drove for thirty to thirty-five years and never had an accident. I still have my license. My wife does all the real driving, but when I do drive I put it [the hearing aid] on.

But why I am telling you this is because this was approved by the Motor Vehicle Bureau, that I can drive with a hearing aid, but the driving is minimal, to obey the alternate-side-of-the-street parking rules I park from one side to the other, or maybe go a few blocks within a short radius of where I live. That's about all.

Otherwise, it's of no use to me. In fact, of late, I never use it. I wear it just for one reason. God forbid something should happen to me. I was going along and a car almost hit me. . . .

These few moments, carefully staged by Julien, but real and painful to Coleman, who could not modulate his voice, stunned the courtoom. Coleman's frustration became so apparent that the court interrupted and asked Julien to please stop him and go to something else. Julien smiled compassionately at his deaf client and told him (with exaggerated hand motions) that he was excused.

Next came our experts. One testified to the plaintiff's hearing loss and its accompanying psychological damage—the almost indescribable effects of sudden, total deafness upon personality, and he described the affliction accompanied by tinnitis.

Dr. Dineen, the surgeon from New York Hospital, was then put on the stand. He was a man obviously dedicated to medicine but resigned to fulfilling his obligation. This was no professional medical witness; he had testified in only one case before, and for a defendant at that.

He stated his opinions: (1) Coleman had been suffering from a subhepatic abscess which had required surgical draining; (2) when the patient postoperatively developed high fever, high white blood count, and suffered a wound dehiscence, cultures should have been taken immediately; (3) Neomycin, if not effective in ten days, would never be effective; and its administration in this case, for such long periods of time, was a departure from common, customary, and accepted medical practice within the City of New York.

Dineen testified that Neomycin was accompanied by its manufacturer's brochure containing acceptable suggestions for its use which should be heeded by physicians. The brochure was received in evidence against all defendants, with Julien twinkling at the jury as though to say, "Look what I've done for you. I didn't let them get away with it!"

Next on the stand came Coleman's wife, followed by their daughter and a friend, all of whom testified as to the changes in his personality and physical appearance as the result of his hospitalization. We heard about his discomfort and pain while in the hospital and about his former earning capacity, gone now that he was deaf. His wife denied having conversations with the physicians about the hazards of Neomycin.

Julien finally rested plaintiff's case, after putting in medical bills and testimony concerning prospective future medical bills.

The court refused to grant defendants' motions to dismiss the case against all the defendants. (It did, however, grant them as to two less important doctor-defendants, holding that no case had been made out against them sufficient to go to the jury.)

It was now time for the defense to be heard, although it was apparent that little evidence that in any way implicated the hospital had gone into the record.

Mr. Treanor called Dr. Carpenter as the defendants' first witness and elicited a most impressive list of credentials from this surgeon-teacher-author of numerous medical articles. Slowly and very effectively, Treanor brought out the medical history surrounding Coleman's treatment. He asked in minute detail about virtually every entry in the hospital record, what each one meant. Apparently, Coleman was at no time abandoned or left uncared for during the course of his hospital stay. We were given a description of his operation, the countless tests that were administered, the X-rays taken, and the thousands of entries that made up the hospital record were referred to in detail.

The history of Coleman's treatment was developed on an almost day-to-day basis, and on some dates, hour-by-hour. When his condition became serious (heavy emphasis on this point), daily consultations with other experts were held (their names, prestigious positions, and credits given).

Under Treanor's detailed questioning, Dr. Carpenter—the teacher

174   ALFRED JULIEN

—now provided us with a learned dissertation on the functions of various drugs of the mycin and other unpronounceable family names. Why, in this case, was one given rather than another? Why intravenous solutions of this or ampules of that? Why this test and that one? Well, it seemed just about all of Coleman's organic functions were being tested and performances measured—and everything was being reviewed by other experts and teachers.

Carpenter testified that during the whole time, he visited Coleman daily, sometimes more than once a day—"some of which appear in the nurses' notes and sometimes when it couldn't, because I was back and forth too often." Did the other doctors on the case visit him frequently, too? They did. And were they all in touch with each other and discussing the case, considering the possible diagnosis, as well as treatments to be administered? They were. And these treatments were consistent with accepted medical practice? They were.

By the end of Carpenter's testimony, it became apparent that the man the jury was judging was a serious, careful, well-educated, and skilled physician who had not neglected his patient.

Now was the time for Julien to cross-examine. Had the jury forgotten his earlier examination? Better remind them by repeating some of his earlier questions. . . . He dusted off that suspicious squeezed-in entry so atypical of the surgeon's notation style. He reminded the doctor that first he had testified that there was no rule at his hospital requiring him to write up operative charts immediately after surgery; and then he extracted from him an admission that there *was* a rule at the hospital requiring the completion of operative notes immediately following surgery.

Then Julien took off, a step at a time, on the failure to take cultures:

J.: Doctor, can we agree that cultures and sensitivity tests are very valuable diagnostic aids?

C. (agreeing): They are.

J.: And the sooner these tests are made and their results obtained, the earlier the physician gets this valuable diagnostic information?

C.: True enough.

J.: And the earlier he gets this information, the better equipped he is to evaluate the infection?

C.: Not necessarily.

(Julien wouldn't buy that, and the answer was changed to "No.")

J.: All right, how about: the earlier the information, the better equipped you are *in general*?

C. (begrudgingly): In general? Perhaps yes.

J.: Well, Doctor, don't you agree it is better to treat an infection in its earlier stage with the medication to which the bug is sensitive than before the bug has had a chance to fulminate? Isn't that true?

C.: Most of the time.

Now the judge found this curious and asked, "When is it not true, Doctor?"

"Well, for example, if you get misinformation."

Julien just couldn't let this go by: "You weren't assuming back in June that you were going to get incorrect information, were you?" No comment.

Dr. Nelson was called to the stand next. Carpenter's credentials had been impressive enough, but this man's were downright staggering. Pathologist, research scientist, specialist in internal medicine, pioneer in antibiotics and chemotherapy, author-contributor to textbooks and medical journals, teacher. . . . How could the jury help but be impressed with his erudition? Treanor got it all in, and Julien was powerless to stop it. The stage was set, and the star specialist was graciously going to lecture the jury and the court on the complexities of the Coleman case and how miraculously this man's life was saved.

Treanor was savoring this one and his questions, in a subdued, respectful voice, were measured out clean and small. But they added up, and we learned from Dr. Nelson that *all* antibiotics are toxic and can cause a variety of allergic reactions (ticking them off in detail)—mild or severe reactions, and sometimes even death. No antibiotic, no drug, no chemical is completely innocuous.

What about the toxicity factor of the drugs in this case—Neomycin and the others that were used? The specialist really put his back into this one and may very well have told the jury a lot more about drugs than they needed to know. But his professionalism could not be denied. On and on he went, describing the properties of drugs in a formal but enthusiastic way. He spoke of the seriousness of Coleman's illness, and the danger of attempting to be too decisive too quickly.

He was making a splendid witness. He relived the tremendous concern that he and the others felt as Coleman's condition worsened, and poignantly he recounted his conversation with Mrs. Coleman:

"I told her I didn't think we would be able to save her husband, that I thought he was desperately ill. . . . That since the relatively nontoxic drugs had failed, we would try to use these more toxic agents in an attempt to save his life. I told her Mr. Coleman suffered from multiple conditions involving his brain, lungs, intestinal tract, bloodstream, and liver, and that there was surely not an optimistic case or much hope for recovery; and that is what I believed at that time."

He also told her, he said, that one of the effects of these toxic drugs might be loss of hearing; another might be kidney damage. But the doctors were warranted in taking this chance to save her husband's life.

Of course, he made it clear, when he came into the picture on June 16 Coleman was suffering from an extremely serious and fatal disease (sixteen-syllable name, patiently spelled out for the court reporter)—a disease that destroys the whole lining of the intestinal tract, often right up to and including the stomach. "Untreated, it has a hundred-percent mortality."

Using terrifyingly big technical terms, Nelson continued explaining (*and* spelling *and* interpreting for the jury) why he chose Neomycin above all other drugs to treat this dying patient in a last-ditch effort to snatch him away from imminent death. His reasons, if not perfectly clear, sounded good enough. After eight days, he stopped the drug because Coleman, though critically ill, was improving very gradually; and Nelson wanted to see if, without the drug, the patient could hold the ground he'd gained.

At this point, Julien looked barely awake. Periodically, he would rouse himself from him boredom long enough for his eyes to tell the jury, Wait, I'll show you; he's trying to put one over on you. But he knew that with each question and answer, the venerable doctor was reaching this jury.

Nelson said he was well aware of Neomycin's side effects, and during the eight days Coleman was receiving the drug, he did attempt gross hearing tests such as clapping his hands and shouting at the man. There was no other way of reaching him, he claimed, because the patient was either comatose, semicomatose, irrational, or disoriented. Further, the patient was often in an oxygen tent that made a hissing noise, and he had nasal catheters with oxygen bubbling through fluid.

Also, he said, in view of the difficulty he was having testing Coleman's hearing with a watch and hand-clapping, he did not think an audiometer would be useful.

On June 29 the patient's condition demanded the resumption of Neomycin, Nelson thought, since there was no other effective antibiotic that could have been used (in his judgment). This time, the drug was given in a lesser dosage.

Julien had implied earlier in the trial that Nelson should never have gone on vacation on the very day that Neomycin was being restarted on a critically ill patient; and Treanor, with an ace-up-the-sleeve kind of assurance, now referred to that. Why indeed had he gone away? Wouldn't you know?—he had suffered a heart attack several years before and doctor's orders were to take frequent vacations. Naturally he made sure to see Coleman on the day he left and on the day he returned. Nelson maintained that with the new Neomycin program the patient gradually became better, and on July 9, the dosage was cut down even further.

And now, of course, Treanor and Nelson had the big hurdle to leap, the thorn that had been in their sides since the pretrial examinations months before: Why did they stop giving Neomycin on the very day the nurse noticed that Coleman had lost his hearing? If his deafness was cause for discontinuing the drug, why hadn't it been stopped earlier?

No one ever knows if the jury, before summation, is ready to understand the significance of each part of the testimony; but Judge Nunez and every lawyer in the room, including Julien, listened intently for what Treanor was about to go into and the crucial answers Nelson would be giving.

"Why was the Neomycin dosage reduced on July 9?"

"Well," said the specialist, "he had gradually improved, and we were trying to see if he could be removed from the drug a second time . . . how he would do with the lower dosage."

Treanor then asked him to explain why, when Coleman's hearing difficulty was discovered on July 12, the drug was discontinued altogether. Because Coleman, though still very sick at that time, was holding the ground he'd made; and they figured if he'd lost some hearing at that point, it would be worth a trial to stop the medication completely . . . and restart it if he slipped back.

Under further questioning, we heard, Nelson last attended the pa-

178   ALFRED JULIEN

tient on July 12, with the understanding (with Dr. Carpenter) that if the medicine had to be restarted, he would come back on the case. In how many cases, before Coleman's, had he used Neomycin intramuscularly?

"About a hundred to a thousand."

Never did he see Coleman in condition to receive an audiometric test. Every time he did see him, however, he made an effort to test his hearing, "as is routine on all these cases." How? "Well, in the early stages I made loud noises, shouting, clapping, et cetera, to see if I could attract his attention." He also tried loud watch-ticks, but couldn't really tell if anything was reliable. "I wouldn't want to base any judgment on his hearing up to that point (July 12)."

As Dr. Nelson also recalled, under questioning, that the nurse who first noted the loss of hearing on that date also noted in the hospital record that she'd had some difficulty with Coleman's responses the day before. . . . Was there any way to determine when his loss of hearing began? The doctor didn't know of any way. He himself could not detect it, "but I will say they were very gross tests because of the patient's condition; and I don't know, frankly, when he started to lose hearing."

Was it possible that just a few doses might have done it? Julien objected to the "possible" and was sustained.

"Bearing the patient's condition in mind, Doctor, assume that an audiometric test had been made, say, on the twenty-ninth—before Neomycin was resumed—and it showed some loss of hearing. Would you have changed the medication in any way?"

"We would not."

"Why not?"

"Because the hearing was not the primary consideration here." (Here we go, with the line of defense!) "We were trying to save this man's life. We had decided originally that we would push this as far as we had to to save his life, and that was the decision."

"Which applied right down to the time the drug was finally discontinued?" (You bet!)

At last, Treanor was laying it on the line, and he was going to rely on this witness to drive the defense home. He had turned this defendant into an expert—an expert for all the defendants. Before continuing, he stopped long enough for a slightly triumphant and somewhat disdainful look at Julien, whose bland expression in no way betrayed the computerlike clickings going on in his head.

Now Treanor wanted to know, when Nelson originally came into the case did he review the antibiotics that had been given the plaintiff up to then? He did. He saw them on the hospital record and discussed them with Dr. Carpenter.

"And in your opinion, Doctor, with reasonable medical certainty, were the method of treatment and the antibiotics given in this case in accordance with sound and accepted medical practice?"

"They were."

Next, he was asked to assume that cultures and sensitivity tests *had* been taken a few days before he was brought into the case, and that they knew then just what organism was involved. . . . Would it have been accepted medical practice to order drugs other than the ones being used at that time? No; they try to give the least toxic antibiotics first, before switching to the more toxic ones—because the correlation between the test tube and the human body ranges somewhere between 70 and 80 per cent.

Would he now explain the time period for giving these less toxic drugs? Yes; it takes between two to four days to determine how an antibiotic is doing. You don't change drugs in less than four days because it may take that long for the major effects to become evident. (Small clinical lecture here about why this is so.)

Up until the time Nelson came into the case, were there any lesser toxic antibiotics that hadn't been used that might have been effective? He didn't think so.

Treanor then reviewed Nelson's testimony concerning the specific quantities of Neomycin that had been injected into Coleman from start to finish. "In your opinion, Doctor, was the administration of fourteen grams of Neomycin over a period of twenty-two days contrary to accepted medical practice?" It was not. Was it a medical necessity? It was.

Assume again, Treanor asked of his witness, that the brochure states that no more than one gram should be given in any one day, and that the medication period should not run beyond ten days. . . . On the basis of your clinical experience with Neomycin, are there occasions when it is proper to go beyond ten days? "Yes," said Dr. Nelson, upon which Treanor turned the witness over to Julien.

With a conspiratorial glance at the jury, Julien rose and walked quite slowly to the stand. He began his cross-examination by demonstrating that although this doctor was the only antibiotics specialist with clinical

ALFRED JULIEN

experience at the hospital, there were others in the city. Yet (he got Nelson to concede) when he left for vacation, he left the drug therapy in the hands of a surgeon who had never administered it before and an internist who had only recently been licensed to practice and whose experience with the drug was limited. Nelson agreed that he could have called in other doctors from other hospitals to watch Coleman and administer the drugs during his absence.

Julien dealt next with Nelson's notion that the patient was too sick for audiometer tests:

J. (thundering): Neomycin is always given to very sick people.
N.: Yes, it is.
J.: And when the manufacturer recommends with respect to very sick people that audiometric tests be given, it is understood that they are given to people who are critical; isn't that so?
N.: It is by me, anyway.

(Julien was scoring heavily.)

J.: Did you say to Dr. Carpenter or some other doctor before you went on vacation, "If his condition permits, take an audiometric test"?
N.: I can't remember.
J.: During a short period of lucidity, Doctor, if there were a standing order to take such a hearing test, it could be done; isn't that so?
N.: Not necessarily.
J.: I didn't ask you "necessarily"—I am asking whether it *may* be done.
N.: No, it may not. . . . During the first period of Neomycin therapy, I tried clapping my hands at Coleman.
J.: Was he responding?
N.: Sometimes.
J.: You *say* you shouted at him?
N.: Yes.
J.: Any *record* about shouting or clapping hands or any record of his response anywhere at all in the records?
N.: No.
J.: Had it ever occurred to you, Doctor, that you may not have

gotten response to the softer sound because perhaps the patient wasn't hearing it?

N.: It occurred to me.

J.: Did you get response to the loud sounds?

N.: At times, yes.

And now Julien was ready to spring his trap. Addressing the doctor in a very conversational and low-key manner, he asked if he had correctly understood him to say that sputum cultures were of no significance in treating pneumonia or infections of the respiratory tract and that the taking of cultures was not important generally in treating infections. Cultures *might* be important, agreed Nelson, but not necessarily so. Would the doctor say that *without* cultures, diagnosis could be hit-or-miss or uncertain? No, he wouldn't say that at all.

The hapless victim had taken the bait. . . . Julien sprang into action, waving in the air an article from a Mt. Sinai medical journal written by Dr. Nelson himself:

J.: Didn't you say in this journal that "the use of smears in diagnosis is of special value with infections in the upper-respiratory tract"?

N.: I did.

J.: And didn't you say in this 1953 article that "the nature and cause of an infectious disease cannot be determined with certainty without the assistance of appropriate laboratory tests"?

N.: Yes, I said that.

J.: Did you say in this article, "In order to treat properly, it is *imperative* that the nature of the invading organism be ascertained, and only the isolation and identification of the etiological agent provides the physician with an exact diagnostic measure"? Did you say that?

N.: May I see it, so I can see where it's in context, Your Honor?"

J.: I would just like to know whether or not you recognize the language which you yourself employed.

N.: I would like to see it there in the book.

(The article was handed to the witness.)

ALFRED JULIEN

J. (repeating himself): Did you say what I just read?

N. (in a clipped voice): I did.

J.: Did you say in this article, "Without the benefit of sensitivity studies, the clinician [attending doctor] may be at a loss as to which antibiotic to prescribe; and the patient may be obliged to undergo a series of therapeutic trials with various drugs until the hoped-for response is elicited. In addition to the cost and discomfort involved, such a procedure is not without risk, since very valuable time may be lost in some instances where early and vigorous treatment is essential to effect a cure." Did you say it?

N.: If it's in there, I said it.

J.: Don't you recognize it?

N.: It sounds—it sounds like I said it, yes.

The defense counsel huddled over the article (a copy had been handed to them), and Julien, from the corner of his eye, watched as they pored over it, looking for some portion that Julien had not read— *something* they could read to the jury in the hope of vindicating their witness.

Julien, having finished with the article, continued with the attack. He went on to the nurse's note of July 12:

J.: "I have noticed *since yesterday* [Julien emphasized] patient seems to have difficulty in hearing me. I must repeat a request several times. Ate fairly well this a.m. Seen by Dr. Nelson."

J.: Did you see him on the eleventh?

N.: Yes, I did.

J.: Clap your hands for him on the eleventh?

N.: Imagine I did.

J.: Did he hear?

N.: I can't recall.

J. (sarcastically): A record would help, wouldn't it, Doctor—*if* you had recorded it?

N.: It would help.

J. (voice vibrating with sarcasm and disbelief): Did you shout at him on the eleventh?

N.: I imagine I did because we did all the tests.

J.: Did he respond?

N.: He might have. I don't know.

J.: If you had a record, we would know, wouldn't we, and you could make a comparison?

N.: Yes.

J.: Did you clap your hands on the tenth, on the ninth, and on the eighth?

N.: I imagine I did.

J.: You imagine?

N.: I did.

J.: Got no record?

N.: No.

J.: Don't know whether there was response or not, do you, Doctor?

N.: Mr. Julien, there was no way of knowing whether there was response half the time. You couldn't tell.

(Julien went on to the two other drugs for which Coleman had been tested and which the laboratory showed might be effective. Why hadn't he been given these drugs [which Nelson admitted having used on other patients, and which could have been used on Coleman, with proper monitoring]? As a matter of fact, continued Julien, when Nelson found out—from a gross test, just mere conversation—that Coleman's hearing had been affected):

J.: You immediately stopped the Neomycin and substituted another drug, didn't you?

N.: I did; yes, I did.

J.: The man's condition did not deteriorate, did it?

N.: No, luckily.

J.: While, as you say, he remained critical?

N.: That's right.

J.: Without Neomycin he continued that month and the next month; isn't that so?

N.: That's right.

(Julien then questioned Nelson concerning the dramatic conversation he testified to having had with Mrs. Coleman in which he claimed to have told her that Neomycin had serious side effects involving loss of hearing and kidney damage. Julien asked the doctor if he remembered

ALFRED JULIEN

having said, "It may affect his kidneys." Yes, he repeated, he remembered saying that.

Out came the transcribed pretrial examination of Dr. Nelson and, with it, Julien's reminder that two years before, when Nelson's memory presumably would have been much fresher, he had been asked whether or not he had warned Mrs. Coleman that Neomycin therapy might result in kidney damage to her husband; and Nelson had answered, "I might have, but I don't remember.")

J.: When you advise a patient or his family about the potential dangers of a drug that is being used on him, isn't it common practice to inscribe that in the hospital record?
N.: We do it at times, yes.
J.: Did you do it here?
N.: No.

With this "No," Nelson's examination was over, its value tarnished, to say the least.

It had taken several days, but Drs. Morton, Carpenter, and Nelson, the principal defendants in the case, had been heard—and listened to with obvious interest by the jury. The surgeon and the specialist particularly were men of great presence and had an aura of authority about them that engendered instant respect.

And now the time had come for them to produce their expert witness, the distinguished Dr. John Reed, known from coast to coast as "The Million-Dollar Hands." He was reputed to be one of the finest surgeons ever to practice. He had specialized in surgery for forty-three years and had performed an estimated three thousand gall-bladder operations.

Neither Julien nor I had had any idea who the defendants' expert would be; and as we sat there listening to this eminent practitioner reeling off his qualifications, my body sank lower and lower into my chair—along with my spirits. Professor of surgery for twenty-five years, member of all the important societies, and founding member of too-many-to-suit-me boards of surgery.

Sensing my apprehension, Julien leaned over and said, "Don't let it bother you. This son-of-a-bitch will be sorry he ever came here today." When Julien is on trial, all opponents and hostile witnesses are sons-of-bitches, rotten bastards, or liars at least.

Reed testified that he had read the records of the Coleman case, and he approved of the defendants' practices and techniques. "It was quite evident," he said, "that an attempt was being made to have a survived patient, a living patient; the only way this could have been done in this particular instance was with the use of an antibiotic. And the only effective one was Neomycin." He went on to add: "I think the question of deafness should have been completely disregarded in an attempt to save this patient's life."

As for the various drugs and treatments (dealt with individually) that had been administered in this case, Reed concurred that they were the proper ones to use.

Treanor had no sooner sat down than Julien was on his feet. Firing a barrage of questions at the expert, he established that Dr. Carpenter had been Reed's assistant for ten years, they'd known each other since 1942, and were close and good friends. And what about Dr. Nelson? Yes, they were associates at the hospital and they, too, had known each other for many years.

Slowly but forcefully, Julien coaxed Reed into admitting that in diagnosing an infection, it is always better to have cultures than not to have them, and that the earlier you have them, the better equipped you are to deal with it.

Next came the operative note. Why had Carpenter not dictated the report right after or soon after the operation, as required by the hospital regulations? "Incidentally," Julien asked (making it sound as incidental as possible), "in these operations which you perform, do you write them up, Doctor?" "Yes, sir." Did the doctor dictate his reports? No, his resident did. When? Usually the same day. Is that because that's the time when a busy surgeon remembers and knows all the details of his operative procedure? "I should think so, yes."

Dr. Reed, like the other witnesses, attempted to evade Julien's questions about the advisability of taking cultures earlier. They wouldn't "necessarily" help, he said; they might not "be of assistance."

But Julien, in a series of questions with built-in affirmative answers, cajoled him into agreeing with him:

J.: I appreciate your saying "not necessarily," because medicine is not an absolute science; true?

R.: True.

J.: But when you're operating with the laboratory tests before you, you at least have more information about the patient than you would otherwise?

R.: Naturally.

J.: And the more information you have, the better your elective choice?

R.: Yes.

J.: Therefore, the earlier you get this laboratory assistance, the better off you—and the patient—may be; true?

R.: As a general rule, that's correct.

(Julien now asked if Reed had indeed said that he'd seen entries in the hospital record about certain hearing tests that were given Coleman—the whisper or watch test. Well, if he had said that, he now said he was mistaken; rather he was relying upon what Treanor had told him.)

J. (pressing on): In order to evaluate hearing on a day-to-day basis, comparisons—findings from one day to another—become important, do they not, Doctor?

R.: Yes.

J.: You cannot evaluate or make comparisons unless there are entries in the record; true?

R.: I should think so, yes.

J.: Doesn't common and proper practice require you to record the results of any hearing tests you were taking?

R.: I should think it ought to be recorded, yes.

Finally Reed conceded that in all the gall-bladder operations he had performed, none of his patients had ever lost his hearing. Julien stared with satisfaction at the defense table, then at the jury, and last at Reed, whom he then excused.

Defense's last witness was an internist—some kind of specialist in electrolytes—who, if anything, worsened the defendants' position. His expertise was hardly reflected in the hospital notes and was totally uncorroborated by the other doctors. Nice, but inconsequential, try. . . .

Counsel for Mt. Sinai now made a motion to dismiss the case against the hospital. Julien did not oppose the motion, for very little evidence had been introduced that implicated the hospital.

The attorneys would be summing up following the afternoon recess. Throughout lunch with our client and his family and the usual well-wishers who attend trial conducted by Julien locally, the grand master was all smiles. If he was at all nervous about his all-important summation, he certainly didn't show it; he was far too busy with Coleman. They "talked" together animatedly and Julien seemed fascinated with him. (Years later I realized that in almost every case he tried, sooner or later Julien will visit his clients' homes, go to dinner with them, become real friends with them, simply so that he can feel closer to them and even more immersed in their causes. The deeper the relationship he developed, the easier it seemed for him to communicate with the jury.)

After lunch, defense counsels' summations again focused on how hard these doctors had tried. Physicians dealing with patients listed as critical should not have to worry about lawyers peering over their shoulders at some future time, second-guessing them. The years of study, experience, discipline, the years of self-denial, are rewarding to these doctors when they can cure disease and thwart death.

Death in this case had been faced not only by these doctors but by other doctors and nurses who had assisted; and the major battle had been won. The larger portion of credit should be gratefully bestowed upon these front-line defendants who had won the war with death and saved Coleman's life. The tragedy of his deafness was the price that had to be paid. And nobody regretted it more than these doctors—or these lawyers who were privileged to represent them.

The implication was clear. These men should be honored, and it was a disgrace to drag them before a court of law. It was their knowledge, experience, their selflessness that saved the life of the man who was now looking to punish them.

It was our turn now. The court was able-to-hear-a-pin-drop quiet as Julien arose and looked at Coleman. "Looking to punish," was he? Julien opened on that one. . . . The last thing Harry Coleman wanted to do was punish anybody. Punishment wouldn't restore his hearing. And sympathy?—sympathy is something you get used to, and then you get sick of.

Nobody in that courtroom was making accusations against or questioning these doctors' capabilities. The issue was simply: what had they done—or *failed* to do—as far as this plaintiff was concerned?

Julien reminded the jury (several times) that it was "their" investiga-

188   ALFRED JULIEN

tion, along with his—the one he'd promised them he would make—that had been completed. From the very beginning, they both knew—he and the jury—that what these doctors said might be quite different from what they had written. Which do you believe: what was placed in those records when Harry Coleman could still hear (and when there was no reason to believe there would be a lawsuit) or what was said here by people who stand accused of carelessness—not a *crime*, just carelessness—after they have talked among themselves, after a lawsuit has been started, after they have conferred with their attorneys?

Bit by bit, Julien reviewed and pointed out contradictions in what the witnesses had said and what they or others had written; what they failed to put in the hospital record and what they claimed happened later on.

Next came the questionable "coincidences": Carpenter's squeezed-in entry after the second operation; how much time passed before he dictated his surgical report, and how much longer still before it was transcribed. And wasn't it interesting how Dr. Morton said he'd seen the operative report before Carpenter had even dictated it?

He excoriated Carpenter and Nelson for having the temerity to suggest to a jury that it *wasn't* better for a doctor to have at his fingertips whatever cultures, sensitivity tests, and other aids he can get from a large metropolitan hospital when waging war against a disease that is ravaging his patient's body. (Phew! Exhale . . . But that's Julien.)

And let's not forget the doctors' testimony that Coleman could not be given an audiometer test. . . . As Julien read from the hospital notes, the jury was reminded how often the patient was improving and was out of bed and reading. He invited the jury to go through the doctors' notes, as he had, and look in vain to see when any of them had ever visited Coleman after midnight. (Sarcastically): Do the patients of these doctors conveniently die for them only during the daytime?

From irony, he switched to terrible melancholy: "In the same hospital, a short elevator ride away from this man, from whom pus and bile and sputum could be taken at any time, was that laboratory. It wouldn't 'necessarily' help, they said, it 'might not' have done any good, they claim; but [looking pleadingly at the jury] didn't they owe it to Harry Coleman to *try*, if it might have saved his hearing? Not if it 'necessarily' would have made a difference, ladies and gentlemen, but if it might have, shouldn't they have *tried*?"

Harry Coleman could no longer work. The horrors of tinnitis and deafness were portrayed. They had seen for themselves the frustration of a man who desperately wanted to communicate with them but could not.

Coleman had only one chance in this world to receive justice for what had been done to him—justice for the things that had not been done *for* him—and for which he certainly paid. "Oh, how he has paid, ladies and gentlemen!" If the jury did not award him enough damages now, he could never come back to them again. They could never rectify any mistakes that they made now. Coleman could never reconvene them and say, "Look, you made an honest mistake, but you did not give me enough. I can't support myself or my wife."

He called the jury's attention again to the brochure (holding it aloft)—this silent witness that the defendants tried to sweep under the rug. (Pointing to the defendants scornfully): "*They* know more than the men at the laboratory who test this drug and put it on the market! Only one of them knew anything about this drug, and *he* went on vacation."

Remember Dr. Dineen. . . . "What did that doctor have to gain by coming here and telling you folks what really happened in this case?" Had he ever testified in court before? "You all heard that he had only testified once, in defense of a doctor. He did not even submit a bill for his services to us and Mr. Coleman. He came because he is dedicated to medicine and because he refused to cover up what had been done in this case."

Julien asked them to return a verdict for $150,000. No other sum of money could repay Coleman for his pain and suffering and future expenses. "Anything less is insufficient." He was finished, and the only sound to be heard in the courtroom was the sobbing of Mrs. Coleman. Court was recessed until the next morning.

At 10:00 a.m. the next day, Judge Nunez charged the jury, carefully instructing them upon the law and reminding them of his recollection of the testimony. But he stressed it would be their recollection, rather than his, that controlled. At noon, the jury retired to consider its verdict.

Two alternate jurors had been discharged after hearing all the testimony in the trial. Judge Nunez now called them to the bench for an exchange of whispers, after which they left. Julien asked the judge to let us in on the secret: "How would they have voted?" The defense attorneys wanted to know, too. "For the plaintiff," said Nunez. My jubi-

ALFRED JULIEN

lation was cut short by Julien's curt "Forget it, it doesn't mean a damned thing."

2:40 p.m.: All counsel were asked to reappear in the courtroom. The jury had returned and asked to hear again a portion of the judge's charge, one which seemed very much to favor the defendants. The portion was read, and defense counsel left the room elated. We sat there enveloped in gloom.

4:30 p.m.: Jury returned with a unanimous finding for the plaintiff—$150,000.*

Coleman rushed to Julien and these two old friends clutched each other like long-lost brothers. The jury, wordless and exhausted, filed silently out of the courtroom. As Julien watched them go, he said, "God damn it, I love them; they never fail, I just love them."

---

* Subsequently, a motion was made to reduce the verdict on the grounds that it was excessive. Motion granted and verdict reduced to $100,000.

DIVORCE, JULIEN STYLE

One weekend several years ago, while Julien and his wife were guests at our country house, I found myself worrying aloud about an impossible case I had to try early on Monday. Encouraged by my sympathetic wife and a couple of curious Juliens, I aired the facts of the matter:

I had been retained by a twenty-odd-year-old man (let's call him "Bob") who had been married to (shall-we-say "Amy") an extremely wealthy young lady for whose father he worked. Bob was a bit of a philanderer, not much of a worker, and something of a cad. They had two children.

From the first, it was not what one would call a "marriage made in heaven," and parenthood did little to elevate the relationship. Minor bickering, in time, mushroomed into fairly major battles; and on several occasions, Amy alleged (and several witnesses were willing to corroborate) that Bob had physically assaulted her.

Amy had a good deal of money in her own name. Over a period of time, Bob began withdrawing increasingly larger sums from his wife's account and putting it in their joint account. There is some confusion as to whether or not he had any authority to do even that at this point. But as time went by, all of Amy's money found its way, first, into an account in Bob's name only, then into new accounts whose whereabouts Amy did not know, then into cash, and then into an account belonging to Bob's father.

When Amy's parents learned about all this money manipulation, a lawyer was hired, Bob was fired, and his wife sought a divorce on grounds of cruel and inhuman treatment; she also sought the return of her money.

During the course of the lawsuit, Amy made a motion for support for herself and the children. The defense, of course, was that Bob was hardly in a position to pay it, since his father-in-law had fired him. The judge who heard the motion and read the wife's supporting affidavits was apparently convinced that Bob had, in fact, done all the things of which he had been accused. He granted the wife's motion and directed Bob to pay a whopping sum of support. His decision was no doubt based on the theory that even though Bob had been fired, he had peculated enough money to pay the award.

And that's where the matter stood as of this pretrial weekend evening.

Having summed up my story with a statement that it was the worst case I had ever agreed to handle—one that *nobody* could win—I settled back to wallow in condolences. The ladies came through and commiserated with my plight. Julien, with characteristic modesty, said, "If there is a jury, I can win it."

Since there *was* going to be a jury, I challenged him to try it and he said he would love to. He hadn't tried a case in weeks (it was summertime) and he thought it would be fun—if I could get an okay from my client.

Since my client, I felt, was halfway to the gallows anyway, I assured Julien that there would be no problem about it, and that was that.

On Sunday evening, as he was leaving for the city, I asked if he wanted to take along the file. "No," he said, "I didn't promise to work for you, I just promised to win your case."

I arrived in court early next morning and met my opponent ("Edwards"), who asked if I was ready. I explained I was not going to be trying the case. "Well, who is?" he wanted to know. So I told him.

"*Al Julien!*" Edwards shrieked. "You mean somebody from his office?" No, just Julien, himself. My opponent blanched and bordered on fainting. Then he rushed off to consult with his client and her parents.

When Julien arrived, I introduced him to Edwards, who extended his hand. Julien looked scornfully at him and, pointing his finger two inches from the man's nose, said, "Now look here, my friend, I want you to know why I am trying this case. I read your goddamn papers and they are a pack of lies. They are not at all the kind of papers a lawyer has the right to file in this court. And when I get through with you,

you'll never try any cheap shots like this any more."

Mr. Edwards, stunned, wanted to know what Julien meant. It meant the harangue wasn't over: "Don't try that innocent bullshit with me. Let's just pick a goddamn jury and get it over with."

With that, Julien started to walk away, then looked back and said, "You ought to be ashamed of yourself."

Back in the conference room next to the courtroom, I asked him why he had berated Edwards so harshly. He smiled and said, "He is a son-of-a-bitch. I don't like him at all. I think he is the guy that picked on one of my friends a few months ago."

Now he met our client for the first time—and our client met Mr. Charm-Hyphen-Warmth. I had told Julien that Bob was a terrific golfer, and the two began talking about golf as though it were their only concern. Within fifteen minutes, Julien was taking a putting lesson right there in the conference room. Within twenty minutes, Edwards was knocking on the door with the first of (what was going to be) several offers to settle the case.

> J. (going into his act): I am a trial lawyer, I don't settle cases. If you want to settle the case, we keep the money and you get the divorce. No money, that's it.
>
> E.: She doesn't want much, but she does want support for the children.
>
> J.: Daddy broke up the marriage, let Daddy pay.

Edwards left and soon returned—and left and soon returned—while Julien chuckled. "I don't think he wants to try this case."

Finally, when our case was called, Julien leaped to his feet and raced toward the bench yelling, "Both sides ready"; and then, waving to his opponent, said, "Edwards, get over here."

Edwards trotted up behind him and when they arrived at the bench, Julien said:

> Your Honor, this is a divorce case in which my client is supposed to have beaten his wife and done a lot of other terrible things. Incidentally, he didn't do any of them. Those are issues for the jury to decide. He's also accused of having stolen his wife's money, but the question of money goes to how much support should be paid, if any. That's for Your Honor to decide.

Now, I want to tell you something, Judge. I know this other lawyer, and I know he is going to try to tell the jury about all of that money business, and it's wrong, its prejudicial, it's unfair, and before he gets a chance to poison the jury, I want to tell him not to do it.

By now, Edwards was so intimidated that he said, unthinkingly, he was planning no such thing. (In fact, it could have been argued at least that if the thefts were proven, they alone might constitute cruelty.) But poor Edwards, with rivulets of perspiration streaming down his face, was simply trying to defend himself against Julien's attacks.

The judge said, "Well, apparently you both agree that the question of what happened to the money is for me to decide, after the jury decides the divorce action. That's it."

"I understand that," said Edwards.

Julien, staring at him, lashed back with: "See to it that you do."

Counsel was directed to pick a jury. When it was Julien's turn to talk to the proposed panel, he was patience personified. He told them that he represented an extremely nice young man who was being sued by an extremely nice young lady:

Regardless of what happens in this case, you won't find me or my client saying one nasty word about this young lady. This unhappy situation epitomizes what happens to marriages when outsiders meddle into relationships they know nothing about.

This is a very simple case. I am here to save the marriage and I need your help. And that man [pointing accusingly at Edwards] is here to destroy it. And after you have heard the evidence, I don't think you're going to let him get away with it.

Julien then told the jury what was wrong with the marriage: rich in-laws who tried to buy a son-in-law who was not for sale. And even when the marriage stands before them in ruins, the wife suffers the final indignity of having her daddy's lawyer shoved down her throat.

On and on went Julien. Actually, he was delivering an opening address or a summation to a prospective jury, but at this point Edwards hadn't the gumption to try and stop him. At one point he did rise and start to object, but Julien cut him short with, "Will you please sit down and behave yourself and let me talk to these people." He did.

Julien reminded the jury that in this state, divorces are not handed out for the asking. He supposed that they, just like him, had rough periods in their married lives, but they stuck them out. And who knows, perhaps they wouldn't be married today if they had had the misfortune, as poor Amy had, to have a father who couldn't tell the difference between money and love.

Out in the hall, after the jury was selected, Julien, with a nod toward Edwards, said to me, "He'll never try this case; he just hasn't got the stomach for it." He asked what I thought we should settle for. I suggested that Amy and Bob split the money and that he support the children. Julien just smiled.

Later, after two trips between the in-laws and Julien:

E.: What do you want? My clients want to avoid all of this.

J: Does she really want the divorce?

E.: Yes, the marriage is over.

J. (magnanimously): She can have it, but my client needs the money.

E.: All of it?

J.: Yes, I'm afraid all of it.

E.: What about support?

J.: Nothing for the wife, twenty-five dollars a week for the children.

E.: Both of them?

J.: Well, I don't know; I'll talk to Sheresky here. Maybe I can get you twenty-five dollars for each of them. What do you say, Norm?

(I counted to five under my breath, and allowed as how the client might accept that.)

J.: All right, but before I make this deal, I have to talk to Sheresky alone.

We walked off to a corner of the courtroom. Julien was earnest: "Look, I don't want to do this if there is any doubt in your mind that I can win the case." I assured him that Edwards and I both knew that he could.

ALFRED JULIEN

"All right, see if the client is happy and ask him when we're going to play golf together."

Julien was through and home in time for lunch. And the worst case I had ever had had been won.

Rehashing it all later, I asked Julien what would have happened had we been up against a better trial lawyer than Edwards. He said there would have been a terrific trial, but he thinks he would have won.

And what if Williams or Foreman or Belli or Nizer or Bailey had been his opponent?

All he would say was, he would have had more fun that morning, although he might easily have lost. "We're like professional football teams playing against each other, Norm. On any given day any one of us can win and any one of us can lose."

MELVIN BELLI

Mel Belli is the senior partner of Belli, Ashe & Choulos. His main office is in the "Belli Building," in San Francisco, and it is one of the most beautiful law offices in the world. If his stationery means anything he is also senior partner in a firm entitled Belli, Weil & Jacobs, in Bethesda, Maryland, and senior partner in a firm entitled Belli, Shairshon, Carner, Thierman & Steindler, in Forest Hills, New York. And, according to his stationery, he is associated with other law firms in Sacramento, California; Munich, West Germany; and Tokyo, Japan. He is certainly controversial; he is flamboyant; he is a character. He makes enemies as fast as he makes headlines. He is also a writer, a teacher, a television personality, and one hell of a good lawyer. Unfortunately, Belli is known more for his questionable antics—and his tactics in defending Jack Ruby—than he is for his accomplishments in the law over a lifetime of dedication to it. As his stationery indicates, Belli is all over the place, and his "proper place" as a trial lawyer becomes less definable because it is so often blurred by his activities outside the courtroom.

The first time I met Belli was at 7 o'clock in the morning, one dreary and chilly day in San Francisco. To my surprise, he was a guest host of a television interview program on which I was to appear and discuss a book I had written with Marya Mannes on the subject of divorce. My preconceptions about him were the same as most Establishment lawyers; he was perhaps the "king of torts" (i.e., "trivial" things—such as negligence, medical malpractice, and so on) and a well-known character, but not *really* a trial lawyer. At that first meeting, when he was interviewing me, I noticed two things about him that so predominate the mystique of the grand masters: he charmed me and in ten minutes got more information out of me on the subject of divorce than other interviews, television, and press had been able to do in hours.

Belli, like other grand masters, has an incredible curiosity about absolutely everything. I have seen it operate in countless situations. For example, when he invited me to the courthouse in San Mateo to watch him try a civil lawsuit, his curiosity about the architecture of the building, which had been designed by Frank Lloyd Wright, far exceeded the enthusiasm about his case. He spent close to an hour looking at the courthouse, examining each of the courtrooms, visiting the library (asking how many books it had), and going through the cafeteria (inquiring how many people it could seat). His desire to find out all there was to know about the new courthouse was intense. When his curiosity was satisfied, his concentration returned to the case he was trying.

On the early-morning television show in San Francisco I asked him whether he thought he qualified as a grand master.

"Shit, yes," he said. "Although I'm not so sure some of the ones you mentioned qualify."

He agreed to see me at my convenience, and several weeks later we met.

Belli's office reflects the man perfectly. It is flamboyant, overdone, but a true marvel. The Belli Building is really a complex of offices, with the main building housing the reception area, library, and other partners' offices. The building is separated by a gorgeous courtyard from another building, the one that Belli's office is in, and he has his own entrance. The offices in both buildings are richly Victorian, and the Belli Building is one of the true "musts" for tourists in San Francisco.

That first interview began in Belli's office, lasted through a long lunch in his favorite restaurant next door, and continued back in his office. That day, I was introduced to his new, young, and beautiful wife, two of his partners, two secretaries, and a group of associates. They were all told that I was writing a book about great trial lawyers, and he invited me to speak to any or all of them whenever I wanted. During the course of the interview I learned about the history of San Francisco, San Francisco politics, national politics, great wines, the dangers of "screwing" (in the sexual sense) your own client or witnesses, the evils of the American Bar Association, the treachery of Nixon, the ineptitude of McGovern, the history of Mel Belli, the boy, the young man, and the master trial lawyer, and many of the do's and don't's of trial practice.

Most of the time my tape recorder was on, and I asked Belli whether it bothered him and if he was curious about what I was going to write. As had *every* grand master I interviewed, Belli said he didn't care what I wrote. Although some of the grand masters asked to see any quotations, simply to make sure they were accurate, Belli didn't ask even for that. Like the others, Belli is a raconteur. He told me about a time many, many years ago, when he was trying a case in another state which he was sure he had lost. While the jury was out, Belli was dallying with a waitress from a local bar in his hotel room. The court clerk called Belli's room at the most inopportune moment to announce that the jury was back in, and that everybody was waiting for him. Belli didn't think there was much sense in interrupting what he was doing to go across the street to hear how he had lost a case, so he finished what he was doing. "Shit, was I surprised to hear that I had won the goddamned case!" When I asked him whether he would object to my using such material, he told me that if someone is dumb enough to grant an interview to a writer, he ought to at least be smart enough not to try to control what they wrote.

It is easy to criticize Belli from a distance; it is not hard to find fault with many of the things he has said and done as reported in the press, but, faced with the man and with some of his accomplishments as a lawyer and as a teacher, the verdict is far from clear. As we shall see, even the verdict of the legal profession in general, that Belli "blew" the Ruby case, in the light of what we now know, may be largely erroneous.

Belli is the author of several books, some for laymen and others that are "standard works" in the field of law. His six-volume *Modern Trials and Modern Damages* is as good an encyclopedia of trial practice as anything available. He has repeatedly made new law in the personal-injury field, as well as in other fields. He has taught young lawyers the art of trial advocacy, and has written countless articles on that subject for more than two decades. Anybody who makes light of Belli's talent as a lawyer doesn't know what he is talking about. There is surely plenty of room to criticize him as a personality, or even for the way he practices law, but the man is able: there can be no doubt of that.

Belli is an only child. His father was a wealthy banker in Sonora, California. "I remember when I was a kid, my father used to say, 'Go down to the bank,' and I'd go down there and think all that money was his." But, before he graduated from Boalt Hall Law School in San Francisco, "My father disposed of that impediment, if it is necessary to my greatness to be a pauper." He regrets being an only child. He said, "I suffered from that, it makes for selfishness. Now, as I get older, I see a lot of the attributes of selfishness which I am trying hard to squelch. I'm trying to become more mellow. I'm trying to become a good guy and more of a conformist. Every day that the bar association doesn't file an extra complaint against me makes me think that I have mellowed."

When he was young, Belli loved to act in school plays. Once, in high school, he gave a speech during which there was a lull. He remembers saying, "It's not that I have forgotten what I was going to say. I've got so much to say I don't know what comes next." And he remembers making a speech in college during an oratorical contest. Explaining why he came in second, his professor said, "His historical facts were in-famous—Belli's got the Russian before the American Revolution. He's got Genghis Khan going through Africa. All of which is horrendous. But he's a spellbinder." Belli says, "I think the law is like acting . . . every time I try a new case I get a new script."

Like most of the other grand masters, Belli knew he wanted to be a trial lawyer from the very first. He loved being one from the first day he ever walked into a courtroom. He wasn't interested in anything else.

"If somebody had come into my office and told me he wanted me to draw a contract of a construction of a building bigger than the Empire State Building and told me that my fee would be ten per cent of what was spent, I wouldn't have cared. Money didn't interest me in those days. Shit, I remember in the early years of my marriage—as soon as I got out of law school—my wife was working for Travelers' Aid and she was making about a hundred and fifty dollars a month and we were living on that."

He said that he started out in criminal law and loved it, but, "I got to the point in criminal law where I realized that if I stayed in it I would have ended up in the bucket because everybody was bribing every-body. The cops in San Francisco were arresting people and then going to jail bond brokers and lawyers and telling them that for five hundred dollars (which was like five thousand today) that they would swear that it was so dark that they couldn't really see what happened and the defendant would get off. In a rough sense, justice was done because the defendant ended up paying a five-hundred-dollar fine to the cops and to the lawyers but nothing to the state. As a matter of fact, it probably made them more careful. And who's to say, in the nature of things—maybe it worked out all right.

"I like it so much that if I couldn't try cases, I couldn't live. If that bar association ever bumps me for having a lecture agent or criticizing some dumb son-of-a-bitch judge or anything like that, I'm going to be in a helluva fix."

And like so many of the other masters, he began taking any case he could. Earl Warren, long before he became Attorney General of the State of California and then a Supreme Court Justice, was a friend of Belli. They both attended Boalt Hall Law School. Also, Warren was some years older.

In the early days Belli says Warren used to like to have Belli speak at various political rallies. "The only reason Warren asked me to make a speech for him was because of his introduction. He'd say, 'I'm going to introduce a real comer, a young lawyer who, when the trap sprung last week at San Quentin, had half his practice wiped out,' and I'd get up and say, 'The District Attorney [Warren] isn't telling the truth. I had my whole practice wiped out.' "

Discussing the difference between the advantages of a young trial lawyer against a veteran, Belli said, "A young lawyer is sharper. He is more in tune semantically and knows what the jury is familiar with. If you get a younger jury, he knows their language." But he points out that hiring the veteran trial lawyer has the same advantages that you get when you hire the veteran surgeon: "The appendicitis operation may be pretty routine, but yet the patient may develop a problem that you see only once in thirty years in medicine. Well, the guy that's been practicing for over thirty years is going to be able to handle it better." And he points out that it takes a while to develop the killer instinct that a trial lawyer has to have. "Your opponent may be your good friend, but never in the courtroom. Fuck'em if you can. They expect you to do it. Friends of mine, like Bob Lamb, who represents Lloyds of London and who is the best defense trial lawyer around here, would never speak to me again if I pulled a punch against him in court."

Belli says that he tries to avoid introspection about himself in the courtroom. "You keep away from all that stuff when you're trying cases," he says. "You've got to be a mechanic. The niceties of why you do things, who you are, where you belong in this life, interferes with your being a mechanic."

When I asked him why he and Hallinan and so many of the others seemed to be so tolerant of their own clients, he said: "We've never had a client who's perfect. And we're impressed with that. We try to build him up to perfection but we see the frailties of mankind."

I asked Belli what was the most important part in trying a case, the opening, the cross-examination, the final summation? He answered, "What's the most important part of the man, his heart, his eyes, his legs?" Belli stressed that a true trial lawyer has to have, in addition to a sense of legal history and in addition to the ordinary skills of voice, grace, timing, and so forth, a true warm feeling for the client. "It's a great nostrum that money can bring when it's put on your desk and you realize you've got to think for the person who put it there. You pay money and I'm with you. Shit, I wouldn't think of changing sides. It's just sheer bullshit when people come in and say to me, 'I had a good lawyer but he sold out.' Lawyers don't sell out. We don't sell out because we don't make money doing it, but, more important, we don't sell out because our own egos and our own personal feelings are involved. We marry our clients . . . my feeling about a client has never been, You bum, I made a case for you. I think my clients are beautiful. I have more of a director's pride than an author's pride. . . . I simply couldn't be objective about a client after the first couple of hours. And that's why I've lectured that it's so terribly important that when you get a client you have to make notes immediately about your impression of him, if his hair is too long or if you don't like his mustache, or if you don't like the way she wears her nails or hair. You better make note of it on that first visit. That's the way the jury's going to see your client."

Most of all, Belli thinks that a great trial lawyer has to be warm and have jury presence: "You have got to have warmth and you've got to be alert for that one break in the case." He tells the story of a doctor that he represented in Indiana in a small town: "The filthiest damn case I ever had. I was getting the shit beat out of me. My goddamn client was no damn good. This client was charged with sodomizing some girl who testified that she had come to the doctor's office with her girl friend. The girl friend testified that she had waited a considerable time in the waiting room and that she didn't do anything—even though she was afraid that the doctor was attacking her friend. Finally, the girl friend testified, 'I put my head in the door and I said, "Shit, Doctor, you've been in here long enough." ' I asked her, 'You said, "Shit, Doctor, you've been in here long enough?" ' She said, 'Yeah.' "

Belli said, "I closed my case. When it came time to argue that case, the only thing that I argued to the jury was: 'I want to tell you that sometimes we may be guilty of breaches in grammar. But I've been in your community now for about a week; I've been here to your fried-chicken place; I've been out to your wonderful ranches, and I've met a lot of your wonderful fine people." And he named several of the local establishments that he had been to. He then said, "Never once while I've been in your community, never once when I've been waited on by any of your neighbors—perhaps even by some of your daughters, never once would any one of them ever say to me, 'Shit, Mr. Belli, we ain't got no more bacon,'; 'Shit, Mr. Belli, we ain't got no more fried chicken.' And I continued to sum up like that and, by God, I got the son-of-a-bitch off." He continued, "What's the most important part of the case? It depends on the case. The most important part of that case was when that witness said, 'Shit, Doctor.' "

Inevitably any introduction about Belli or with him brings up his role as chief defense counsel in the Jack Ruby case and about that there is much to be said.

The State of Texas V.
Jack Ruby AND Melvin Belli V.
The City of Dallas

In a way it is typical of Melvin Belli that he supplied me with a maze of material concerning his defense of Jack Ruby. And most of the material that he gave me was highly critical of him.

At the first meeting I had with him I told him that as a trial lawyer it seemed to me, as it seemed to most lawyers, that the defense he put up was plain lousy. Belli agreed that he should never have taken the case; that he was the wrong lawyer for a city like Dallas. He thinks somebody like Percy Foreman, or some other Texan, would have been acceptable.

On the other hand, he forcefully argued that his defense of Ruby was as good and as innovative as could have been put together by anybody.

On November 22, 1963, President John F. Kennedy was shot and killed by Lee Harvey Oswald. And while most of us remember that Jack Ruby shot President Kennedy's assassin, Lee Harvey Oswald, on November 24, 1963, and that Melvin Belli unsuccessfully defended him, we never knew—or have forgotten—much else. At approximately 11:17 on the morning of November 24 a third-rate night-club operator, known as Jack Ruby, found himself wiring a $25 money order to a strip-tease artist who had worked at his night club under the name "Little Lynn." Across the street from the Western Union office was the Homicide Bureau of the Dallas Police Department and a crowd had gathered because Lee Harvey Oswald was being held there. Ruby walked up a ramp leading from the street, stepped through the door, and walked toward a crowd of newsmen and police. Ruby made his way through the crowd and saw the manacled Oswald about to be led out of the station. In the glare of floodlights, popping flash bulbs, and in the midst of confusion and excitement, unfamiliar in the life of most of us, one of the newsmen asked Oswald, "Do you have anything to say in your defense, Lee?" Before he could answer, Jack Ruby had shot him dead. Less than four minutes had passed between the time Ruby shot Oswald and the time he had left the Western Union office.

In Texas, you don't shoot manacled men, and insignificant Jewish night-club operators don't deprive a whole city of the opportunity of avenging the death of a President. As much as District Attorney Henry M. Wade and the other law-enforcement officials of Dallas wanted the blood of Lee Harvey Oswald, they came to want the blood of Jack Ruby even more.

How would you find twelve good citizens and true, in the city of Dallas, who would give Ruby his constitutional right to a fair and impartial trial, when in fact everybody in Dallas and indeed the entire country saw Jack Ruby shoot Oswald on national television in front of their very eyes. The answer was becoming clearer every minute and every day, until March 14, 1964, at 1:06 a.m., when Ruby was found guilty of murder with malice of forethought and when it was decided that he should suffer the penalty of death. The answer was simply that the provisions of the United States Constitution, the Constitution of the State of Texas, and the decisions of the Supreme Court of the United States—in a variety of criminal cases—were going to be suspended as far as Jack Ruby was concerned. And in as miserable and disgusting a travesty of justice as has ever been perpetrated in any court of law, Jack Ruby was denied the most fundamental and elementary principles of justice by a publicity-seeking and inept judge; by a talented, resourceful, and unrelenting team of prosecutors without a smidgin of conscience and regard for the law; by a panel of jurors more intent upon getting a seat for the hanging than finding out what the hanging was all about; and by the passions, guilt, remorse, and thirst for revenge which seized us all in the aftermath of the slaying of our own King of Camelot.

Within a week of Ruby's killing Oswald, there entered on the scene the least likely gladiator of defendants' rights to curry favor with a Texas jury, Melvin Belli. Nobody likes a fight better than Belli, unless it's an enraged Texan. The citizens of Texas charged with the responsibility of seeing that justice was done to Jack Ruby made as tragic an assessment of Belli as Belli made of them.

Just who did this little, gaudily dressed San Francisco dude think he was, trying to disguise Jack Ruby—"Jew-boy" night-club operator—by using meaningless psychiatric words, like "episodic control," "organic brain damage," "psychomotor epilepsy"? What business did a California negligence lawyer have coming to Dallas, shooting his mouth off that his client couldn't get a fair trial? And what on earth made Belli believe that the people of Texas were going to be any more amenable to his fancy notions of psychiatry and constitutional law when, wearing $400 suits, he spouted them down at the people from a pedestal upon which he was perched, and without any trace of a drawl? The people of the State of Texas and Melvin Belli were on a collision course. When they met and collided, the laws of the State of Texas and of the United States lay in a shambles beneath their feet.

There is a regrettable tendency among the press, the public, and, surprisingly, even lawyers, to judge the trial bar solely by what they read in the press about trial lawyers. Famous cases seem to make famous trial lawyers, and that is so even when the trial lawyer "loses." Williams, Nizer, Sears, Belli, and the rest have lost many cases; but, long after their defeats, all we tend to remember is that they were involved in them. Sometimes the losses are truly brilliant, as when Darrow lost the Scopes case, and when Williams lost in his epic defense of Senator Joseph McCarthy. In retrospect it can easily be seen that Darrow never had a chance with the kind of defense he put up in Tennessee. And although Williams was justifiably commended for his brilliance in defending McCarthy, the facts of the case and the uncontrollability of the client made the loss inevitable. And each grand master has days when he is terrible. There are cases in which he is ineffective, and there are times when almost any experienced trial lawyer could do better.

In the Ruby case, the curious thing about Belli is that in my view he has been excoriated unjustifiably by those who should know better and by those who should not. The defense he chose to assert on behalf of Jack Ruby was brilliant. His summation, as we shall see, was masterful. The trial record he made was not only adequate but it supported fully the contentions of his successor counsel in the Appellate Court in Texas—which *reversed* Jack Ruby's conviction, and which did so for the very reasons Belli was screaming about throughout the trial.

Belli's mistakes in the Jack Ruby case had nothing to do with his inability as a trial lawyer. They had more to do with his ego and keeping it bridled when the world spotlight was on him. In a carnival atmo-

MELVIN BELLI

sphere, Belli succumbed, and matched TV interview with TV interview, ill-advised statement with ill-advised statement, and antic with antic. The net result was that Belli contributed as much as anybody to creating and nourishing the very atmosphere which made it impossible for him to be heard by a Dallas jury in a Dallas courtroom.

But the facts remain that Belli's basic contentions, which he consistently made prior to trial and during it, were upheld on appeal, and are now obvious, even to Belli's worse detractors. From the very beginning Belli said that it was impossible for Ruby to get a fair trial in Dallas. He immediately made a motion for a change of venue, and a hearing was held in which the defense contention was overruled. The Court of Criminal Appeals in Texas found that the refusal to grant a change of venue was an error.

From the outset Belli took the position that Article 616 of the Code of Criminal Procedure of Texas precluded the seating, over the objection of counsel, of a juror who had witnessed Jack Ruby shooting Lee Harvey Oswald. Eleven of the twelve Ruby jurors admitted to having been television witnesses to the shooting. Article 616 provides as follows:

A challenge for cause is an objection made to a particular juror, alleging some fact which renders him incapable or unfit to serve on a jury. It may be made for any of the following reasons:

    6. *That he is a witness in the case.*

  112. That he has a bias or prejudice in favor of or against the defendant.

Belli, in a personal brief filed with the permission of the Texas Appellate Court, wrote:

While many Dallasites did see Jack Ruby apparently shoot Lee Harvey Oswald (and *discussed this*—as they testified on *voir dire*), they also heard the announcer giving his verdict before the trial. It was impossible for these eleven witness-jurors to have considered whether Jack Ruby was in an epileptic fugue state when they had already seen the apparent deliberate *manner* and *demeanor* and calculating method, from the edited film clips, in which he shot Lee Harvey Oswald. When the defense mental experts took the witness stand they were not describing *de novo* an event, *they were rebutting evidence* (i.e., *apparent deliberate manner*, etc.) in which Ruby shot Oswald for these juror-witnesses. . .

In the Ruby case it was *doubly* prejudicial (one, the event—two, the state of mind) to have had witness-jurors.

> Exigency and catastrophe cannot warp, expand, waive, or suspend constitutional safeguards and due process of law. One exception to some guarantees, perhaps, is a state of siege in which martial law is declared. But there was no state of siege or declaration of martial law in Dallas either before, during or after the Ruby trial. . . . The tragedy of the assassination of a beloved President did not warrant a suspension of Article 616, Code of Criminal Procedure of Texas.
> Is Article 616 valid, i.e., that a witness cannot be a juror, only when a *few* witness an event and an exception made when *many* witness it?

One of the judges on the Court of Criminal Appeals accepted Belli's view that all of the jurors who witnessed the shooting of Oswald should have been disqualified, and the other two, while disagreeing, agreed that the particular jury which heard the case was not in a position to be even minimally dispassionate within the meaning of the constitutions of Texas and the United States and many decisions interpreting those constitutions.

During the course of the trial, an alleged confession by Ruby—made somewhere between ten and forty minutes after Oswald's shooting, depending on the conflicting stories of Dallas policemen—was admitted into evidence. The "confession" was admitted, despite Article 727 of the Code of Criminal Procedure of Texas, which provides:

> *When confessions shall not be used:*
> A confession shall not be used if, at the time it was made, the defendant was in jail or other place of confinement, nor while he is in the custody of an officer, unless made in the voluntary statement of accused taken before an examining court in accordance with law, or be made in writing and signed by him, which writ-

ten statement shall show that he has been warned by the person to whom same is made:

First, that he does not have to make any statement at all, second that any statement made may be used in evidence against him on his trial for the offense concerning which the confession is therein made; or, unless in connection with such confession he makes statements of facts or circumstances that are found to be true, which conduce to establish guilt, such as the finding of secreted or stolen property, or the instrument with which he states the offense was committed. If the defendant is unable to write his name and signs the statement by making his mark, such statement shall not be admitted in evidence, unless it be witnessed by some person other than a police officer who shall sign his name as a witness.

And Article 727-A provided:

Evidence not to be used:
No evidence obtained by an officer or other person in violation of any provision of the Constitution or laws of the United States or of this State shall be admitted in evidence against the accused on the trial of any criminal case.

Concerning the alleged confession by Ruby, the Texas Appellate Court said: "Obviously this statement constituted an oral confession of premeditation made while in police custody and therefore was not admissible. The admission of this testimony was clearly injurious and calls for a reversal of this conviction."

It is certainly fair to say that the Court of Criminal Appeals of Texas fully vindicated Belli the lawyer. Judge W. T. McDonald, in a concurring opinion supporting the reversal of Ruby's conviction, said, as did Belli time and time again before and during the trial:

It is apparent . . . that President Kennedy's assassination occurred at a site on a Dallas Street so close to the Ruby trial courthouse that it could be seen daily by the jurors. . . . This location was being visited by the public who were placing wreaths at the historic spot out of respect to President Kennedy. Traffic was even then becoming jammed in the area by spectators.

Dallas was being blamed directly and indirectly for President Kennedy's assassination and for allowing the shooting of Oswald by Ruby. The feeling and thought had been generated that Dallas County's deprivation of prosecuting Oswald could find atonement in the prosecution of Ruby. . . . The citizenry of Dallas consciously and subconsciously felt Dallas was on trial and the Dallas image was uppermost in their minds to such an extent that Ruby could not be tried there fairly while the state, nation and world judged Dallas for the tragic November events.

The press had a field day with stories stating directly, indirectly, by hints and innuendoes that a Communist conspiracy existed between Oswald and Ruby. Ruby was referred to as a "tough guy," a "Chicago mobster," "a strip-joint owner." Anti-Semitism against Ruby was sparked by pretrial publicity that Ruby's name had been changed from Rubenstein to Ruby.

The strong local prejudice against Ruby was reflected in the refusal of the County-operated Parkland Hospital to permit Ruby to undergo neurological testing for the purpose of determining his organic brain condition for trial purposes.

The trial judge retained the services of a prominent public-relations counselor to handle the courtroom seating, the press, the trial publicity, and public relations in advance of the venue hearing and for the entire trial. Some three hundred members of the news media occupied most of the seats in the courtroom.

The fact of the shooting of Oswald had been seen on television many, many times on that fateful day, November 24, 1963, in the Dallas County area, by countless thousands of citizens. This alone precluded Ruby from receiving a fair and impartial trial by a Dallas County jury. A fair and impartial trial is the rightful boast of Western civilization.

Against such a background of unusual and extraordinary invasions of the expected neutral mental processes of a citizenry from which a jury is to be chosen, the Dallas County climate was one of such strong feeling that it was not humanly possible to give Ruby a fair and impartial trial which is the hallmark of American due process of law.

MELVIN BELLI

And then Judge McDonald cited a Supreme Court decision by Mr. Justice Felix Frankfurter* frequently relied upon by Ruby's defense counsel, including Belli:

". . . rudimentary conditions for determining guilt are inevitably wanting if the jury which is to sit in judgment on a fellow human being comes to its task with its mind ineradicably poisoned against him. How can fallible men and women reach a disinterested verdict based exclusively on what they heard in court when, before they entered the jury box, their minds were saturated by press and radio for months preceding by matter designed to establish the guilt of the accused? A conviction so secured obviously constitutes a denial of due process of law in its most rudimentary conception."

Surely, then, Belli's legal arguments were not only sound but virtually all of them were accepted by one or more of the judges of the Texas Appellate Court. He brought to Texas an eminent psychologist from Yale, Dr. Roy Schafer, and a highly regarded neurologist from the University of Texas, Dr. Martin L. Towler, who diagnosed Ruby as a "psychomotor epileptic." He also brought to Texas one of the world's most eminent electroencephalographers, Dr. Frederic A. Gibbs, and a world-renowned psychiatric expert, the late Dr. Manfred A. Guttmacher of Johns Hopkins University.

Over defense objections at 8:04 p.m. on Friday, March 13, 1964, Judge Joseph B. Brown, brushing aside the notion that it was unfair to everybody to begin to sum up a major American criminal case in the evening, began giving "instructions" to the jury. At 8:22 p.m. the jury began hearing summation from four lawyers representing the prosecution and from the three defense lawyers, Phil Burleson, Joe Tonahill, and Mel Belli (in Texas, everyone uses his nickname).

Belli's summation was hardly perfect. Perhaps his critics are right that it was too long in view of the hour at which he was forced to make it. He has been criticized for asking too much of the jury—an acquittal. And it is true that he rambled at times. But in the light of the facts that, close to midnight, he was addressing a hanging judge, and a

* *Irving* v. *Dowd,* 366 U.S. 717, 729, 730, 81 S. Ct. 1639, 1649, 6 L. Ed. 2d 751.

weary hanging jury in a hanging community, I think Belli's summation was superb. In part, this is what he told the jury:

May it please you my brother Tonahill, may it please Your Honor, may it please you officers of the state, may it please you ladies and gentlemen of the jury: my mother always told me that when I came to a strange place, if I was treated graciously, to thank my hosts.

And that I do here and now first; I have been treated graciously here from the high to the low, from the taxicab driver to the waitress, from the millionaire to the pauper, the rabbi and the reverend; all individually have treated me graciously.

But my mother also told me not to be a hypocrite in what I said. You know all too well what I have said to you, that I thought it was impossible for any one of you to sit on this jury, because of the events that happened in your own city and because of the unconscious pride that you have in your city.

But let us now see in these beginning small hours of this morning, early-morning hours when great discoveries in the history of the world have been made in garrets and attics and basements and even caves, if here, in your own temple of justice in Dallas, we can't rediscover something that has never really been lost in your great city of Dallas; that we may rediscover justice!

And let me say at the very beginning that I do not speak for Judge Lynch or lynch law. I couldn't because my life has been dedicated to the true law. Except for when the great Howard Naffziger urged me to leave the law and go into his specialty of neurosurgery, other than for those few months, I think I have dedicated my whole life to my discipline, the law.

So this is what I now tell you of my law in these small hours of this morning that we are creeping into about this case:

You've heard everyone from the "Weird Beard" to the great Dr. Gibbs. How shall you know whom to believe? Whom shall you cast aside, and in whom shall you find the truth? Some of you, individually, on *voir dire*, expressed that concern. How shall we know in whom to believe in this great assembly of scientific men?

Well, here is one infallible test that I give to you at the start: If there were someone near and dear to you, a mother who was

MELVIN BELLI

sick, if a little one at home in the crib was convulsing, and you called your doctor in, you'd called someone in and talked to him and asked him, "Who shall we send our child to? Who may we call that we may honestly know before operating on his brain?" I think then you will get your answer. Would you be satisfied with an ultimate opinion on life and death of your loved one, from the man to whom doctors all around the world send their electroencephalograms, the man, the year before I was graduated from law school—and I graduated from Boalt Hall at the University of California in 1933—the year before I got out of law school, was just inventing the electroencephalogram which gives us our diagnosis of brain damage?

Would you settle for less than he for someone near and dear to you if he were fortunately available to you in your misfortune?

When they look back at us forty, eighty years from now, when they look back at us and see how we sat here and tried to look into the brain of Jack Ruby, this sick man here, how will they shake their heads in pity at our clumsy medical contrivances. But we do the very best we can for you.

I can't find it in my heart that you want the blood of this sick man on your hands, or even that you want one year of his life. You can't give him a "suspended sentence." He's already been in jail four months. You know what one minute, one hour, one day, one week, two weeks, three weeks can be in partial confinement, as you have been locked up during your jury duty.

When the historians look back at us and see what we were trying to fathom about the recesses of this man's brain; when they see that we've only gone to the cortex, the outer surface of it, trying to determine whether this man was sick, whether he was well, whether he did an act that was responsible or was irresponsible; they may laugh at us from their vantage point of history in retrospect, as we laughed at those who, not so many years ago, tried to transfuse sheep blood into humans. And that wasn't so very long ago. These yesterday doctors knew nothing of the Rh factor which today would be malpractice to ignore. They didn't even know the classifications of blood at the beginning of this century—A, B, O, and so on.

What I tell you here is that you can now discover justice this wakening morning in Dallas, the justice of science and the law;

the science of a great doctor whom we brought to your city and to whom are sent all their electroencephalograms from all over the world for him, alone, to read and decipher.

If you believe this great man, Dr. Frederic Gibbs, the man to whom I would say, "Send your child, your patient," then this man has given you your answer for Jack Ruby: Jack Ruby has rage states.

Then also you must believe this great man from Yale University, Dr. Roy Schafer, if you will follow the test that I laid down for you, whom you would want to examine your child, in, God forbid, your misfortune, and then you must add to these great scientists the name of that other savant who came here from distant Maryland, Dr. Manfred Guttmacher, the psychiatrist from the Supreme Bench of Maryland.

Do you know what we did in this lawsuit in your State of Texas? Probably for the first time, and against the advice and criticism of my brothers of the bar, I placed Jack Ruby in the electroencephalographic laboratory for any work the state or court wanted so that we could all see. Every test the district attorney wanted of this defendant was available to them and the court's appointed psychiatrist. I was sure what we would find. And we found it unequivocally—psychomotor-variant epilepsy.

Dr. Roy Schafer first came to Dallas at my request and tested Jack Ruby for hours on end. Then he took his test, and after a hundred hours' work put all the facts together and came up with his conclusions. You remember Roy Schafer on the witness stand, and in my home state of California we instruct our jurors that one way to determine truth is to remember the appearance of the witness on the witness stand, how he answered up, whether he rang true to you, whether he appeared to be an honest witness. You remember now, and when you go to deliberate in your mind's eye, that tall, great psychologist from Yale University, Roy Schafer, and in his testimony you will find the truth because he prognosed what the laboratory would find, a feat I cannot recall in the annals of criminal investigation and trial:

So when Roy Schafer came to Dallas and again I say I got the very best psychologist I could in the world, and he is Roy Schafer, and Dr. Schafer examined Jack Ruby with his Rorschach and his other tests, and he is doing specialized work at Yale University with the Rorschach tests and epilepsy and electroencephalograms, Dr. Schafer said to me, "The man doesn't have schizophrenia, he is not paranoid; he has organic brain damage: I'm so sure of it that if you will get an electroencephalographic test, his organic brain damage will show up on the electroencephalographic test!"

Now remember that Dr. Schafer told me this and you have his report, and the date of his report, where he told me this, long before this trial and long before the electroencephalographic examination. He said, "Jack Ruby has organic brain damage." He also told us that Jack Ruby will be given to rage states and despondency; and Jack Ruby will attempt suicide, and that will be our big problem in caring for him in the future. Dr. Walter Bromberg told you the same thing, organic brain damage, and this is the organic brain damage that manifests itself functionally or clinically in the psychomotor-variant type of epilepsy which accounts for the "blackouts" or the "rage states."

We have our diagnosis from our doctors; we have our prognosis. We know why Jack Ruby shot Lee Harvey Oswald, and we know he wasn't responsible at the time. So in all honesty and sincerity and fairness, probably for the first time in Texan legal history, we go to the judge and the district attorney and tell them to get any doctor they want in the world, and we send our defendant over to their laboratory for them to examine him. There was no way that these examinations could have been done or obtained by the state or the district attorney under Texas law, unless we suggested them and agreed to them. We knew we had a sick man, and it was proved. We've brought before you now a man who is sick. And even Dr. Holbrook, who I told you is referred to as the "jailhouse psychiatrist," went over to participate in the examinations and even he had to tell you that Jack Ruby had an "unstable personality."

Then Jack Ruby was put under the electroencephalographic machine to have his brain-wave tracings made. Dr. Martin Towler, your own Texan who teaches at your own University of Texas down at Galveston, read those tracings and said, "This is what we have. We have a psychomotor-variant type of epilepsy, given to rage stages." He corroborated precisely and conclusively what Dr. Roy Schafer and Dr. Manfred Guttmacher said would be found if this man was sent to the laboratory!

Belli went on to discuss at great length the meaning of the psychiatric testimony that the jurors had heard. He then told the jury that it was obvious from the testimony that Ruby was not a "normal person" with a "normal breaking point." He said his client was a psychotic, and portrayed him as the "character," the "village idiot":

Ah, what great sport to have in our community "the character." In the old days we used to call him the "village clown," "the village idiot." There's a chained wolf to be tormented, there's the hunchback of Notre Dame, there's our own Emperor Norton in San Francisco, the old humpty-dumpty who, for fifty cents, would bend over and allow people to hit him on his backside with a board. Ah, what great sport for this . . . troubled human being we're trying, until something goes wrong. There's trouble. Then the cry goes out, "Who do you suspect the most; who would do an unusual thing like that?"

The answer: "The village idiot." You substitute the village clown, the village idiot—Jack Ruby! The man who is always around the police station bringing the coffee, the man who brings the doughnuts, the sandwiches, who can be sent out . . . for the cold beer. . . .

Publicity he wants? Publicity he seeks? Ah, ladies and gentlemen of the jury, I suppose before that handful of dust that is each of us settles down on the plain to be scratched by the dancing tumbleweed, that we'd all like to engrave our initials in some big oak tree, that we'd like maybe to be in [gossip] columns. There are some of us even who want to have our faces immortalized on Mount Rushmore. There are some others of us who want to write as well as the immortal Shakespeare, or be able to compose Gray's "Elegy in a Country Churchyard." There are others of us who seek more humble forms of immortality. There's this lonely craving that we all have. . . .

Jack Ruby: this poor sick fellow—and sick he is. And you know he's sick, every one of you in your heart, every one of the twelve of you know he is sick. . . . There cannot be any doubt that there is something wrong with Jack Ruby. Every one of the state's doctors told you that the electroencephalogram was unusual. And even the man whom they rely on the strongest, Dr. Holbrook, tells you that Jack Ruby was "unstable, brittle." God forgive us, for we know not what we do, when we fracture this brittle personality of our village idiot, our village clown whom we tolerate—until something goes wrong, and then we search for something to pin our blame on him!

Who of all the people in this troubled city of yours on that tragic weekend was a candidate to do what Jack Ruby did? He did this for money, for glory, for heroism, for a messianic purpose? In one breath the district attorney says, in many breaths they say, "Lee Harvey Oswald was manacled." Sure he was manacled, you saw the picture; there is no question that he was manacled. But then, in the next breath, they say that Jack Ruby shot him to "show what guts a Jew had." Why, the very manner in which it was done, before the television cameras, with a manacled man, doesn't that—of itself—show the bizarre nature of the conduct of the act? And as I ask this of you, there comes popping into my head so, so much of the testimony. Don't you remember the little girl whom the state asked, "What did you see when he was there?" And her answer, "He was staring, staring, staring off into space!"

Finally and dramatically, after a long analysis of the testimony the jury had heard, he ended his summation to the jury:

You can't arrogate unto yourselves, you good jurors of this town, the right to put a sick man in jail for six months, or to put a stigma on him by a suspended sentence. He is sick. Give a just and fair verdict compatible with modern science. That's what the world wants to see in justice from this community. Not that we have to wash any sins away and say, "Well, we've got to give him one year, five years or a suspended sentence, so the rest of the world will know that we're a law-abiding community." Anatole France wrote in *Penguin Island* that when the people got up on the shore and saw the gallows, the gibbet, with the bodies hanging from it, they fell down on their knees and thanked God for having cast them upon a civilized shore.

You're an intelligent jury, and I don't want to butter you up. That's always my problem: that I'm a little too direct. I don't butter any of you up. I tell you, use your God-given intelligence in this case.

They'll look back on this verdict in forty, fifty, maybe even eighty years from now. They may laugh at us at what we are trying to do with these poor tools that we have at our command, but don't stigmatize a sick man—the village idiot, the character, the village clown, or whatever you will—by any jail sentence or any suspended sentence. . . .

And as I started, thank you. Thank all of you for your attention.

Two hours and nineteen minutes from the time the jury commenced deliberation they reached a verdict of guilty. Before Jack Ruby could ever be brought to trial again he died of cancer.

MELVIN BELLI

ET AL.

An anthology of great arguments and speeches, collected in 1881, was published in 1918 under the title *Great Speeches by Great Lawyers*. It paid tribute "to the memory of the eloquence of Ogden Hoffman and David Graham" and to the "forensic utterances of Dexter and Otis, of John Adams, Joseph Hopkinson, Jared Ingersoll, Seargent S. Prentiss, Robert Goodloe Harper, Luther Martin, Edward D. Baker. . . ."

These past grand masters of the English and American courts are now forgotten and unknown to the public and to the vast majority of the trial bar. In reading some of the great speeches and arguments of the past two hundred years, it becomes obvious that history has not neglected these heroic verbal gunfighters of the past. Today, their style, brilliant in its time, seems stilted, cumbersome, and very often dull. "The old order changeth, yielding place to new," said Tennyson, and so it is with trial lawyers.

Each generation thinks its actors, actresses, trial lawyers, or musicians are the best. And there has never been a generation in which some law professor or trial lawyer or judge has not said that the trial bar is going to pot; that there is a dearth of quality trial lawyers; that there will never be another Williams or Sears, Nizer or Belli. But there will be, and there are.

Each grand master has pointed out that there is always some ambitious talented youngster looking to make his reputation by doing battle with giants, and, as in any profession, there are those who make it. Nizer pointed out that there is far more room at the top of any profession that there is in the middle. With the proper blend of courage, passion, talent, zeal, and experience, a great trial lawyer is somehow made, and they will continue to be made, no matter how the system operates.

In labeling some members of the trial bar as grand masters, we are only scratching the surface. There are so many more: in New York—Simon F. Rifkin, Frank G. Raichle, William G. Mulligan; in Florida—Perry Nichols and Marion Sibley; in Montana—Moses Timer; in Boston—James St. Clair and James Hennessy; in Texas—Leon Jaworski and Percy Foreman; in Phoenix—Henderson Stockton; in Los Angeles—Arthur Groman and Warren Christopher. In any so-called list, there would be glaring omissions. Indeed, the designation of many of the men already mentioned will stir controversy within the trial bar and among trial buffs, among whom passions seldom lie dormant. I can hear it now: "Julien's just a negligence lawyer; he's not nearly as good as Harry Gair or Jim Fuchsberg." "What do you mean, 'Belli is a grand master'? He blew the Ruby case, didn't he?" "What about Joe Doakes from Idaho?"

Well, I don't know Joe Doakes from Idaho, and I don't think there has ever been a grand master who has not botched up a trial. Harry Gair is as good as Julien, and on the right day and in the right case either one of them might even surpass Williams or Sears.

The analogy between the trial lawyer and the gunfighter may be picturesque, but as Judge Herbert Stern, a fine trial lawyer and an avid student of trial advocacy, points out, the analogy is far from perfect. The favored gunfighter had to stay alive to uphold his reputation. The great trial lawyers do not. They win and they lose.

However you feel about your favorite, perhaps you will enjoy a few more stories about some of mine.

In appearance, demeanor, and style, Louis Nizer resembles the distinguished trial lawyers of the past more so than many of the others mentioned in this book. Like Lloyd Paul Stryker or Max Steuer or Barnabas Sears, Nizer conveys the impression of seriousness and studiousness. There is none of the Willy Fallon, the Jake Ehrlich, the Foreman, or the Belli in *Mr.* Nizer. Indeed, the gunfighter image applied to him seems ludicrous, and he rejects the analogy.

Nizer believes that his status as a grand master has been achieved through work, preparation, more work, and more preparation. Some trial lawyers may be suggestive of the trickster or magician, but this one may be better characterized as an elegant producer or maestro.

I first met Nizer about fifteen years ago, when I was a young, very junior associate helping another lawyer engaged in an extremely important antitrust case brought against several large corporations, including United Artists, who were all charged with "block booking" of television programs. Each of the joint corporate defendants was accused by the government of forcing television stations to accept inferior motion pictures in order to get better ones for use on television. Nizer was the chief counsel for the defense, and I marveled then as I marvel now at the enormous amount of work he puts into the preparation of a case. The actual trial lasted well over a month, and, needless to say, the preparation for trial took longer than that. I doubt that anyone would disagree that among all the attorneys involved in this case, including associates and junior associates, the one who worked the hardest was Louis Nizer.

At one point before the trial began, Nizer appeared before the U.S. District Judge Archibald Dawsen, a brilliant but irascible disciplinarian. Nizer complained that the government had not produced all the documents that it had been directed to and he requested an adjournment. A young U.S. attorney told Judge Dawsen that he could not consent to an adjournment unless he first called Washington. The judge slammed his hand down on his massive desk in chambers and bellowed: "God damn it, Washington is dead! In this court I give orders." And he granted the adjournment.

During the course of the ensuing trial, the less experienced U.S. attorney made several procedural blunders, and one day irked the judge so much that he was the victim of one of the most intemperate judicial blasts I had ever heard. There was not a lawyer or a spectator in the courtroom who did not feel enormous sympathy for the young government advocate, who may have erred but who surely did not deserve the berating he took.

After a short recess and despite the risk, Nizer rose before Judge Dawsen and said he spoke only for himself and not for his client or the other lawyers. He told the judge that in his view his opposing counsel in no way merited the rebuke that the court had dealt him; that he could not idly sit by without observing how strenuous the case before the court was, how complex the issues, and how courteous and able he himself had found the government attorney to be. In one of the most polished and spontaneous speeches I ever heard, Nizer so influenced the judge that he immediately apologized to the young government attorney and made the day more pleasant for everybody.

In that trial, one of the most damaging witnesses for the government was the vice president of a large television station who seemed to testify against each of the defendants with such enthusiasm and in such infinite detail that all the defense attorneys wondered what on earth they could come up with to diminish his credibility. Typical of the Nizer thoroughness, his office had uncovered the unlikely fact that this particular witness had a hobby of flagpole-sitting. Nizer conducted the cross-examination for most of the defendants and his examination was short and brilliant. He brought out that the witness knew that if the government were to win the case, his television station might institute a suit for damages against these same defendants and might reap a windfall. He then questioned the witness about his hobby. "My hobby?" answered the witness. "Sir, don't toy with us. You know what a hobby is, don't you? Tell His Honor what you do for fun."

When the witness explained that he loved flagpole-sitting, Nizer snapped, "You simply like sitting way up there as high up as you can get, looking down at all the little people?" And before government counsel's objection could be sustained, Nizer sneered at the witness and said, "You disgust me!" thus dismissing him as though he were the largest wart on the rump of society that Nizer had ever seen.

Bruno Schachner is a crusty old trial warhorse. I once explained to him what great difficulty I was having in cross-examining a crucial witness and asked for his advice. When he heard the facts of my case, he said, "My dear fellow, cross-examination isn't what it used to be in the good old days when we had torture."

In a prolonged proceeding involving the custody of a twelve-year-old boy, Schachner found himself opposed by David Bress, a leading member of the Washington, D.C., trial bar. During the course of Schachner's scorching cross-examination of the mother (which had gone on for days), the concerned grandmother, seeing her daughter being cut to ribbons, fainted in the courtroom with the loudest thud imaginable. With his black robes flowing, the judge, the court clerks, and most of the spectators rushed to the aid of the stricken woman. I, as an associate counsel, looked first to make sure that the woman was not too seriously injured, and then I went in search of Schachner. Neither he nor Bress was in the courtroom. I went out into the corridor and there was Schachner with a smile on his face, and there was Bress proudly lighting Schachner's cigarette. The Washington lawyer was telling Schachner that he himself had never gotten a spectator to faint. Then he told him how on one occasion his tactics were so exciting that a juror fainted. Each man was so lost in respect for the other that the plight of the poor woman inside could not have mattered less.

During the same trial, Schachner was pointing out to the hapless mother that on numerous occasions she had taken the child from New York to Washington, although a separation agreement between the parties stipulated that she was not to remove the child from New York beyond a radius of two hundred miles. The cross-examination went something like this:

S.: You are aware, madam, that the agreement between you and your former husband provided that you were not to remove your son beyond two hundred miles outside of New York City?
M.: Yes.
S.: And you now live in Washington, D.C.?
M.: Yes.
S.: Are you not aware that Washington is more than two hundred miles from New York?
M.: Not as the crow flies, I don't think.
S.: And when you take this boy to Washington from New York, madam, do you often take a crow?

One of the most flamboyant, successful, and notorious lawyers of the trial bar is Percy Foreman. No book about American grand masters would be complete without a Foreman story. While there might be some doubt as to how effective he would be trying a securities case against Williams in Washington or Nizer in New York, there is considerably less doubt about the outcome of almost any jury case against Foreman in Texas, regardless of whom the opponent was.

My favorite Foreman story happened in his early years, when he served as defense attorney for hundreds of bearded Jewish peddlers who found themselves being prosecuted by the local police in Houston, Texas. It appeared that without licenses they had been peddling groceries at cut prices. The story, as reported by Michael Dorman, goes as follows:

The established stores found business dwindling and vowed to get even. At their insistence, the police launched a massive crackdown on members of the pushcart brigade for peddling without the necessary licenses. The peddlers were hauled away to jail by the dozen.

"They finally came to see me and offered me a hundred dollars a week to represent them," Foreman recalls. "I accepted. And that may have been when I learned it could be better to fix a high fee and lose a client than to fix a low fee. Some weeks I would get thirty to fifty of these peddlers out of jail. But I finally put a stop to the mass arrests.

"I let two hundred or three hundred cases accumulate, then agreed to try them all on the same day. The crime was peddling vegetables without a license. Like any criminal case, the complaining witness had to identify the person accused of the crime. So I brought in about sixty or seventy of my clients and they sat down—all looking very much alike, with their long beards. As soon as the first officer took the stand, I asked him if he could identify the accused. He took one look at all of them, with their beards, and gave up. Ralph Fowler (now a United States commissioner in Houston) was the judge handling the cases. He turned all of my clients loose except one."

The one unlucky peddler was a man who was all too cooperative with the minions of the law. Foreman asked the arresting officer in his case: "Can you identify Muscowitz?" At this point the client stood up and announced: "Muscowitz, dot's me!" The officer promptly identified him as the defendant, and Muscowitz was convicted.

"I must have had nine hundred cases for those peddlers and that's the only one I lost," Foreman says.*

* *King of the Courtroom: Percy Foreman for the Defense* (New York: Delacorte Press, 1969), pp. 50–51.

ET AL.

Marion Sibley is one of the established leaders of the trial bar in Florida. Many years ago I asked him to represent one of my New York clients who was being sued by his wife for a Florida divorce. It seemed that during the course of a stormy marriage, my client's wealthy father-in-law had used the joint account of my client and his wife as a conduit for tens of thousands of dollars, which would be deposited on one day or during one week and then withdrawn and made payable to various payees of the father-in-law. All in all, over $100,000 had been put into the joint account. My client reasoned that since his wife was deserting him, he should get some money out of the transaction.

When I spoke to Mr. Sibley about the case, he told me he would take it—as an accommodation to me and because he had known my family for some time—but only on the condition that he could be forthright with the judge. And indeed, when asked what the case was about, Sibley did forthrightly tell the court: "Your Honor, I represent a blackmailer, but we are being sued by a thief, and I think everybody ought to get a little something."

In actuality, Sibley speaks with about as much of a Southern accent as does Peter Lawford; but when he is on trial, especially in front of a jury, his Southern drawl carries one back to the cotton mills of Old Virginia. Once during a trial, Sibley's opponent shouted "I object!" Sibley shouted back, "You are overruled"—and then looking impishly at the judge, he said, "Isn't he, Your Honor?" The judge smiled and agreed.

Bert Fields is a senior partner and chief litigator in a Beverly Hills, California, law firm. Curiously, he is one of the few very successful trial lawyers who does equally well behind a desk representing commercial clients—a diversity of them, such as Cardinal Spellman, Japanese Motion Picture Studios, Jack Webb, Elaine May, Peter Falk, James Caan, and Mario Puzo.

During the trial of a matrimonial case, Fields represented a husband whose wife claimed that her and her husband's community-property business was worth $10 million, in which case (according to California law) she would be awarded $5 million. The husband had calculated that the business was worth somewhere between $700,000 and $800,000 and produced testimony supporting that range of value.

Much to the surprise of Fields and his client, the wife produced a distinguished professor of economics with impressive credentials. He testified at great length, supported by an elaborate report, that in his opinion the business was worth between $7 million and $10 million. After the to-be-expected cross-examination of this expert by such a seasoned trial lawyer, Fields took a different tack:

F.: Professor, you've told the court this business was worth seven to ten million dollars. Will you buy it for just *one* million?

(This led to strenuous objection from the other side. After argument, the line of questioning was permitted.)

F.: Professor, I'm authorized by my client to offer you this business today in open court for one million dollars cash, the same business you said was worth seven to ten million. Do you accept?

P.: I'm a college professor. Most of us don't have that kind of money.

F.: That's no problem, Professor. I'm authorized to give you time to raise the money. Will you buy it for one million?

P.: Well, I'd have to know much more about it.

F.: Professor, you said this business was worth seven to ten million. You now have a firm offer to buy it for one million and you can have time to raise the money. Do you accept that offer or not?

P.: Well, I am not in the business of running corporations. I don't know if I could find a buyer. . . .

F.: That's all I have for this witness, Your Honor.

That's all he needed. The court found that the value of the business was $700,000.

On another occasion, Fields represented a businessman who had been arrested by two policemen and charged with indecent exposure in a Los Angeles pornographic movie house. One of the policemen testified that in the men's room of the theater the defendant not only propositioned him but also proceeded to stroke the policeman's penis for about forty-five seconds.

Fields's cross-examination was a masterpiece of self-control. He did bring out that the arresting officer was a recent addition to the vice squad and that he wanted to remain on the squad. It was only during summation that Fields reduced the policeman's story to nonsense. Producing a large clock with a second hand, Fields passionately told the jury that his client was a husband and a father with no criminal record, and that his reputation might be sullied by a conviction on the testimony of an overzealous policeman. When he addressed himself to the policeman's forty-five-seeconds penis-stroking story, Fields started stroking the jury rail . . . while he talked and kept talking about the basic inherent improbability that a police officer, supposedly trained in making accurate observations, would wait a full forty-five seconds before making an arrest of somebody soliciting him in a men's room.

"Can you imagine only fifteen seconds have gone by?" said Fields, still stroking the jury rail. "And the policeman still has not made his arrest. . . . And now only twenty seconds . . ." and so on, for forty-five interminable seconds.

Fields's client was acquitted.

Just as the golf and tennis professionals sit around exchanging ideas on how to improve their tactics or strokes, trial lawyers do the same. They lend each other mind-bending phrases they use before juries. They tell each other what works or does not work in front of a particular judge. They tell each other what kind of arguments appeal to different juries. For example, at a seminar held by the New York State Association of Trial Lawyers, dealing with the "Art of Summation," the great Moe Levine discussed the subject of drama and emotion in jury summations with Jacob D. Fuchsberg (now Justice of the Court of Appeals, New York's highest court), James Dempsey, and Herman B. Glaser. The lawyers were discussing how to sum up to a jury on behalf of a man who had lost both his arms in an accident case. Levine told the other lawyers that in such a case, rather than belabor the obvious suffering of his client, "The only thing I said was that it would be an insult for me to tell them [the jury] what it could mean to have both arms off; all they had to do was close their eyes and think of all the things during the day requiring at least one arm. Then I said, 'You know, I had lunch with him. He eats like a dog.' Then I continued and concluded my summation. Believe me, no more was required."

Later during the seminar, the discussion turned to how to ask a jury for money for the death of a parent. On this subject Dempsey said, "I find that now instead of quoting Shakespeare and the Bible many lawyers in summation quote Chinese and if I have heard it once I have heard it a thousand times that 'One picture is worth a thousand words,' and other Chinese proverbs.

"As I listened to Jack Fuchsberg try to tell you how you could highlight the death of a parent, I thought of a Chinese story that they tell about this man who was very much in love with some woman. She was extremely envious of the love that the man had for his mother. Finally she said the price of her hand was to have the son bring to her the mother's heart. Overwhelmed with love, he went and killed his mother, and he carved out her heart. As he was running headlong back to the girl of his choice, with his mother's heart in his hand, he tripped and fell. The heart rolled out and spoke up and said, 'Did you hurt yourself, my son?' "

Ken Knigin, a New York trial lawyer, tried a long and somewhat boring commercial case before a jury. His client had entered into a contract with a man who had claimed during his testimony that he had read only part of the contract but not all of it before he signed it. In summation to the jury, Knigin remarked that this was the first contract he had ever read as a veteran lawyer which came with its own set of stop lights. "Imagine," he told the jury, "the stop light was set for green when Mr. Jones read the parts of the agreement that were favorable to him and then . . . conveniently, very conveniently . . . the stop light turned red before it got to the part which favored my client."

From Abraham Lincoln to Daniel Webster to Rufus Choate to Darrow to Steuer to Williams and all the rest—fascinating stories of what the great trial men have done and can do pass from generation to generation. So long as the drive for excellence continues among the trial bar, grand masters will continue to appear and be recognized.

Melvin Block, a distinguished New York trial lawyer, put it this way: "It is a sad but nevertheless verifiable commentary that some attorneys, after having divested themselves of the fact that a certain motor vehicle traveling at a given rate of speed will come to a halt in such and such distance, have then exhausted what approximates the sum total of their human knowledge. It is ironical that these very same lawyers yearn for immortality, yet do not know what to do on a rainy Sunday afternoon. To be more than a mere 'claims broker,' the true advocate must attempt to keep the cosmos in his head. It has been said that a lawyer without history or literature is a mechanic, a mere working mason; if he possesses some knowledge of these, he may venture to call himself an architect. His sphere must be from Genesis to genetics."

THE SEARCH FOR
TRUTH

Justice Jerome Frank said that "our contentious trial method has its roots in the origin of court trials as substitutes for private brawls." Professor Edmund Morgan of Harvard said (in favorably reviewing a book on trial work): "If only a reviewer could assert that this book is a guide not to the palaces of justice but to the red-light districts of the law." And many critics of the American judicial system agree with Damon Runyon's assessment of trials as little more than sporting events with the outcome largely dependent upon the lawyers' skills and far less affected by the facts of the particular cases.

The assemblage, presentation, and resolution of factual disputes is far more complicated than most people imagine. Countless studies have pointed out how frail our memories are—as honestly exercised by most of us. Ten people witnessing a single event, for even a short period, will give vastly disparate views of the details of that event. And what happens when the fact-finding takes place long after the event? Such fact-finding is often based on the testimony of witnesses who are either interested in the outcome of the case or in how well "informed" they appear; and their testimony is given in an unfamiliar, bewildering, and seemingly hostile atmosphere in which at least one lawyer's job is to discredit them. How much further and further away from the truth do we get then?

If the process by which facts are resolved in an adversary system of justice seems grossly unfair, it's because it is unfair. I doubt whether that process is greatly enhanced by the skill of our great trial lawyers. A careful distinction must be made between the enormous art of advocacy and its effect on the theoretical goal of trials—the search for truth. This pursuit of truth is only part of the law's ultimate goal, which is justice. Justice depends on, and is a function of, the wisdom and richness of our body of substantive law. But the most effective application of the law depends on how well we use it to find out the truth about the controversy, whether civil or criminal. That is the purpose of trials.

In this search for truth, the skill of the advocate takes on such overriding importance that we must ponder whether more evil than good is done. Today, more than ever before, many teachers, trial lawyers, and judges, such as the Chief Justice of the United States, are once again calling for the enhancement of the trial bar. They are claiming that we should adopt the English system of solicitor and barrister, with the right to practice in our courts given only to those of proven skill. The notion that a young lawyer, recently admitted to practice and with no experience, should be permitted—theoretically, at least—to try a murder case or an antitrust case seems patently unfair.

But, do we need more and more skillful "mind-persuaders" or "testimony-cosmeticians"? Or do we need an overhaul of a system too dependent on what lawyers feed into it and too little dependent on what should go into it?

The Chief Justice and other observers of our trial bar are quite correct. Under our system the trained and talented advocate grinds out just the right kind of gruel to make our system *appear* to work magnificently. *Williams* v. *Nizer, Sears* v. *Belli*—how superb! The line-up is perfect. The facts will be presented skillfully, the issues will be clearly defined and passionately espoused, and the trial will doubtless be a masterpiece. But will the truth emerge any better?—better than if *all* the facts were investigated and less artfully presented to the same jury by mouths other than hired ones whose duty and livelihood depend on partisanship?

It would be puerile to suggest that our system be turned over to amateurs whose lack of skill would then be considered an asset. It is apparent that the system itself, rather than the trial lawyers who work within it, needs to be vastly overhauled if the search for the truth is to be less haphazard.

The fact that a genius such as Williams or Nizer believes passionately in his cause is relatively meaningless. Passionate belief in an unjust

THE SEARCH FOR TRUTH

cause is no more socially advantageous than the nonpartisan or dispassionate presentation of a doubtful cause or even a just one. Manifest injustices are certain to abound in a system that permits a grand master to align himself with one litigant while the other is represented by the average trial lawyer—and while twelve sincere amateurs are struggling with the business of fact-finding.

Nor is it any more just to have a system in which the government with all its investigatory resources should be permitted to use them in a too often one-sided contest with its opponents—especially when its opponents are indigent with no counsel or with court-appointed counsel with no funds to prepare a defense properly. Studies have shown that court-appointed counsel suggest and urge guilty pleas far more frequently than do privately retailed counsel. The problem, in part, was stated by Professor Leonard W. Levy in criticizing the opinion of Mr. Justice Byron R. White in *McMann* v. *Richardson:*

One of the worst features of the court's decision in the plea-bargaining cases was its unrealistic assumption that indigent defendants receive effective representation from court-assigned counsel. In White's romanticized Perrymasonland, there dwell many an F. Lee Bailey and Edward Bennett Williams. No doubt there are court-assigned counsel who are zealous and conscientious in the discharge of their duties, but many are inexperienced in the field of criminal law and lack the time, money, will, and investigative facilities to prepare a case effectively. Representing an indigent defendant for some modest, fixed fee entails financial sacrifice; counsel would rather get on with his regular practice and make a living. The pressures are on him to plead his client guilty, and the system is structured to expect that of him and to expect his cooperation. There are assigned counsel who are regulars within the system, friends of the trial judge and of the prosecutor's office; they tend to be Stakhanovites who work as if on a piece-rate basis. If they can persuade the defendant to plead guilty, they save themselves the labor of investigating and trying the case; the guilty plea permits counsel to collect his fee and turn expeditiously to the next case. Court-assigned counsel tend to be mediators between the system and their clients rather than champions and representatives. They operate on a presumption of guilt and mute the adversary features of criminal justice. They play Russian roulette with other men's lives.

Court-assigned counsel too often develop a stony indifference toward their clients, akin to the attitude of a physician toward a patient with a terminal or incurable disease. The one observes, "You have cancer, go to the hospital"; the other, "You are guilty, go to jail." In *McMann,* one attorney allegedly conferred with his client "only ten minutes prior to the day the plea of guilty was taken." In that brief time the defendant told his story, how he had been beaten into a confession and did not want to plead guilty to a crime he did not commit; and in that same brief time counsel made an on-the-spot decision to waive all his client's constitutional rights and cop a plea to a lesser charge. Counsel for another defendant in the same case ignored his alibi defense and supposedly misrepresented the charge. Query: How much skill, time, and care must counsel devote to an assigned case in order to fall within Justice White's range of acceptable competence? The Court in *McMann* found no violation of the right to effective counsel.

Counsel's performance in *McMann* was apparently par for the course. Various studies tell us that defense counsel, especially court-assigned counsel, rather than the police or prosecution, are the ones who by far the most frequently suggest to the accused that he plead guilty. One investigator found that the suggestion to plead guilty came from defense counsel five times more often than from police and prosecution combined. Moreover, privately retained counsel suggested the guilty plea on first contact in almost 35 per cent of the cases, while assigned counsel did so in almost 60 per cent of the cases. Another study showed that retained counsel did so on first contact in only 25 per cent of the cases, compared to 71 per cent for assigned counsel.*

Isn't there a better system than this? I have asked each of the trial lawyers interviewed for this book and have spoken to dozens of others about this enormous inequity in which the odds are so heavily rigged in favor of one litigant. They simply shrug their shoulders, and invariably point out that the law, like life, has its imperfections. Why shouldn't everybody have the right to the best surgeon, the best law-

* *Against the Law* (New York: Harper & Row, 1974), pp. 108–09.

THE SEARCH FOR TRUTH

yer, the best accountant, the best whatever? Because, they say, there are not enough to go around. They point out that juries are becoming more sophisticated, that judges are being appointed or elected on the basis of merit, and that more judges are intervening in the trial process to protect litigants—litigants who are either underrepresented or are well represented but facing staggering mounds of evidence collected by financially uninhibited governmental agencies.

Much reliance has to be put upon juries, and it is almost inspirational to see how well and effectively they work in attempting to resolve factual disputes. In England (at least in the higher courts), the quality of judges and their method of selection are so superior that the right to a trial by jury in civil cases has been sharply reduced. And where that right exists in criminal and in civil cases, it is very often waived because the parties and their attorneys are willing to rely on the integrity and expertise of trial judges to resolve factual disputes.

If one were to be able to assume a highly trained, effective, and impartial judiciary, as well as an equally highly skilled trial bar, the adversary system would obviously work a great deal better.

Until that time, fortune will continue to smile on those who can afford the grand masters and on those with sufficient financial resources to protect themselves against the government's unlimited funding of the investigation and presentation of its cases.

INDEX

A

Adams, John, 221
Advocacy, art of, 4
Against the Law (Levy), 236–37
American Bar Association, 107, 109, 200
American Civil Liberties Union, 123, 128, 135
American College of Trial Lawyers, 107
American Colonies, 5
Armed Services Committee (House of Representatives), 34, 51, 53
"Art of Summation" (New York State Association of Trial Lawyers), 229

B

Bailey, F. Lee, ix, 5, 197, 235
Baker, Edward D., 221
Barrister and solicitor, British system of, 5, 234
Barry, Treamor, Shandell, & Brophy, 160–61
Belli, Marvin, 11, 13, 14, 139, 141, 197, 199–220, 221, 222

background of, 202–203
reputation of, 199–200
Ruby case, 199, 201, 205, 206–20
Belli, Ashe & Choulos, 199
Belli, Shairshon, Carner, Thierman & Steindler, 199
Belli, Weil & Jacobs, 199
Belli Building (San Francisco), 199, 200
Bickford, Mary, 2
Black Panther case, 121–37
background of, 121–23
Illinois Supreme Court and, 128–29, 132–36
results of, 136–37
Blackmun, Harry A., 109
Blackstone, Sir William, 105
Block, Melvin, 230–31
Boston Strangler, 31
Brady, Michael J., 68–88
Brandeis, Louis, 105
Bress, David, 224–25
Bridges, Harry, 64, 65
Brougham, Henry Peter, 1
Brown, Joseph B., 213
Buchwald, Art, 39
Burke, Ed, 107
Burleson, Phil, 213

C

Caan, James, 227
California Supreme Court, 65, 70
Campbell, Lord John, 105
Cardozo, Benjamin, 105
Caroline (queen of England), 1–2
Carpenter, Dr., 161, 166–70, 174–76, 185, 186, 189
Caruso, Enrico, 33
Castro Convertible Corporation, 20
Catt, Carrie Chapman, 83
Cedarquist, Weyland B., 136
Central Intelligence Agency (CIA), 19, 28–29
Chaney, James, 83
Charlemagne, 13
Chicago Bar Association, 123, 128
Chicago Council of Lawyers, 123, 128, 135
Chicago Daily News, 124, 129–30, 133
Chicago Police Department case, 110–20
 background of, 110–11
 closing argument, 111–20
 verdict, 120
Chicago Police Internal Investigations Division, 123
Chicago Sun-Times, 131–32, 135
Chicago Today, 135
Chicago Tribune, 122, 135, 136
Childers, S. J., 24
Chinese jurors, 12
Choate, Rufus, 2, 230
Christopher, Warren, 222
Chrysler Mission (World War II), 33, 34, 35, 38–39, 43, 46
Cicero, Marcus Tullius, 1
Civil Rights Division (U.S. Department of Justice), 29
Civil-rights movement, 83
Clark, Mark, 122

Code of Criminal Procedure of Texas, 209, 210–11
Cole, W. Sterling, 34, 36, 50–60
Communist party, 22, 38, 46, 47, 48, 64
Connally, John B., 4, 19
Cook County Democratic Central Committee, 128
Cook County Democratic Organization, 123
Copernicus, Nicolaus, 84
Corrasa, Inspector, 91
Costello, Frank, 28
Credibility gap, 10
Cunningham, Patrick, 20

D

Dairy industry, 19
Daley, Richard, 123, 124, 128, 134
Dallas Police Department, 206
Darrow, Clarence, 2–3, 208, 230
Davis, John W., 105
Dawsen, Judge Archibald, 223–24
Dean, John, 19
Democratic National Committee, 20
Democratic party, 20, 32
Dempsey, James, 229–30
Dickinson, Angie, 20
DiMaggio, Joe, 20, 31
Dineen, Dr. Peter, 148, 155, 173–74, 190
Dittstein, Dr. Harvey, 90, 92
Divorce case, 192–97
 background of, 192–93
 jury selection, 195–96
 results of, 196–97
Donovan, Justice, 114, 119
Donovan, General William J., 37
"Dope sheet" on jurors, 12

Dorman, Michael, 226
Dukhobors (religious sect), 101

E

Ehrlich, Jake, 222
Election of 1976, 32
Emerson, Faye, 26
Emerson, Ralph Waldo, 82
England, 1–2, 4–5, 13, 234, 237
Epting, Officer, 82, 83
Erskine, Lord John, 108–109

F

Falk, Peter, 227
Fallon, Willy, 222
Fascist party (Italy), 38, 41
Federal Bureau of Investigation (FBI), 30
Feeley, Diane, 69, 71, 78, 79–80
Fields, Bert, 227–29
Finian's Rainbow, 142
Fitzpatrick, Tom, 131–32
Foreman, Percy, ix, 5, 197, 206, 222, 225–26
Frank, Jerome, 233
Frankfurter, Felix, 105, 213
Freedom of Information Act, 29
Fuchsberg, Jacob D., 229, 230
Fuchsberg, Jim, 222
Fugitive Act, 82

G

Gair, Harry, 222
Gaius Verres, 1

Garrison, William Lloyd, 82–83
George IV (king of England), 1
Georgetown University, 20
Gibbs, Dr. Frederic A., 213
Glaser, Herman B., 229
Gold cart fall case (out-of-court settlement), 143–45
Goodman, James, 83
Göring, Hermann, 4
Graham, David, 221
Great Atlantic & Pacific Tea Company, 107–108
Great Speeches by Great Lawyers, 221
Groman, Arthur, 222
Gutierrez, Norbert, 68–88
Guttmacher, Dr. Manfred A., 213, 216, 218

H

Haldeman, H. R., 19
Hallinan, Terence, 64
  trial of, 68–88
Hallinan, Vincent, 7, 63–103, 105, 139, 142
  convicted for contempt of court, 64
  dissenter case, 68–88
  indicted for conspiracy, 65
  public fight against Supple, 97–103
  unconscious killer case, 89–96
Hallinan, Mrs. Vivian, 63–64, 65
Halpern, Isidore, 141
Hampton, Fred, 122
Hanrahan, Edward V., 122, 128, 130, 134, 136, 137
Harper, Robert Goodloe, 221
Harry Coleman v. Carpenter, 146–90
  background of, 146–49, 153–54
  first day of trial, 156–165
  jury selection for, 149–53

Harry Coleman v. Carpenter (cont.)
  plaintiff's testimony, 171–73
  statements to the jury, 156–60,
    163–65, 188–89
  testimony of witnesses, 155–56,
    161–63, 166–87
Hearst, Patricia, 20, 64
Hefner, Hugh, 20
Helms, Richard, 19, 28–29
Hemingway, Ernest, 33
Hennessy, James, 222
Hitler, Adolf, 30, 38
Hoffman, Ogden, 221
Holbrook, Dr., 217
Holmes, Oliver Wendell, 105
Holohan, Major William, 33–34, 35,
    36, 39, 42, 43–44, 45, 46, 48, 50,
    51, 52, 55, 60–61
Hoover, Herbert, 85
Hopkinson, Joseph, 221
House of Lords, 1
House Un-American Activities Com-
    mittee, 35–37
Huss, Stephen, 77–78

I

Icardi, Lieutenant Aldo, 33–62
Illinois Defense Project (Northwestern
    University), 136
Illinois State Bar Association, 107
Illinois Supreme Court, 120, 128–29
Industrial Workers of the World
    (IWW), 80
Ingersoll, Jared, 221
Inns of Court (England), 4
International Longshoremen's and
    Warehousemen's Union (ILWU),
    83
Irving v. Dowd, 213

J

Jackson, Robert H., 3–4
Japanese Motion Picture Studios, 227
Jaworski, Leon, 222
Jehovah's Witnesses, 100
Jews, as jurors, 11
Johns Hopkins University, 213
Julien, Alfred, 15–16, 139–97, 222
  background of, 140–41
  Coleman case, 146–90
  divorce case, 192–97
  golf cart fall case (out-of-court set-
    tlement), 143–45
Jury system, 10–17
  opening address and examination of
    witnesses, 16–17
  origin of, 13–14
  selection of jurors, 10–13

K

Keech, Richmond B., 36, 61
Kennedy, John F., 80, 206, 211, 212
Kilday, Paul J., 34, 36, 52,60
King, Martin Luther, Jr., 83
*King of the Courtroom: Percy Foreman
    for the Defense* (Dorman), 226
Kleindienst, Richard G., 109
Knigin, Ken, 230
Korff, Rabbi Baruch, 31

L

La Buy, Judge, 119
Lamb, Bob, 203–204
Lancaster, Burt, 20
Lawford, Peter, 227

Lawyers' Committee for Civil Rights under Law, 128
Lee, Byron, 71–72
Levine, Moe, 229
Levy, Leonard W., 236–37
Lewis, John L., 83
Lincoln, Abraham, 230
Lion in Court, A (Hallinan), 97
Listen to Leaders in Law (Love and Childers), 24
Little Lynn (strip-tease artist), 206
Lives of the Chief Justices (Campbell), 105
Lives of the Lord Chancellors (Campbell), 105
Lloyds of London, 203–204
LoDolce, Sergeant Carl, 34, 39, 45, 46
Louis I (emperor of Rome), 13
Love, A., 24
Lovejoy, William, 83
Lowell, James Russell, 79

M

McCarthy, Joseph, 36, 208
McCarty, Francis, 70
McDonald, W. T., 211, 213
McGovern, George, 201
McMann v. Richardson, 236–37
Magna Carta, 4
Mandel, Marvin, 20
Manfredi, Henry, 34, 47, 52, 55–66
Mannes, Marya, 199
Mansfeldt, Irene, 89–96
Mansfield, Lord William, 105, 108–109
Market Street Railway Company, 97
Marshall, Thurgood, 109
Martin, Luther, 221
May, Elaine, 227

Mencken, H. L., 65
Military Code of Justice, 59
Mitchell, John, 31
Modern Trials and Modern Damages (Belli), 201
Molino, Edward, 48
Moral judgments, 23–24
Morgan, Edmund, 233
Mormon Church, 100, 102
Morrison, Richard, 110, 113, 117
Morton, Dr., 162–63, 164, 165, 170, 185, 189
Moscatelli, Vincent, 47–48
Motion Picture Association, 20
Mulligan, William, 222
Musmanno, Mike, 31
Mussolini, Benito, 38, 39

N

Nazi party, 39, 41, 43
Nelder, Al, 74
Nelson, Dr., 155, 161, 165, 170–71, 176–85, 186, 189
New York State Association of Trial Lawyers, 229
Nichols, Perry, 222
Nixon, Richard M., 19, 30, 31, 109, 200
Nizer, Louis, ix, 7, 28, 140, 142, 197, 208, 221, 222–24, 225, 234
Northwestern University, 137
Nunez, Emilio, 146, 147, 149, 150, 166, 167, 190
Nuremberg trials, 3–4

O

Office of Strategic Services (OSS), 33, 34, 37, 38, 46, 49

Oswald, Lee Harvey, 206, 207, 209, 210, 212, 219

P

Pacific Coast Club Championship, 97
Parks, Rosa, 83
Penal Code of the State of California, 75
People v. Irene Mansfeldt, 89–96
  background of, 89–90
  examination of witnesses, 90–96
  verdict, 96
People of the State of Illinois v. Barnabas F. Sears, 128–29
Peremptory challenges, 11
Phi Beta Kappa, 64
Pierce, Colonel Ralph, 35
Pottinger, J. Stanley, 29
Powell, Adam Clayton, 26
Power, Joseph A., 123–25
Prentiss, Seargent S., 221
"Present Crisis, The" (Lowell), 79
Progressive party, 64, 65
Psychology, 8, 10, 17
Puzo, Mario, 227

Q

Quakers, 100
Quintus Hortensius, 1

R

Raichle, Frank G., 222
Reardon, Michael, 74

Reconstruction Finance Corps (RFC), 54
Reed, Dr. John, 185–87
Reserve Officers' Training Corps (ROTC), 81, 82
Ribbentrop, Joachim von, 4, 30
Rifkin, Simon F., 222
Roman Catholic Church, 97–103
Roman Catholic jurors, 12
Romiti, Philip, 135, 136
Roosevelt, Franklin D., 37
Ross, Robert, 25
Royko, Mike, 124–25, 133
Ruby, Jack, 199
Ruby case, 199, 201, 205, 206–220, 222
  background of, 206–207
  jury selection, 209–210
  publicity, 208–209, 212
  summation to the jury, 213–20
  verdict, 220
Runyon, Damon, 233
Rush, Charles M., 111, 112

S

St. Clair, James, 222
San Francisco State College, 79, 84
San Francisco State University, 68, 70
San Francisco Street Railway system, 97
San Francisco Tactical Unit Squad, 68–69, 70, 72
Schachner, Bruno, 12–13, 224–25
Schafer, Dr. Roy, 213, 216–17, 218
Schwerner, Michael, 83
Scopes trial, 102
Sears, Barnabas F., 105–37, 140, 208, 221, 222
  background of, 106–107
  Black Panther case, 121–37

Chicago Police Department case,
110–20
Shakespeare, William, 230
Sibley, Marion, 222, 227
Sixth Amendment, 22
Speer, Albert, 4
Spellman, Francis, Cardinal, 227
Stanton, Elizabeth, 83
Stern, Herbert, 8, 28, 222
Stern, Michael, 34, 51, 52, 55
Steuer, Max E., 72, 105, 222, 230
Stillman's Celebrated Freckle Cream,
108
Stockton, Henderson, 222
Stryker, Lloyd Paul, 105, 222
Suffolk University Law School, 29
Supple, David, 97–103
Sweet, Henry, 1–2

T

Tennyson, Alfred Lord, 221
*Terence Hallinan v. Michael J. Brady,
City and County of San Francisco,
and Norbert Gutierrez*, 68–88
background of, 68–70
examination of witnesses, 71–73, 77
summation, 73–88
verdict, 88
Timer, Moses, 222
Tirrell, Alfred, 2
Tonahill, Joe, 213
Towler, Dr. Martin L., 213, 217–18
Treanor, James, 160–61, 174, 176–85
Trial lawyers:
introduction to, 1–8
jury selection and, 10–17
selection of, 9–10
See also names of cases; names of
lawyers

Trial transcripts, reading of, 17
True (magazine), 34, 52
Truman, Harry, 85
Twain, Mark, 103

U

United Artists Corporation, 223
U. S. Constitution, 22, 50, 207
U. S. Criminal Investigation Division,
34, 46, 47
U. S. Department of Defense, 48
U. S. Department of Justice, 29, 54, 58
U. S. Department of State, 48
U. S. v. Icardi, 32, 33–62
background of, 33–50
cross-examination testimony, 50–60
verdict, 61–62
U. S. Supreme Court, 22, 64, 82, 84,
103, 109, 125, 136, 207, 213
United States Supreme Court Reporter,
85
University of California, 64, 90
University of Frankfurt, 20
University of Pennsylvania, 64
University of Pittsburgh, 37
University of Texas, 213, 217–18

V

Vesco, Robert L., 20
Victor Emmanuel (king of Italy), 38
Vinson, Carl, 34, 51

W

Wade, Henry M., 207
Ware, Mitchell, 130, 131, 134, 135

Warren, Earl, 203
Washington Post, The, 20
Washington Redskins, 20
Watergate scandal, 19, 29–30, 109
Webb, Jack, 227
Webster, Daniel, 230
White, Byron R., 236–37
Who's Who, 32
Wickersham Committee, 85–86
Wilde (burglar), 113
Williams, Edward Bennett, ix, 4, 7, 19–62, 105, 139, 140, 197, 208, 221, 222, 225, 230, 234, 235

background of, 20
Icardi case, 33–62
Wilson, William T., 107–108
Witch hunts, 36
World War I, 37
World War II, 37, 67, 81–82
Wright, Frank Lloyd, 200

Y

Yale University, 8, 20, 213, 216